Piaget, Jean, 1896-

Morphisms and categories

DATE DUE

MORPHISMS AND CATEGORIES
Comparing and Transforming

STATEMENT OF SPONSORSHIP

The Jean Piaget Society and the Fondation Archives Jean Piaget encourage translations of important works not yet translated, support retranslations of inadequately translated texts, foster consistent translation of technical terms, and provide translators with expert consultation. Their goal is to promote easier access to and better understanding of Piaget's ideas by English-speaking scholars. This translation of Jean Piaget's *Morphismes et Catégories: Comparer et Transformer* reflects the efforts of these scholarly organizations.

MORPHISMS AND CATEGORIES
Comparing and Transforming

JEAN PIAGET

Gil Henriques   Edgar Ascher

Translated and Edited by Terrance Brown

Preface by Seymour Papert

LEA
1992
LAWRENCE ERLBAUM ASSOCIATES, PUBLISHERS
Hillsdale, New Jersey   Hove and London

Lawrence Erlbaum Associates, Inc., Publishers
365 Broadway
Hillsdale, New Jersey 07642

Library of Congress Cataloging-in-Publication Data

Piaget, Jean, 1896–
[Morphismes et catégories. English]
Morphisms and categories : comparing and transforming / by Jean Piaget, Gil Henriques, Edgar Ascher : translated and edited by Terrance Brown : preface by Seymour Papert.
p. cm.
Translation of : Morphismes et catégories.
Includes bibliographical references and index.
ISBN 0-8058-0300-9
1. Genetic epistemology. 2. Categories (Mathematics)--Psychological aspects. I. Henriques, Gil. II. Ascher, Edgar. III. Brown, Terrance. IV. Title.
BF723.C5P5213 1992
155.4′13—dc20 91-19072
CIP

Printed in the United States of America
10 9 8 7 6 5 4 3 2 1

Table of Contents

About the Translation

Bärbel Inhelder informs me that the investigations published in this volume were carried out at the International Center for Genetic Epistemology during 1973 and 1974. The work itself was finished by Piaget, Ascher, and Henriques in 1975, but was not published at that time. It forms a natural sequel to *Recherches sur les Correspondances* published in 1980. That volume, number XXXVII, was the last of the *Études d'Épistémologie et de Psychologie Génétiques*. It remains untranslated.

The present translation began before *Morphismes et Catégories* was published in French (1990) and was translated from the manuscript itself. Because the French edition appeared before the translation was completed, it was possible to identify, correct, and incorporate important changes from that edition into this publication.

As in my other translations, I have strived for fidelity and clarity throughout this project. The first is a matter of understanding, a formidable challenge in parts of this work; the second is a matter of editing. By the latter, I do not mean that I have deliberately omitted, added, or rearranged ideas or data. I mean that I have tried to present what Piaget expressed in endless, complex sentences in a simpler and more natural way.

If this translation proves at all successful, it will in large part be due to the encouragement of Bärbel Inhelder and Jacques Montangero, to the patience of Judi Amsel of Lawrence Erlbaum Associates, and to the wonderful spirit of cooperation shown by Piaget's co-authors and collaborators. My burden was eased substantially by having several of the scholars who actually carried out the experiments or who wrote chapters in the original version (several of whom are members of the Translation Advisory Committee of the Jean Piaget Society) check various parts of this translation. Not only have they corrected errors and suggested improvements, but in one case, they have even added new material. In particular, I am grateful to Edgar Ascher for carefully examining key theoretical sections in addition to his own chapter. I am also grateful to Gil Henriques for vetting the chapter he contributed, to Annette Karmiloff-Smith and Edith Valladão-Ackermann for reviewing chapters and reporting on their experiments, and to Angela Cornu-Wells for her work on the impossible chapter 1.

—Terrance Brown

Preface

Studying this volume has been a very special experience for me, and I think it will also be for all those who take seriously Piaget's commitment to finding continuities between the psychogenesis of children's thinking and the historical development of ideas. This volume contains a particularly clear statement of his mature position on continuity, with biology as well as with the history of ideas; it also offers a rich description of one of the most interesting attempts to use a very sophisticated form of the continuity hypothesis as a guide to experimentation. Let me quickly note, because such issues sometimes make for hard reading, that this book, like much of Piaget's writing, and like all the best literature, can be read profitably on several different levels.

Who has not picked up a new volume by Piaget and made a first pass at it by savoring the poetry of the dialogues with children, skimming lightly over the intervening prose discussion of abstruse issues? Doing so does not necessarily mean missing the essential: To a surprising extent Piaget's theoretical positions are brilliantly embodied in these concrete instantiations. Many Piaget-watchers who never go back for a second pass still take profound lessons from the masterly choices of situations and interchanges. The series of experimental studies described in the following pages can be recommended as an exceptionally rich source of pleasure, information, and ideas for those who prefer this style of reading as well as for those who want to follow him through every turn of thought.

This series of studies is also outstanding in the extent to which it allows the intellectual personalities of the individual experimental collaborators to shine through Piaget's integration of their work as part of his larger theoretical perspective. Although I do not know all the collaborators well enough to comment on each individually, I am struck by the consistency over many of the books from Geneva of such features as the crisply logical style of Berthoud-Papandropolou's experimental studies, the real-world rootedness of Karmiloff's, and the fascination with mechanism shown in Blanchet and Ackermann-Valladão's. The role of the collaborators, as individuals, as more than just names listed as footnotes to each chapter, had received very insufficient attention in the discussion of Piaget's methodology.

I see this as absolutely capital. I hope that one day a historian of Piaget's work will capture the importance of the cycle in which a very general idea, such as *causality* or, in this case, *categories,* put out by Piaget, is picked up, Rorschach-like in different ways, by the various members of the team of collaborators who feed back to Piaget what they, and the children they worked with, made of the idea: It is hard to imagine a situation richer in the interplay of assimilations and accommodations than the *genèse* of a study such as the present book. But without waiting for this historian, the alerted reader can piece together the traces of the process sufficiently to read the book as more than the homogeneous intellectual product of a single brilliant mastermind.

My own experience with this book was not without some pain. The pain of being reminded the *"le patron"* is no longer with us was the more acute because this volume is so pervaded by aspects of his thinking that are least represented in contemporary Piagetian discussion, the ones most likely to fall by the wayside as Piaget the epistemologist is himself appropriated by psychologists and educators. But besides this pain of loss, I also experienced an intellectual pain of struggling to find meaning in texts that go dizzyingly in and out of focus. Do I really know what makes a transformation *"morphismique"* and can I really see Piaget's use of quite deep and quite technical mathematical ideas as more than superficial metaphor? I am not alone in being sometimes beset by such doubts; indeed, I know more than one among those who were closest and are most loyal to Piaget, and most grateful for what they have learned from him, who have long ago decided (at least in private) to treat this side of Piaget as the kind of obsessional quirk of mind one tolerantly humors in friends and family. But if you recognize yourself in this description, I urge you to try one last time to go with the flow of Piaget's thought: In addition to its important new theoretical advance, this volume offers an excellent exercise ground for coming to grips with the side of Piaget, in his view a vitally important one, that so many have found hardest to appropriate.

Buried deeply in the concluding section of the book, Piaget offers one of the clearest statements of the centrality to his work of the search for connection with what is most fundamental in science and mathematics: "A genetic epistemology only has meaning on two conditions. One is if it demonstrates a continuity between 'natural' thought and scientific thought. The other, just as essential, is if it explains natural thought in terms of its biological formation by reattaching it to the organic processes of life itself."[1]

---

[1]See chapter 15, p. 215. Note the use of the word *continuité,* a much more subtle statement of a principle in question than any allusion to the hackneyed recapitulation of phylogeny by ontogeny.

In itself, the idea of looking for a relationship between the development of natural thought in childhood and the development of scientific thought in history, is not troublesome. Simple examples abound: For example, the key role of conservations in both, or the ways in which children's notions of physics can be described as pre-Galilean. But Piaget has tougher stuff in mind, and most of us, even (and in some ways, especially) those trained as mathematicians, get into trouble when we meet discussion of the relationship between psychogenetic studies and often controversial issues in contemporary mathematical thought. The theme of the present book is the appropriation by genetic epistemology of one of the most formidable products of post war mathematical research: a body of results, some would say an ideology as well, known by the deceptively unformidable name of "category theory." I look first at the relatively clear-cut way in which this fits with the first of the two conditions, and then turn to the more obscure ways in which Piaget uses it to show relationship between psychogenetic development and the process of life.

One could imagine an unkind critic reacting to this side of Piaget by branding him a mathematical faddist: Whatever mathematical methodology happens to be in vogue comes up a little later in Piaget's writing as a proposed theoretical framework for understanding genetic epistemology. The 1930s was the heyday of universal algebra, and Piaget's search for a general framework naturally ended with an algebraic type of structure, his *groupements.* After the war Bourbaki was in vogue, especially in the French world, and we see Piaget reformulating his approach to mathematics in line with the Bourbaki theory of structures. By the 1960s the original Bourbaki framework was being challenged by the increasing acceptance of the theory of categories. And once more we see Piaget's focus shifting to where the mathematician's fashion lies.

But I mention this unkind interpretation only in the spirit of following Piaget's own well-known advice about the value of using a *téte de Turque,* in this case an imaginary one but one that nevertheless draws attention to a problem that is easily neglected: Might there not be a deeper reason for the fact that mathematical thinking has progressively thrown up a series of ideas that fit so neatly with the unfolding of Piaget's own enterprise? The answer of course lies exactly in the principle of continuity: Mathematical thought is following an evolutionary track that, if seen through the right prism, will be recognized as closely related to that followed in psychogenetic development. And this parallelism is ultimately responsible for the circumstance that Piaget was able to find the right mathematical concepts when he needed them. Let me oversimplify, in the following way, the version of history I am proposing here, going only slightly beyond what I think one can read in Piaget: The mathematics of the 1930s from which was born the *groupement* was the "right" mathematics for the early development of children's thinking, that is to say for the preoperational stages and for their transition to operativity; the structuralist mathematics of Bourbaki provides the "right" conceptual framework for a deepr understanding of the concrete operational stages; and finally the theory of categories provides the "right" frame for understanding the transition to the formal stages, a richer model than the traditional INRC group.[2]

I believe that the idea of *groupement* as a general model for intellectual activity was first formulated in 1937[3] and first given elaborated form in the work with Alina Szeminska on *Number* and with Bärbel Inhelder on *Quantities*. This work is characterized by two steps of great originality in relation to the "obvious" approach. First, the focus is shifted from studying entities such as "Number" to studying mathematical systems. Even Bertrand Russell looked for a definition of number and answered something like "a number is a class of equivalent classes." Piaget makes a profound shift, and one that is in line with the mathematical fashion of the time, in saying something like "don't worry about what a number is, worry about what you can do with it." And so he is led to see the object of his study as the development of systems of operations on numbers. But this is only half a step. The second half, also in line with the mathematics of the time, is to look for more elementary, more homogeneous systems. You can do too much with numbers: You can order them, you can add them, you can multiply them, you can count with them. The real stroke of genius was to look for the development of minimal systems of pure operations, for example, seriation or classification. The primary locus of development toward operativity is *within* such microsystems. Of course it would be most uncharacteristic of Piaget to ignore interactions between the systems at all stages, but it is only at a later stage, after the internal development of the systems has stabilized, that the dominant locus of development can be in the transactions *between* the simple systems. But thinking about this later stage takes us into a new mathematical perspective: Bourbaki took the step of revisioning the simple systems by seeing them as "mother structures" out of which the whole mathematical edifice could be built; and Piaget, as far as I can tell, independently had formulated an analogous perspective for

---

[2]Someone in search of a doctoral topic should review Inhelder's classical experiments reported in Inhelder and Piaget, *The Growth of Logical Thinking from Childhood to Adolescence* (New York: Basic Books, 1958), where the use of INRC was first elaborated. In this connection I note that (a) Piaget does not explicitly present the theory of categories as constituting a new approach to the formal and (b) my interpretation does not in any way belittle the many other insights obtained through this theory.

[3]A fascinating, little known minipaper by Piaget is: "La réversibilité des opérations et l'importance de la notion de 'group' ne pour la psychologie de la pensée," *Proceedings of the 11th International Congress of Psychology,* 1937.

natural thought well before his first elaborated manifesto of Genetic Epistemology.[4]

The strikingly natural isomorphism between Piaget's classical picture of psychogenesis and Bourbaki's picture of mathogenesis must stand as a pinnacle of achievement in the quest for continuity. Its crystal clarity pervaded the atmosphere of the first years of the *Centre d'Épistémologic Génétique* in the late 1950s and early 1960s. But both Piaget and mathematics were already in motion toward a next phase of contact: the one that this volume is all about. For me, its spirit is vividly captured by the continuation of the series "within . . . between . . ." by the addition of a third term:[5] ". . . beyond" in a sense of transcending or "getting above." The sense in which the theory of categories,[6] in its technical use in mathematics, can be seen as "going beyond" is explained as lucidly as anywhere by Edgar Ascher in Chapter 14, one of the two chapters in the book not written by Piaget.[7] To summarize here in a nutshell: In the same sense in which treating numbers as elements of an additive group gets away from or goes beyond the specific content of numbers, treating mathematical systems as elements of a category gets away from their specific content; in the psychogenetic use of the concept of category this way of thinking provides a new prism for looking at the passage from the concrete to the formal. I venture to speculate that this new look at the formal eventually will be seen as the major impact of the kind of thinking presented in this volume. The new look is richer than what one could see when the only prisms were "algebraic" (here including combinatorics and Boolean Logic as well as the INRC) and very much more able to place the emergence of the formal as part of an integrative view of the entire process of development.

Treating numbers as elements of an additive group abstracts a particular way of putting two numbers together to make a new number, namely adding them. Treating mathematical systems as elements of a category also astracts certain particular ways of putting them together. Of these, the most fundamental, the one that makes a category a category, is of a different nature from addition in that it puts two elements together to compare them

---

4Jean Piaget, *Introduction à l'Epistémologie Génétique* (3 Volumes) (Paris: Presses Universitaires de France, 1950).

5The prefixes *intra-*, *inter-*, and *trans-* are actually used in the text. More discussion of this series can be found in the two books with Rolando Garcia, *Les Explications Causales* (Paris: Presses Universitaires de France, 1971), and *Psychogenèse et Histoire des Sciences* (Paris: Flammarion, 1983), who likes to use the abbreviations Ia, Ir, and Tr.

6Not to be confused with "category" meaning class or type or with Kant's categories or indeed with any ordinary language use of the word.

7The other is a more committed and personal interpretation by Gil Henriques of the relationship between the theory of categories and genetic epistemology.

rather than to make a new element; in mathematical texts[8] one sees the two elements represented by dots linked (or "tied together") by arrows representing mappings or *"morphismes."* Is an operation that only compares rather than makes something new still an operation? Questions like this, though more subtly put, figure prominently in Piaget's text. Is a comparison a transformation? Out in the physical world one might say: "Obviously not. When I compare thee to a summer's day you are still you." As Piaget points out: "Insofar as one is inclined to consider knowledge in general as a copy . . . of reality . . . , the role of correspondences or morphisms as instruments of comparison could only be overestimated whereas transformations would themselves be reduced to metaphors . . ."[9]

But for a poet, for a lover, or for a constructivist epistemologist, things can be very different. Bringing two epistemological objects together, two things in the mind, might change them forever. But not always. "Love is not love," says Shakespeare, "that alters when it alteration finds." And in Piaget's lifelong saga of trying to understand change, a major theme has been the need for enough stability, even rigidity, in the system to support the orderly and meaningful regulation of change. This theme, already present in the ideas of assimilation and accommodation, has always been prominent in his thinking. In this volume its discussion reaches a new level of energy and detail.

These remarks about what changes and what stays the same when a system develops bring us to the second continuity, *"toute aussi essentielle,"* to be investigated by genetic epistemology: continuity, not this time with human-made mathematics, but with the process of life itself. In earlier works[10] this continuity typically has meant arguing that biological and cognitive processes share concrete mechanisms such as equilibration of the phenocopying process or that they share functional phenomena such as anticipation. The presentation of continuity in this volume is of a radically different kind. One might say that it has moved from the concrete to the formal. The argument here does not point to mechanisms they share but rather shows that an isomorphic formal structure fits both. I found myself toying with the idea of applying the language and mode of analysis of the book itself to the way Piaget discusses the relationship between these two systems and came up with formulations such as saying that Piaget's discussion of the correspondence between the two systems, cognition and life, has advanced from being "intermorphic" to being "transmorphic." I do

---

[8]Peep at Ascher's chapter in this volume (chapter 14) if you are not familiar with these diagrams.

[9]See chapter 15, p. 215.

[10]Jean Piaget, *Biologie et Connaissance* (Paris: Gallimard, 1967), and *Adaptation Vitale et Psychologie de l'Intelligence: Sélection Organique et Phénocopie* (Paris: Hermann, 1974).

not want to argue that this self-referential point can really be sustained. But I found it a useful way to appropriate the ideas of the book by playing with them, and would recommend to the reader this end-of-the-chapter exercise: Compare and contrast the discussion of how children compare two machines in Chapter 12 and the way Piaget compares the two "machines" to which he has devoted his life's work.

—Seymour Papert

Introduction

As instruments of comparison, correspondences are both transformable with regard to their form and nontransforming with regard to their contents, and that is true whether their contents are states or unmodified transformations. In consequence, the study of correspondences, epistemological as well as psychogenetic, raises two great problems among many others. The first of these has to do with the relationship of correspondences to their contents. Although it is clear that putting static figures into correspondence does not modify them but only enriches them with comparisons, things become more complicated when morphisms consist in comparing transformations to one another or to their results. While acknowledging in such cases that transformations are not changed simply by being compared, one still must wonder whether transformations create morphisms, whether transformations themselves result from previous correspondences, or whether, care being taken to distinguish operations preparing the way for transforming operations from the morphisms resulting from them, both are true. Even if such questions have no interest from the point of view of mathematical technique, they are important from the point of view of constructivist epistemology which must distinguish and even oppose the two principal functions at work in rational creation: comparing and transforming. This leads to the first great problem brought up by the analysis of correspondences and morphisms: the problem of how they relate to their content. In particular, when they bear on transforming actions or operations, it leads to the problem of how they relate to transformations. A preceding work has been devoted to that topic.[1]

There is, however, a second great problem having nothing to do with relationships between correspondences as form and transformations as content. This is the problem of how the forms of morphisms develop. Although correspondences do not transform anything, they do undergo developmental transformations. Thus, the object of the present volume is to study a new type of transformation, that is, the transformations involved in

[1] Jean Piaget, "Recherches sur les correspondences," *Études d'Épistémologie et Psychologie Génétique, XXXVII* (Paris: Presses Universitaires de France, 1980).

the evolution of morphisms as such rather than the transformations involved in transformatory operations linked to one another by correspondences.

This second type of transformation consists, essentially if not exclusively, in progressive compositions linking correspondences or morphisms to one another. As we stressed in our work mentioned previously, the three permanent and specific forms of correspondences or morphisms evolve very little in comparison with the unlimited production of new transformatory operations of whatever nature. From the bijections, surjections, or injections already at work in the sensorimotor period up to the isomorphisms, epimorphisms, and monomorphisms of the mathematical theory of categories, these forms do not differ as elements but do vary considerably in their increasingly refined modes of composition. The chapters that follow, therefore, focus on the problem of how compositions among correspondences or morphisms develop, because it is from this point of view that one sees the most evolution from noncomposable forms to forms with the organization characteristic of "special categories."

Although the two principal problems that we have identified are quite distinct, they are not entirely independent of and, at times, even interfere with one another. In order to demonstrate this, we need to introduce certain terminological conventions. We call *operatory transformations* those trnsformations that are used without recourse to morphisms and that modify their extramorphic objects or contents at every level. An example of this sort of transformation might be $7 + 5 = 12$ when, with Kant, such an operation is considered synthetic rather than analytic! We also employ this term to designate transformations that generate their own content, for example, the operation $n + 1$, whose constructive power extends to infinity. By contrast, we call *morphismic transformations* those transformations that modify instruments of comparison themselves and that can generate new ones from them, especially through compositions. From this point of view, such transformations are analogous to operatory transformations, but they are distinct from them in that the elementary instruments they compose or link together are not themselves transforming. In other words, where morphismic transformations are concerned, it is necessary to consider how contents are included in one another. (Given the relativity of form to content, this is not surprising: In every form-content hierarchy, every form except those at the extremes is also content and vice versa.) However, their originality with regard to the construction of new instruments of comparison is that, although being transforming by the fact of this construction, they create instruments for putting things into correspondence that are not themselves transforming. This amounts to saying that they bear on elementary correspondences or morphisms that do not modify their contents insofar as objects to be compared are concerned, even if those objects are operatory transformations. By contrast, at higher levels one sees morphismic compositions of different degrees which are the source of transforming constructions insofar as compositions or new formations of morphisms are concerned. In brief, then, basic extramorphic contents, that is, objects to be compared, are not modified by elementary comparative forms, whereas such forms are modified by higher forms bearing on them, the contents in this case being morphisms to be improved or even created.

Returning to psychogenesis and formulating our two great problems as previously mentioned, several possible relationships emerge. The first is that of the relationships between correspondences or morphisms and extramorphic contents including operatory transformations. The second is that of the nature of morphismic transformations and how they relate to operatory transformations, no longer in terms of content but in terms of processes of equal rank. Are they independent and parallel, does one of them determine the other, or do they progressively converge? Such questions appear quite different from the first problem because they have to do with the ways in which morphisms are composed with one another. Nevertheless, they are closely related, as is evident from the following considerations.

Investigations of the relationship between correspondences and extramorphic contents have demonstrated the progressive reversal of the relationship between correspondences and operatory transformations. Correspondences begin during the initial developmental stages and prepare the way for the operatory transformations in the sense that they lead to their discovery. Subsequently, correspondences become subordinated to transformations in the sense that they end up being necessary deductions from them. In other words, what was at first a simple comparison of empirically established observables becomes an elucidation of common forms. This occurs because the content of the initial correspondences is structured with the help of these common forms insofar as the reading or recording of facts is concerned but goes beyond correspondences in the direction of understanding the reasons for them, that is, in the direction of an autonomous construction of transformations. Another way this might be stated is that unstructured content becomes an operatory form while remaining a content of correspondences. If the latter have undergone transition from a pretransformational variety to intertransformational or cotransformational varieties, they are not for all that a source of transformations. To put a final state into correspondence with an initial state or to put transformations into correspondence with their results does not involve generating transformations themselves. However, the forms taken by transformations and the related forms taken by correspondences become more and more solidary. It is evident, therefore, that where compositions among morphisms are concerned, analogous processes will be found. These, however, will be more complex for the simple reason that two transformations, some operatory (in the restricted sense allowed by our conventions) and others morphismic, are involved. This is because the formation of new, in the sense of composed, instruments of comparison does not constitute a comparison as such but rather constitutes a transformation in the sense of a construction.

Even so, the question of the relationship of new comparative instruments to operatory transformations is far from resolved. Although some elementary morphisms can be deduced from such structures, it is still possible for morphismic compositions to acquire a growing autonomy. In that case, the most likely solution to the problem of the relationship between morphismic and operatory transformations would seem to lie in the direction of progressive convergence and even reciprocal assistance between the two. In fact, such a solution is suggested by the existence in mathematics of common forms of higher rank such as groups of automorphisms or certain rings of endomorphisms, and so forth.

In order to study these problems, we are going to analyze compositions of correspondences or morphisms that are linked to well-defined operatory structures. We do so by beginning with spatial compositions. The advantage of proceeding in this way is that it combines logical difficulty with figurative facility. We then continue with problems of reciprocities and symmetries which are essentially inferential and end with questions of causality.

What we find in each of these cases, but in very different forms, is that morphismic transformations proceed through three stages. In order to facilitate interpreting the facts, I describe these stages now. The first is called "intramorphic" because it does not yet include compositions. In this case, it is a matter of simple correspondences, not all of which will consist in mappings because they sometimes are neither exhaustive nor univocal. The only characteristic they have in common is that they all bear, either correctly or incorrectly, on observables, especially predictions of observables. The lack of composition can lead to contradictions that the subject does not feel. In short, it is still only a matter of empirical comparisons, whether bearing on transformations or on simple states.

The second stage is designated by the term "intermorphic" and marks the beginning of systematic compositions. It involves correspondences among correspondences, particularly in intertransformational situations, which confers a beginning of necessity on these morphisms or premorphisms of second degree. However, intermorphic compositions are still only local and proceed by degrees without ending in a general system capable of closure or, more important, in compositions that are "free" in the sense of "arbitrary" in their starting point and univocal in their endpoint. Nevertheless, such comparisons of comparisons lead to great progress in composition and help in understanding the transformations from which they, in turn, begin to be deducible.

Finally, the third stage in the evolution of morphismic transformations is characterized by an epistemologically instructive reversal. It is not simply a matter of correspondences among correspondences attaining a higher degree—the eventual third degree morphisms will again arise from the intermorphic—but of a new mode of composition. This we call "transmorphic" in the etymological sense where "trans" means "beyond" and not simply "from one to the other." In effect, this is the level where the subject begins to "operate" on morphisms. In other words, it is the level where the subject begins to compare morphisms by means of operatory instruments obtained through the generalization or explanation of transformations constituting the content of prior morphisms and, therefore, of Stage II compositions. Here we have the beginning of a complex situation whose even more elaborated and refined functional equivalents are found on the plane of scientific thought (see Henriques's chapter later in this book). To take a simple example, the structure of a "group" is made up of "operatory transformations" that, as such, remain "extramorphic." A set of morphisms can be associated with these operatory transformations without in any way transforming their group structure. At the same time, these morphisms can be constructively composed with one another and, consequently, they are transformable up to the point of generating the "category" of this group. That category has the morphisms that it coordinates as morphismic contents, but, at base, it has the operatory structure of a group as extramorphic content.

In sum, the interpretation that guides us in the course of the discussions that follow is this. Operatory and morphismic transformations progressively converge, but this convergence does not necessarily dissolve the autonomy of these two vast constructions. Morphismic transformations aim at comparisons or comparative transferences; operatory transformations aim at the creation and transformation of objects or contents; and their convergence ends in the elaboration of general common forms, for example, monoids, groups, rings, lattices, and so on, of all logicomathematical transformations that have achieved a sufficient degree of reflective abstraction.

1 Rotations and Circumductions

Jean Piaget
with
Cl. Monnier
and
J. Vauclair

Chapters 2 and 3 have to do with morphisms linked to rotations of varying degree and complexity. In chapter 2, the rotations involve cyclic successions of several elements; in chapter 3, they involve rotations of a cube. It makes sense, therefore, to begin with the simplest situation where the positions of a single object, for example, the head and feet of a doll, vary according to the rotations and circumductions to which they are subjected and where morphisms consist only in linking starting to ending points by means of transformations.

1. TECHNIQUE

The horizontal apparatus consists of a square platform on which is drawn a large circle almost tangent to the edges (Fig. 1.1). On the platform sits a round box containing an unmovable bear lying on its back. The child is asked to indicate the bear's head and hind legs. The box is then closed by means of lids of which there are two sorts. One is attached to a long stick that allows the box to be pushed around the circumference of the circle without changing the bear's orientation relative to the subject (circumduction); the other has a shorter stick that attaches to a pivot in center of the circle so that, when the box is pushed around the circle, the bear's orientation rotates from rightside-up through upside-down and back to rightside-up relative to the subject (rotation). In both cases, the investigator has the child establish the position of the head at the start, for example, toward the subject, toward the window, and so forth. Then the box is

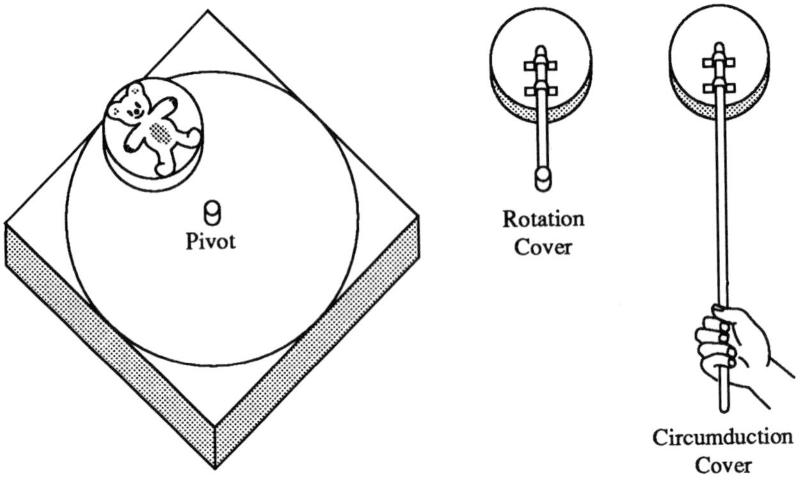

FIG. 1.1. Horizontal apparatus.

closed, and the child is asked to move the box 90°, 180°, or 270° using specific movements of the stick and to indicate the position of the bear after the movement is performed.

The vertical apparatus consists of a little trolley car on rails (Fig. 1.2). On it sits a wooden base holding a picture of a little man drawn on a card. The picture is masked while the investigator performs movements either of circumduction (where the man remains upright) or rotation (where the man turns upside- down at 180° and rightside-up at 360°. After each movement,

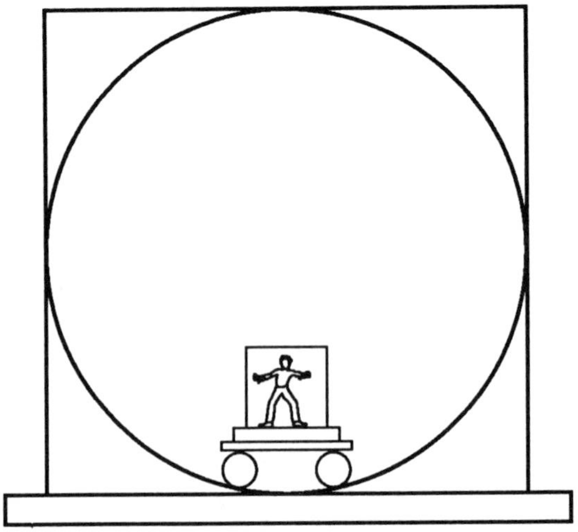

FIG. 1.2. Vertical apparatus.

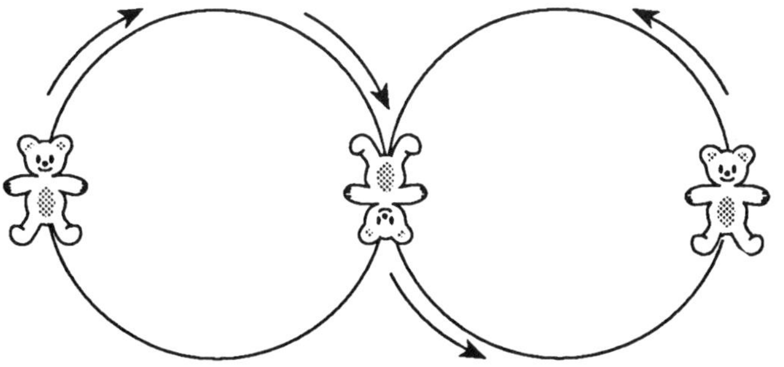

FIG. 1.3. Horizontal figure eight apparatus.

the experimenter asks the subject whether the man is standing, lying down, and so on, and in what direction his head is pointing as well as to give reasons for his answers. Then the investigator takes the card out of the base, hands it to the child, and asks him, by imitating the movements, to anticipate the path to be traversed or to reproduce the path that has been traversed when the little man was behind the screen. The child also is asked to compare the two apparatuses.

Two other horizontal patterns of movement also are used (Fig. 1.3). One is a figure eight (∞) on which different paths, for example, m, ∿, and so forth are followed. The other is a figure made of four 90° arcs of a circle turned inward with the points of contact extended, for example, ⌑. With the latter figure, the bear's head is oriented toward the outside at the starting point to which it subsequently returns.[1]

Finally, let us note that in each situation, orbital rotations can be combined with rotations proper, that is, rotations in place making an object turn on itself. Or subjects even may be asked to perform compositions such as an orbital rotation of 120° plus a rotation in place which compensates for it, all of which adds up to a circumduction.

2. ELEMENTARY OR "INTRAMORPHIC" CORRESPONDENCES

The aim of this work being to study the progressive composition of correspondences, it makes sense to begin by examining those that do not seem to be composed with one another.

---

[1]The description of the experimental procedure is vague, and Dr. Monnier is no longer certain just how this part of the experiment was performed. I have therefore inferred the bear's positions and paths of movement from subjects' responses and Piaget's discussion of them.—Translator

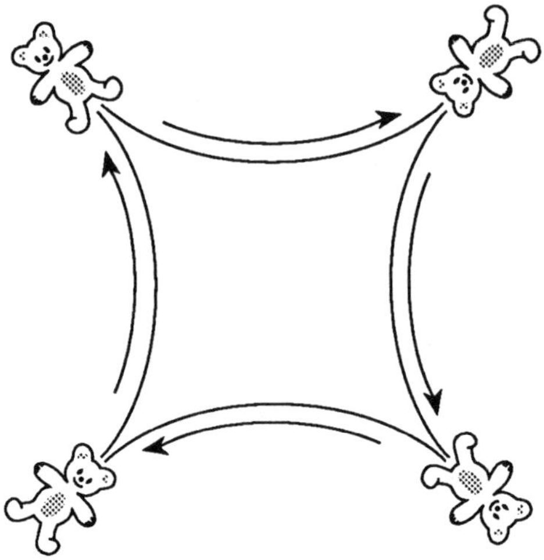

FIG. 1.4. Inverted arcs of a circle apparatus.

VAL (3 years): VAL is shown that, at the start, the bear's head lies in the direction the stick is pointing (horizontal apparatus).[2] After a 90° rotation, she wrongly indicates the opposite of the bear's true orientation, then corrects her answer, then changes back to the incorrect response. By contrast, after a 180° rotation she understands right away ("Toward me, upside down"), but she does not succeed, that is, does not compose the symmetrical of this symmetry, when the box is rotated the other 180° back to the starting point. In the case of circumduction, she likewise believes that 180° brings about an inversion ("Toward me") and fails for other positions.

TIE (4 years, 1 month): After several tries with the the bear visible, TIE succeeds in answering all questions about circumduction on the horizontal apparatus. However, except for 180° he fails on questions about rotation. In the latter case, he turns himself from the bottom to the top of the circle (by moving around the table from 6 to 12 o'clock) and then, starting at 270°, he walks the stick around to 90° in order to find the symmetry. Reinterrogated at 4 years, 5 months, he begins, for rotations, as he had 4 months previously, but subsequently succeeds for 90° because "he had his head there under the board" (stick). In other words, he does so by using the stick as a reference without, for all that, understanding the rotation (failure for a 180° rotation starting from the left-right position). By contrast, he now fails on all problems relative to circumduction, except at 180°.

[2]Say at 12 o'clock using a clock framework (rotation).

OLI (4 years, 4 months): On the vertical apparatus, OLI succeeds on questions relative to circumduction and rotation to 180°. However, he believes that at 90° and 270°, the "little fellow always looks like he's lying down." With respect to the position of the head on the horizontal apparatus, he says that "if you put him like that (90°), the head's there."—"What helps you?"—"The stick." For a rotation of 180° on the vertical apparatus, "he's upside-down," whereas for circumduction, that is not the case because "I held the stick straight." The difference is that "sometimes you can make the little fellow turn on himself." After this false prediction for 90° because "before his head was there," he sees his error, but makes in-place rotations to make things come out alright.

FLO (4 years, 6 months): Starting with circumduction on the horizontal apparatus, FLO makes an error for 180°because "you've changed sides, and so the head's changed sides." Then, after moving on to rotations, she again makes errors for 180° as if there were circumduction and only succeeds for 180° after several tries at 90°, and so on.

MIC (4 years, 7 months): After succeeding on questions relative to 180° rotation on the horizontal apparatus, MIC at first makes mistakes on circumductions from 90° to 270° or from 0° to 180°. When he succeeds, he again is asked about rotation and mixes the two movements, first on movements from 0° to 90, then on others, and so forth.

CAR (5 years, 6 months): For 180° rotations on the vertical apparatus, CAR says, "He's upside-down maybe, because you put him on the bottom."—"And how was he before?"—"Not upside-down. You turned him, and he was put upside down." For 90°, she predicts that the little man will be lying down, but she is not sure what side the head will be on. For 270°, "I think he'll be upside down." By contrast, she succeeds in reproducing the trajectory by following the circumference but thinks that the results change with the direction of movement. For circumduction, 180° first gives "upside down" but subsequently, "I think standing up also. You haven't put him upside down." Interestingly, however, when she is asked later to reproduce this circumduction, she does so as an orbital rotation of 180° followed by a rotation proper (in place) also of 180°. This gives an unintentional composition that would be intermorphic if it were programmed. As it is, only a simple correction is involved (cf. the end of OLI's interrogation).

ARI (5 years, 4 months): ARI succeeds on circumductions with the vertical apparatus, responds correctly for rotations of 180° from top to bottom but hesitates for rotations in the opposite direction, and then constantly makes mistakes by mixing circumductions and rotations.

STE (5 years, 11 months): After two errors, STE succeeds on circumductions as well as rotations of 180° but makes errors for movements from left to right and for other positions as well. In the case of rotation, it is "the box" that moves, but in circumduction "nothing" moves.

It is a matter of course that predictions of the bear's or little man's positions in cyclic succession rest on cotransformational correspondences, because the relationship between one position and the following position results from a rotation. With that in mind, one general fact appears to dominate the preceding reactions. The orbital rotation described by the screened bear at the end of the stick is thought of in terms of rotation proper or, therefore, in terms of rotation in place. This erroneous assimilation of orbital rotation to in-place rotation is natural because, from the first sensorimotor stages, the child knows how to turn an object in place in order to look at its different sides or back, and for a long time he imagines every kind of rotation according to this model. In the case at hand, the subject sees the orbital rotation quite well and even executes it easily on the horizontal apparatus. He does not, however, put the positions into correspondence with the rotation as a whole but instead conceives them as resulting from in-place rotations. As OLI says, in order to differentiate orbital rotation from circumduction, "You can make the fellow turn on himself," or as VAL, OLI, CAR, and so on, say, "He's upside-down" (at 180°) and especially "you turned him, and he was put upside down." OLI makes in-place rotations in order to correct his errors and CAR, in order to realize a rotation of 180°, completes a circumduction by making an in-place rotation at the end. STE says that the box moves during a rotation but that it does nothing during a circumduction. In this case, because he has just effected the movements himself, the "nothing" can only mean the absence of a rotation proper. Another index of this carelessness with regard to orbital rotation is that predictions at 90° are not easier than those at 270°, which would not be the case if the subject were trying to base his correspondences on perceptual pursuit of the circular trajectory.

The first consequence stemming from this essential fact is that, on the average, positions arrived at through circumduction are predicted better than those arrived at through orbital rotation. This is because there is isomorphism among all positions arrived at through circumduction and, therefore, little that is analogous to rotations proper. Even so, several subjects give in to the partial analogy resulting from the fact that the orbital trajectory is the same in both cases (notably for circumductions of 180°). For example, VAL and FLO say "you've changed sides, and so the head's changed sides," and CAR corrects herself by invoking an absence of rotation proper—"you haven't put him upside down."

This occasional contamination of circumduction by orbital rotation (doubtless because of insufficient interpretation) is observed as confusion between two kinds of correspondences. However, with TIE, OLI, and ARI, it appears after initial success with circumduction when questions of rotation are introduced. Only FLO presents this confusion starting with circumduction.

One fact that seems to confirm what has been said about orbital rotation being assimilated to rotation proper is that subjects 3 to 4 years old give better responses for rotations than 5-year-olds do. In effect, the younger subjects care nothing about the trajectory and base their answers on references such as (TIE) "his head there under the board" (indicating the end of the stick) or (OLI) "the little stick" that "helps." Around 5 years of age, by contrast, there are attempts to take account of the orbital rotation as a trajectory (see CAR) but without yet being able to do so successfully for the reasons we have seen.

In sum, the correspondences these children succeed in creating are isomorphisms of position in the case of circumductions and inversions of 180° in top-to-bottom rotations where the precocious role of correspondences by symmetry is combined with interpretation in terms of rotation proper. However, none of these successes may yet be taken as evidence of compositions, because an isomorphism that is repeated cannot yet be qualified as such. Moreover, in the case of rotational inversions of 180°, the lack of composition is so serious that correct anticipation of rotations made in the top-to-bottom direction (from 12 to 6 o'clock) is not always accompanied by its reciprocal (bottom-to-top, from 6 to 12 o'clock) or by a right-left symmetry or its inverse (between 3 and 9 o'clock). We, therefore, can qualify these elementary correspondences as "intramorphic," by which we mean repeatable putting into relationship based on empirical findings but without composition among the relationships created. In intramorphic correspondences, the inferences involved in anticipating the bear's or man's position under the screen are limited to generalizations of previous findings such as in-place rotations acquired at sensorimotor levels or, for circumductions, experience of the fact that lifting a glass of water up and down, with or without curves in the trajectory, does not cause spilling if verticality is maintained.

3. INTERMORPHIC CORRESPONDENCES I

Starting at age $6\frac{1}{2}$ or 7 years, subjects begin by considering orbital rotation as determining a cyclic succession of positions each of which corresponds to the path traveled from the initial position to the position in question. One, therefore, can qualify these correspondences between successors as intermorphic insofar as they are linked to positions that depend on the rotation. Before finding explicit reasons for this, however, one of course finds numerous intermediate cases between intra- and intermorphic correspondences, of which the following are examples:

ISA (6 years, 5 months): With the horizontal apparatus, ISA begins by making errors for rotations of 180° (top-to-bottom), 270° and so on, but succeeds for the 180° bottom-to-top rotation. When the bear's head is to the bottom or to the left, she quite well foresees what will happen when it is rotated to the top or to the right, saying "if you turn it, you change sides." Subsequently, she answers correctly for all questions concerning rotations. Circumduction is understood immediately: "It is because you keep the little stick straight. If you didn't keep it straight, you'd change direction.—"And for the head to be on the bottom (between 3 and 9 o'clock)?"—"You'd have to turn it like that" (shows the orbital rotation).—"What does that make you think of?"—"It's as if he makes a somersault!" A month later, ISA responds correctly to all questions concerning rotations on the vertical apparatus, can reproduce the trajectories, and can explain the positions. The man is then placed head down at 12 o'clock, and ISA is asked where a red spot would have to be positioned so that the man could always see it during a rotation: "At 6 o'clock?"—"No, that won't work."—"And here" (8 o'clock)?"—"That won't either."—"And if I put the red spot at the center?"—"Ah yes, that will always work."

PHI (7 years, 1 month): PHI begins by making errors on circumduction, that is, at 180° on the horizontal apparatus, the bear's head will be "at the bottom, because that (the starting point), it's on top." Subsequently, he succeeds. For rotations, he believes that with the bear lying down with its head to the left, the position will be conserved after a rotation of 180°, and he understands nothing when he sees what happens: "It's magic." But after effecting a circumduction without the screen, he comes to understand the difference between circumduction and rotation. Finally, in order for a red spot to be seen from any position during a rotation, he places it at the center of the circle.[3]

Thus, it is evident how much the consideration of orbital rotation modifies the subject's understanding and permits compositions of correspondences sufficient to affirm that a red spot situated at the center of the

[3]The many references to the direction of the man's gaze are difficult to reconcile with its position, that is, lying on its back and, therefore looking out from the plane of the circle. To make sense, the bear would have to be sitting upright in the box, but if that were the case then the references to the head and feet would be incomprehensible. In the last few paragraphs it becomes apparent that whatever the bear's position actually was, its position in circumduction would not allow a constant focus whereas its rotation would allow focus on a point at the center of the circle.

circle will be seen by the doll from every position, if the doll is looking at it at the start. As for the "somersault" that ISA mentions, it is no longer only a metaphor ("as if") and no longer an affirmation of rotation proper.

Here now are some cases of correspondences that are intermorphic from the start:

NIC (6 years, 6 months): NIC immediately succeeds for circumductions to 180° on the horizontal apparatus "because before he had his head on top (and thus keeps it there)," whereas after rotation "it's on the bottom because he has been turned" (she shows how).—"But before he was also turned (indicating circumduction)?"—"But the stick moved in turning" (shows how). Subsequently, NIC correctly anticipates the position of the man's head in all four positions in random order, saying that "it moves when everything moves." She correctly retraces the trajectories and concludes among other things that "it's the same" in both directions.

SAN (6 years, 6 months): SAN correctly predicts the positions of the bear (horizontal apparatus) after rotations. "And if you don't want it to be upside down here" (180°)?—(She spontaneously makes a circumduction, saying) "You don't turn it." For the horizontal figure eight, she announces right off that there will be a turning upside down at the crossing point and a turning rightside up at the other end of the loop. "Why?"—"I saw" (meaning "followed the trajectory without seeing the man in the box").

SAB (7 years, 1 month): SAB still hesitates for rotations on the circle but for the horizontal figure eight, she correctly predicts the turning upside down at the crossing point and the final turning rightside up: "With the circle the man is upside-down at the other end?"—"Yes, but with the eight it's crossed, and that makes him change position. That makes him get upside down and, after, rightside up."

ANT (7 years, 6 months): ANT is asked what must be done so that the man will not end upside-down at 180°. He first rotates him in place and then makes an orbital rotation to 180°. Subsequently, so that the man will end up upside-down by some means other than orbital rotation, he composes an in-place rotation with a circumduction. For the horizontal figure eight, he correctly shows three distinct positions, but makes an error at the end. However, after recreating the movements, he predicts everything correctly.

PAT (7 years, 1 month): Pat succeeds on the horizontal figure eight. For the ∾ section of the figure going from right to left and starting with the head up, she follows the path with her finger: "There (crossing point) the head on bottom, then the head on top."—"And for the m ?"—(She uses her fingers and makes the correct movement.) She uses the same method for ω.

Did (8 years, 2 months): After having rapid success with the circle, Did sees right off that at the extremities of the ∞ the head is on top, but he adds: "If I've done it correctly, it's the same thing (to the left and to the right) except the left leg and the left arm are outside."—"Why won't the head be upside down?"—He shows the crossing point and the returning upright.

One sees, therefore, that these reactions give evidence of a certain number of compositions. As already mentioned, the first is the morphism of successor which makes each state of the doll after changing position correspond to the state of the doll at the start of the change, and it does so until the starting state of the whole rotation is reached again. What is involved, therefore, is a morphism of successions that is cotransformational relative to rotation, but that is the result of a composition as well. This is because each relationship of successor (from 0° to 90°, from there to 180°, and so on), although being repeatable and therefore constituting a stable correspondence, is different from the preceding and determined by it. A second form of composition comes into play in understanding that, if the doll's head is turned toward the interior, a red spot at the center of the circle is visible from all positions (ISA and PHI). A third form is constituted by the ability to obtain the same result by means of different coordinations, that is, in-place rotation linked to circumduction is equivalent to orbital rotation of 180°, and so forth (see ANT). A fourth form is revealed by the horizontal figure eight (∞) and its sections, where understanding presupposes the composition of correspondences inherent in two circles, but with a crossing point that reverses relationships by passing from one to the other circle.

However, even if the foregoing constitutes evidence of a set of compositions that are unrealizable at the intramorphic level, such compositions are still only inter- and not transmorphic. This is because, although combining several distinct correspondences and by that fact acquiring a necessary character that elementary putting into correspondence does not have, compositions of this sort still can be obtained by simple successive readings (as PAT does by following the horizontal figure eight with her finger) as well as by immediate deduction (as with DID).

With regard to the correspondences between circumduction and rotation that were examined, it is remarkable that not one subject of Level II began by saying that there is a circular trajectory in both cases. All subjects limited themselves to pointing out the difference, to determining whether or not the doll changes absolute position, or even, as SAN says, to claiming that it "does not turn." Now it is clear that each child perceives the circumduction, at least insofar as he follows the form of the large circle drawn on the support, and SAN is the first to do so because she spontaneously discovered circumduction. It is obvious, therefore, that the differences invoked are those between two subclasses within a class of equivalences not made explicit. This implicit class is the class of trajectories imposed on the sticks of the horizontal apparatus by the child himself and consisting in following the circumference given.

4. INTERMORPHIC CORRESPONDENCES II AND THE BEGINNING OF THE TRANSMORPHISM

The figure  is only mastered with a certain delay relative to ∞, due to the fact that, although it also combines circular elements, it does so in the form of four inverted 90° arcs forming four points, as evidenced in the following:

SAN (6 years, 6 months): SAN, whose success with other figures was seen previously, succeeds quite readily in understanding inversions for isolated arcs  or . However, she fails by 180°[4] on compositions of two or three arcs and is, at first, only able to reproduce trajectories by introducing in-place rotations.

LIP (6 years, 8 months): LIP makes the same errors of 180° for compositions and occasionally replaces rotation from one point to the following point by a circumduction. Moreover, he supposes that in passing from Point 1 to its opposite, Point 3, by the intermediary of Point 2 that "it's the same as if you had a straight line going directly from Point 1 to Point 3" (diagonal).—"But do you come to the same position at Point 3 as at Point 1?"—"No, the head is on bottom."

FRA (6 years, 10 months): Although confident about her deductions ("I think, and I follow the road in my head"), FRA nevertheless omits the inversions between successive positions two times out of six.

Such errors are found up to 9 years of age. By contrast, certain understandings are seen as early as age 7 years:

SAB (7 years, 1 month): SAB (also quoted for ∞) succeeds on compositions of two arcs and predicts that 1 → 2 → 3 → 4 will give "the same thing" as 1 → 4. "Is it the same?"—"Because there (3 → 4), that also makes a circle" (like 1 → 4). She succeeds immediately for 1 → 3. In

[4]For the sake of brevity, we speak of an inversion of 180° when passing from the point at one end of an arc to the point at the other end. Subjects themselves sometimes compare this reversal to what one obtains with a rotation of 180° on a circle.

comparing a circle to this figure, she shows that at 180° on the circle, "It's upside down."—"And do you find the same thing here?"—(She indicates the points at the extremities by an arc).

PAT (7 years, 1 month): With regard to the direction of the head, PAT succeeds right away on the composition 1 to 3 (opposite positions). However, when the doll is turned 90° relative to one of the points, she feels a need to follow the whole path of movement with her fingers (as she did for the ∞ in section 3) but still cannot deduce the result of movement along the diagonal from 1 to 3. She has the same difficulties for 2 to 4, but when the doll's orientation conforms to one of the points, she immediately gives correct compositions, saying "I made the movement" (mentally).

LUC (7 years): LUC correctly predicts the result for 1 → 2 and admits that the movement 1 → 3 → 4 → 2[5] would produce equivalent results: "Even so, the head would be toward that corner . . . it has to be toward that corner."—"Why 'has to be'?"—(He shows why with his fingers.) Like LIP, he supposes it would be possible to pass by the diagonal from 2 → 4 but:—"Are 1 → 2 → 4 and 1 → 2 → 3 → 4 the same?"—"No, once the head is on top and once on bottom." By contrast, he does not master problems caused by turning the doll 90° and needs to examine the situation step by step.

DAN (7 years, 5 months): DAN is asked to compare the pointed figure with the figure eight. He responds, "In the ∞, it's the same from there to there (indicating the two extremities) but not in this figure (diagonal 1 → 3)."

MIC (8 years, 8 months): MIC succeeds on all questions. When asked about the diagonal 1 → 3, he indicates the inversion immediately: "Can you explain it to me in terms of the four corners?"—"They both (the two methods) work together."

Once again, then, one finds intermorphic compositions, although more complicated ones than those found in section 3, and that is so whether their construction proceeds by establishing connections successively (PAT, etc.) or by necessary deduction ("has to be" says LUC). At the present intermorphic level, one already sees the rough outline of an analogy between four points on a circle and the figure produced by reversing four 90° arcs of a circle extending their junctions into oblique lines. For example, SAB says of

[5]The text is ambiguous with regard to movements noted 1 → 3, 2 → 4, and so on, and also with regard to the word *diagonal.* At times Piaget appears to speak of direct movements from one point, say 1, diagonally across the figure to the opposite point, say 3. In those cases the position of the bear would not be inverted. At other times, Piaget seems to use the notation and word as a sort of a shorthand for starting and ending positions reached by following the arcs of the figure, in which case the bear would be inverted—Translator.

an arc that "it also makes a circle," whereas DAN opposes going upside down on the diagonal 1 → 3 to returning upright in the case of a double circle ∞, which is another manner of seeing a correspondence with arcs that are not turned backward. The full analogy, however, is only stated explicitly at Level III.

In subjects from 11–12 to 15 years old, there is transition to transmorphism to the extent that the composition of correspondences results from operations inherent in a general system. But in the particular case of the internal correspondences belonging to rotations or circumductions, the only novelty that characterizes Level III consists in coordinating the two reference systems internal and external to the figure:

DOM (15 years, 1 month): DOM answers all the usual questions correctly. When he is asked what the bear is looking at, he responds that it is always what is in front of him, but in one case it will be outside the circle of movement and in the other case at its center.

PAT (11 years, 2 months): By contrast, PAT does not make this remark spontaneously. When she is asked about the positions of the inhabitants of the earth's antipodes, however, she responds that "people's positions are always the same" and concludes, therefore, that "the bear always looks at the same point. Sometimes that point is outside (circumduction), and sometimes inside the figure (rotation)." For m she points to the two extremities and says, "You have made two half circles. It is as if you had made a complete turn."

Thus, development is achieved in three main steps. The intramorphic level is characterized by either correct or incorrect local correspondences without compositions. At the intermorphic level, correspondences that are to be composed rest on operatory transformations from which they can be deduced after having prepared the way for the constitution or comprehension of those transformations. But even in such cases of inter- or cotransformational correspondences, composition at first only consists in linking correspondences together through new correspondences of higher degree (e.g., linking elementary successions). Only later can such correspondences be inferred starting from an operatory calculus. It is this composition of morphisms by means of operatory deduction but based on a general system that characterizes the transmorphism. An example would be PAT's reasoning on the figure eight (with certain responses of Level II). A second example would be where the permanent direction of the bear's gaze toward the same point is understood to be common to rotation (point at the center) and circumduction (external point). This understanding is transmorphic insofar as it is drawn from the operatory coordination of two systems of reference, internal and external. The role of such coordination is seen more clearly in chapter 3, "The Rotation of Cubes," when the subject passes from the six faces of a cube to their 24 possible positions deduced by considering external references.

In a word, this first chapter indicates what we find repeatedly. In general, transformations are prepared by correspondences that (among other things) may later be deduced from them. Similarly, compositions among correspondences, or in other words among morphismic transformations, begin with intermorphic forms that prepare general operatory systems. It is from such general systems that operations will be drawn that will subsequently permit the composition of morphisms in their transmorphismic modes. Thus, the progressive mutual support of elementary correspondences and elementary transformations gradually extends into interaction and, eventually, into interaction in alternate directions between operatory and morphismic transformations.

2 The Composition of Two Cyclic Successions

Jean Piaget
with
D. Voelin-Liambey
and
I. Berthoud-Papandropoulou

In order to help the reader understand the problem of correspondences posed for the child in this chapter,[1] it seems useful to begin with a description of the apparatus used. That apparatus is composed of two concentric superimposed disks. Both can be turned independently of one another in either direction. The disk on the bottom has forms drawn on it; the disk on top is made of colored transparent plastic. The form disk is divided into fourths and the resulting sectors numbered 1, 2, 3, 4. On sector 1 a triangle has been drawn, on sector 2 a star, on sector 3 a square, and on sector 4 a cross. The four sectors of the colored disk are composed of different colored transparent plastic material and are lettered a, b, c, d. Sector a is red, sector b is blue, sector c is yellow, and sector d is green. Moreover, the four absolute positions that the sectors of either disk can occupy are numbered I, II, III, IV. I is at the top, II is to the right, III is at the bottom, and IV is to the left (see Fig. 2.1).

By turning one or the other or both of the disks, it is possible to compose 16 different "global objects," for example, la would be a red triangle, lb would be a blue triangle, 2a would be a red star, 2b would be a blue star, and so forth. In addition to the two disks, the experimenter also uses a circular screen with a quarter sector missing which allows only what is in one of the four absolute positions to be seen.

Using this device, it is easy to have children construct a series of correspondences, that is, nontransformational, intertransformational, or

[1]This chapter was extensively revised (and much improved) for the French edition. I have incorporated the revisions here—Translator.

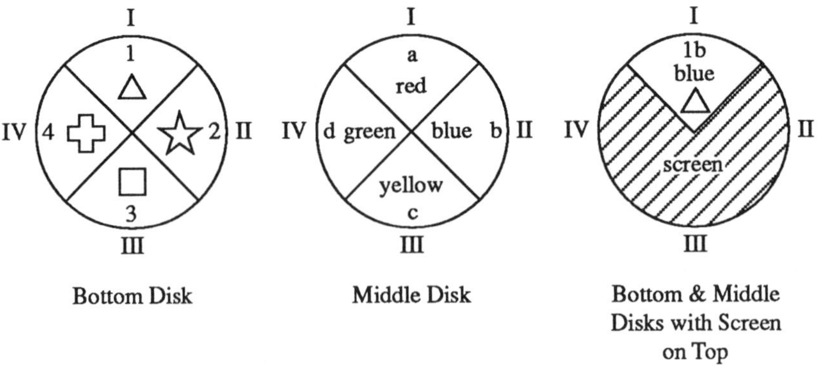

FIG. 2.1. Superimposed disk apparatus.

cotransformational. Even more essential from the point of view of our goals, it is possible, by screening three of the four positions, to have them construct a series of compositions among correspondences. For example, if only position I is visible, the experimenter can replace 1a by 2c in that position and ask what would be found in positions II, III, or IV. To answer correctly, the child must infer from the replacement of 1a by 2c that the disk with the shapes on it has been turned one unit couterclockwise and that the disk with the colors has been turned two units in either direction. Hence, 3d would be found in position II, 4a in position III, and 1b in position IV. The need for inferences of this sort is even stronger if the subject is asked to turn the disks himself in order to obtain, starting from whatever there is in position I, a certain combination such as 3d in position II "at the same time" that 1b is in position IV. And when the investigator asks the child for combinations that cannot be obtained such as 2c in position III at the same time as 4a in position IV, even more complex compositions among correspondences are needed to discover and explain why the task cannot be done. Moreover, in order to concretize their inferences, subjects are provided with memory aids in the form of cutouts of the four forms and four small pieces of colored cardboard. These are discrete elements; no disks are involved. The child can arrange these objects spontaneously to create what one might call an intermorphic model, which we will simply call a "model." Such models permit one to study, in addition to correspondences between the disks, correspondences between the disks and the memory aids. This provides a supplementary and often decisive source of information.

In sum, then, this investigation has to do with the composition of morphisms with one another more than with their respective isolable forms. Because the same subject can present different types of compositions, especially with progress made in the course of questioning, we describe the facts in terms of levels of composition and not in terms of the subject's level.

1. TECHNIQUE

The experimenter begins by familiarizing the subject with the apparatus, demonstrating rotations of one or both disks, and having the child carry out numerous transformations in both directions of rotation. Then, after the subject constructs a model of the apparatus, the investigator introduces the screen. Throughout the experiment, three of the four disk sectors in positions I–IV are hidden; usually only the sector in position I is visible. By contrast, the model remains entirely at the subject's disposition. He can manipulate it as he wishes as questions about the disks are put to him or he can limit himself to visual reference in order to remind himself of one relationship or another (the starting state being 1a in I).

After this is done, the experimenter goes on to question the child about the situation that we call A_1, where only position I is visible and where the investigator rotates only one of the disks in arbitrary fashion (i.e., either $1 \rightarrow 4$, $1 \rightarrow 2$, $1 \rightarrow 3$, or $a \rightarrow c$, $a \rightarrow d$, $a \rightarrow b$ in either direction) thereby changing what is visible. For example, 2a may be seen instead of 1a or 1c instead of 1a.[2] The investigator then asks the subject to infer, using his model as he understands it, what will be found in positions II or IV (neighboring positions) or in position III (opposite).

In situation A_2, the experimenter turns both disks, modifying both the form and color seen in position I (e.g., 2c instead of la). The amplitude of rotation can be different for each disk, which creates new global objects (e.g., 2c replaces la in position I). But it can also be the same for both disks, which only changes the absolute positions, the global objects and their relative positions remaining identical (e.g., 4d instead of la in position I).

By contrast, in situations designated B, the investigator asks the child to form a global object in one of the hidden position (II–IV). The child is, of course, allowed to use his model where everything is visible. It is the child, therefore, who must effect the rotation of one of the disks (situation B_1) or of them both (situation B_2). For example, a child might be given la in position I (visible) and asked to "do what you have to" so that 2c will be in position IV or 3b in position II (positions neighboring I) or so that 4d will be in position III (the position opposite to I).

Situations C again call for rotations to be executed by the child himself, but the goal this time is to obtain a pair of objects in two positions simultaneously. For example, given la in position I, the child is instructed to "do what you have to so that at the same time" you will have 1b in position II and 2c in position III (neighboring positions) or so that you will have 3d in position II and 1b in position IV (II and IV being opposite from one another). It is obvious that, being given a global object in one position, the

[2]Global objects are named "red square," "green triangle," and so forth.

three other global objects are completely determined. The reason for questions of type C is to introduce situation D where the pairs asked for are impossible and where the subject has to discover and explain that fact.

2. INTRAMORPHIC CORRESPONDENCES

As already agreed, by intramorphic correspondences we mean correspondences that are simply imposed by direct readings of empirical content or by direct anticipations based on such readings,[3] but without compositions of correspondences with one another. One observes this lack of composition starting with the explorations young subjects undertake in order to become familiar with the apparatus (where everything is still visible):

CAR (7 years, 3 months): CAR alternates turning the two disks and says, "You can't have the same color and not the same form." She then enumerates both series of four. The investigator shows her the blue square in position IV and asks, "Can you have a green square?"—"Yes" (she correctly turns the color disk). "Is there another way?" After putting the square back in position IV, she moves it to position II which is green, and so on. She seems, therefore, to have understood everything and to be ready to answer the questions that will be put to her in situation B with the screen. But subsequently the interrogation goes as follows: "How many colors can the square have?"—"It can have four."—"And the other shapes?"—"Yes, . . . no, they can't be moved, that can't get up and go there" (she indicates turning the green triangle in position II back up to position I). Subsequently, however, she understands the different possibilities, and the investigator is able to go on to questions with the screen.

VER (7 years, 5 months): In order to change a triangle from red to green, VER proceeds by trial-and-error turning of the color disk. "And without moving the colors?"—"No."—"Try."—"Yes, you can turn the disk with the shapes." She changes the shapes in one direction, then the other. "No, because it's the shapes, and the shapes change if you turn them." Finally, she succeeds. The model at first is constructed without correct succession, then the succession is respected.

These explorations, groping at first but more rapid from age 8 years on, are sufficient to allow the investigator to pose questions with the screen where only position I can be seen. One then can discern a number of correspondences that are evident from the start or that are acquired at the intramorphic level. As predicted, however, these do not yet give rise to the

[3]See the conclusion of this section.

systematic compositions of the intermorphic level and, for that reason, do not make it possible to resolve every kind of problem. In this regard, the easiness of the questions in situation B—and even in C—compared to the relative difficulty of the problems in situation A, already reveals differences between simple correspondences and compositions. In B, it suffices to make a displacement correspond to the absolute position assigned as goal, whereas in A, it is necessary to compose a series of absolute positions bcda or cdab, and so on, starting from the series abcd where a alone is visible in position I. In A, therefore, each series already contains a morphism of succession and the inferences asked for contain, therefore, a composition of those elementary correspondences with one another.

That said, let us try to analyze the correspondences that come into play at the intramorphic level as well as the compositional mistakes that are possible. The first correspondence is, of course, the figural isomorphism between the four shapes distributed on the four sectors of one disk and the four colors distributed on the four sectors of the other. A second isomorphism that is obvious from the start is the one linking the disks to the models constructed as memory aides. If the first of these bijections becomes instructive only when it is composed with correspondences of succession linked to rotation, the same is even truer of the second correspondence. This is because the models are composed of objects that are not drawn on disks, and that do not, therefore, enjoy continuous support. The rotations that eventually will be introduced into the model must, therefore, be inferred from compositions, and the model begins by being only a figurative and static copy. Certain young subjects even place the model elements around the disk apparatus before putting them into an independent circle, and, in any case, the model only represents one particular state of the objects on the disks. The subject, then, has no idea of using it in order to answer the questions put to him because he does not conceive every state as the result of transformation by rotation. This is the reason for the breaks in order that are described later on. At the level of transmorphic correspondences (section 4), we see that subjects 11 or 12 years old no longer need to manipulate the model because they succeed in decentering and in making enough inferences to mentally transform the state represented by the model. The latter, then, is reduced to the simple function of jogging the memory.

A third form of correspondence evident from the beginning is the surjection that makes the four colors correspond to a single form or, reciprocally, that makes four shapes correspond to a single color. Because young subjects lack compositional skills, they do not conclude from this correspondence that there will be 16 distinct global objects as subjects 8 or 9 years old will do.

The fourth type of correspondences, that is, those that link an object (form or color) to its immediate successor, is fundamental. Even though such correspondences are easy to establish empirically at the intramorphic level, mastery of them disappears from the moment that they have to be inferentially composed.

CAR (7 years, 3 months): Before she is asked to, CAR, seeing the yellow triangle in position I in situation A, correctly lists the colors corresponding to the other sectors. "And the shapes?"—"They're always the same" (except in the model, although she follows the succession a → b, and so on, on the partly masked disk). By contrast, as soon as the star is moved to position I, she supposes that the cross will be in position II even though it does not neighbor position I. She also thinks that the square will be in position IV even though it comes after the star in the model. Similarly for the red triangle in position I on both the model and the disks, she indicates that the green cross will be in position IV, saying, "It's in exactly the same order," but the succession and the neighboring relationships are lost when a different object is put in position I.

PAM (7 years, 11 months): After having constructed her model by exactly copying one state of the disks, PAM says, "You can hide and then turn them. Me, too; I can turn them and then find them again." However, she simply permutes the triangle and the cross on her model and then turns both disks simultaneously by a quarterturn. She thinks that this will adjust the disks to her modified model! She even believes so much in the correctness of these operations that when the disk is uncovered she accuses the experimenter: "That's not right because there are the shapes and you've turned there (the shapes) on the bottom and on top (the colors)," as if one could, as she believed she had done herself, alter the relationships of succession on the disks just by rotating them.

In sum, such correspondences of immediate succession are a matter of course insofar as they do not have to be composed with one another except in terms of simple linear sequences. At the intramorphic level, however, they still give rise to difficulties when a given series must be composed with one to be inferred.

A fifth form of correspondences also bears on the invariance of successions, but invariance that is independent of the direction of rotation. In other words, it arises from the fact that one can reach a given configuration whether the disks move in accordance with or contrary to the movement of the hands of a watch. Understanding conservation of this sort requires composition and, at the intramorphic level, is far from being immediately achieved, except by empirical determination, as in the following:

PAM (7 years, 11 months): PAM was just cited previously. When now asked if it is legitimate to permute objects between positions I and II, she responds, "No, because if you turned (indicates clockwise direction) [it was not necessary] to do just that one but also the others" and she moves the blue in the model from position II to position I, the yellow from position III to position IV, the green from position IV to position II, and the red from position I to position III, thus mixing the two directions of the paths. By contrast, she subsequently discovers that one can achieve the same result by adopting one or the other of the two directions without mixing them; and, after having seen the experimenter turn the color disk in one direction in order to bring the green triangle to position I, she correctly reconstitutes the elements of position II, III, IV by following the opposite direction. At the end of her long interrogation, she succeeds at the intermorphic level, declaring with respect to the series 1234, 2341, 3412, and 4123, "It's always the same thing, but you begin with other numbers" and that these successions are found in both directions of rotation.

This question of direction leads to a sixth form of correspondence as general as that of the immediate successor. It has to do with the fact that the direction from which an element moves into a position as well as the direction in which the replaced object leaves it both correspond to the position in question. But this oriented displacement is not necessarily related to the amount of rotation[4] or length of the trajectory, to the overall sequence of successions, or even to the direction of rotation (because permutations may be involved that are not understood to result from such rotations). See the following example:

CAR (7 years, 3 months): CAR succeeds for all manipulations of situation B. Presented with 1a (red triangle) in position I and asked to put 3d in position IV, she demonstrates the transition from position III to position IV (both masked) by saying, "you have to turn the little wheel a half turn" but actually making only a quarter turn. She performs similarly on five other questions of this type. By contrast, when 4a succeeds 1a in position I and she is asked where 3 has gone, she at first indicates that it is between positions I and II, as if it had not been dragged along by the replacing element. She then changes her response, indicating that it is in position II, therefore mistaking the direction, because it has moved to position IV. Then, finding it in

[4]I have translated *écart* as "amount of rotation" because the context here, the first in which it appears, clearly relates the term to the idea of how many quarter turns an element has moved from the starting position—Translator.

position IV, she cannot explain why because she makes no appeal to the general rotation.

Usually, children succeed on oriented displacements of this sort in situation B but not in situation A. In this case, however, they also succeed in situation A (recall that the interrogation always begins with situation A), but only for certain privileged rotations producing permutations along the diameters I–III and II–IV. The problem, then, is to establish whether such successes indicate real understanding of rotational successions and, therefore, composition, or whether they result from simple correspondences by symmetry. What the facts show is that young subjects who discover permutations along diameters also claim that the exchange I ⇆ II is possible, and so forth:

GRE (7 years, 7 months): Situation A: Given 3c in position I, he is asked what is in position III. "A red triangle (1a)."—"How do you know?"—"Because it's upside-down. Before, there (I) was red (a, as on his model), you turned it, now that (I) becomes yellow (c) and that (III) is red (a)." Similarly, he permutes position II and IV "because you've turned them too." He seems, therefore, to understand everything by means of compositions based on rotations. However, immediately afterward for 1d in position I, he cannot say what there is in position IV. "I don't know what it changed with." He tries the permutation I ⇆ IV that he had claimed was possible during explorations without the screen only to be contradicted by the facts.

PAM (7 years, 11 months): We just presented PAM's final successes. Here, like GRE, she easily permutes position I and III, then position II and IV on her model, subsequently applying the permutations to the disk. That, however, does not hinder her on two separate occasions from permuting the objects in position I and IV while leaving position II and III unchanged.

OLI (8 years, 3 months): Situation A: In order to reconstitute the hidden objects when 2a is in position I, OLI immediately permutes position I and III (whence, 4c is opposite), but stops there. "I can't do any more. I don't know what you'll find there and there (positions II and IV)." Subsequently, like previous subjects, he comes to permute I ⇆ II without changing the others. It is only at the end of the interrogation that he conforms to the correspondences of succession.

Thus, we see that in order to reconstitute the trajectory of the visible object as well as the one displaced, the simplest solution is a sort of symmetry or reciprocity between the directions → and ← or ↑ and ↓ , and that this symmetry may be generalized to the point of permutations between neighboring terms. We are, therefore, far from a composition by cyclic successions. Simply regarding the closure of the set, however, we see in three of the four 7-year-olds the construction of a remarkable system. Although the circuit followed is not circular, it is nevertheless closed:

PAM (7 years, 11 months): PAM moves the blue from position II to position I on her model and the yellow from position III to position IV. The two displacements are, therefore, parallel but in opposite directions. She then moves the green from position IV to position II and the red from position I to position III, crossing the two orthogonal diameters. This results in the series bdac that does not conform to circular succession but that constitutes a closed circuit II → I → III → IV → II.[5]

Again, then, we find in these illusory compositions a sort of symmetry between II-I and III-IV and a form of reciprocity between the two subsequences II-I-III and III-IV-II which closes the general circuit. These precocious tendencies toward symmetry can, however, have a positive result. We see this in the case of CAR, who moves on from such beginnings to understand that the same result can be obtained by two different routes, that is, by moving a color over a from or, reciprocally, by moving a form under a color.

The seventh sort of correspondence links pairs of positions to the amounts of rotations among elements. If it is only a matter of the length of a single element's path, the question reduces to the question of successions. When, however, one must reason on the simultaneous positions of two objects, there is the added difficulty of conserving the amount of rotation. This makes this correspondence more complex than that of the direction of movements, especially where questions of situation D having to do with impossible pairs are concerned:

PAM (7 years, 11 months): For the blue star in position II and the green triangle in position III (impossible), PAM realizes the latter position and having placed the blue star in position II on her model imagines that is also that way on the disk. After establishing that this is not the case, she nevertheless tries to turn her disks in order to obtain the impossible configuration.

As for the possible correspondences bearing on relative successions independently of absolute positions—"two places after" as DOM (11 years,

[5]This example from PAM is analogous to that of the same subject cited earlier with respect to directions.

3 months) will say, they belong to the transmorphic level and are not encountered here. The general character of the intermorphic level with which we are presently concerned seems to be, in line with the preceding facts, the ease with which the seven types of correspondences just discussed can be empirically established along with the difficulty subjects have in composing them with one another. However, we have yet to understand this character, because by manipulating his model in order to infer what is under the screen, the subject already composes successions, etcetera. These are read off the model by introducing a morphism between the two. We must, therefore, do one of two things. On the one hand, we might exclude coordinations between correspondences and too-direct equivalences from the definition of the term "composition." On the other, we might take the wiser course of admitting a gradation in the complexity of compositions and the possibility, for each subject, of multiple reactions depending on the problem to be solved. In the latter case, intra-, inter-, and transmorphic levels would be, as mentioned previously, levels of construction in the composition of correspondences and not (or only partially) levels of subjects.

3. INTERMORPHIC CORRESPONDENCES

What the preceding reactions have in common is that they do not result in the constitution of a complete cyclic succession. Despite subjects expressing themselves in terms of "turning" and constructing their model in circular form, they do not succeed in subordinating successive positions to a general rotation that takes account of successions and amounts of rotation. By contrast, intermorphic correspondences lead to that result, even though they still only compare absolute positions without achieving what we call relative successions and the "freedom" that transmorphic correspondences enjoy. See the following case:

TIE (8 years, 5 months): With his first explorations, TIE establishes the existence of four colors and concludes "eight, no, 16" objects because "you turn four times with the green, four with the red (etc.) and all that makes 2 × 8, that makes 16." Similarly, he sees right off that "it's the same whether you turn the shapes or the colors." In situation A with the green in position I, the investigator asks what color is in position IV. TIE begins without compositions: "It should be blue (he indicates position II opposite to position IV in the model), no, red (at position I on the model and, therefore, next to green but in the wrong direction on the disks)." He then goes on to compositions: "You've changed all the colors. The red there (I → II), the blue there (II → III), the yellow there (III → IV) and the green there (IV → I). It makes a complete turn plus one notch (quarter turn) there . . . then five (quarter turns)."—"Then here (IV)?"—"The yellow, and here (III) the blue, and here (II) the red."—"And what form here (in position IV, unchanged)?"—"The cross." They check. "That was right." For 2a in position I, TIE again makes the movements step by step, but he does this mentally by looking at the model rather than by moving the disks. He responds correctly that 3b is in position II, but he produces this response by making a three-quarter turn clockwise instead of a quarter turn backward from II → I.[6] Subsequently, he uses the same indirect method to infer lc in position IV starting from 2d in position I instead of being content with the transition from IV → I. By contrast, by starting from la in position II and basing his reasoning on the successions 1 → 2 and a → d, he quickly agrees that it would be possible to have both ld in position II and 2a in position IV (impossible). For other impossible pairs, he comes back to displacements step by step and empirically establishes what cannot be realized without explaining why.

This beautiful case illustrates both the progress and the limitations of the intermorphic level. The most evident progress is the composition of successions and amounts of rotation at the heart of the displacements. Being given a displacement of a color (green in position I), TIE rapidly sees that the experimenter has "changed all the colors," and he demonstrates this in the order of successions in such a way that he ends up with "five" quarter turns as the amount of rotation. But the limitations of this method are due to proceeding step by step (*groupement!*) rather than in terms of relative positions. The result is that, in certain cases, the subject is so centered on the immediate successors to be composed that he forgets simplifications that might be possible, notably the fact that the product of rotations in the two directions is invariant, as in the following:

MIC (9 years, 5 months): Given a displacement, MIC says "in this direction, all of that is shifted." Nevertheless, he concludes that you can obtain the opposite order by rotating in the other direction. For lb in position I, he infers that in position IV "the cross is red (a) or it's yellow (c); it depends on what direction you turned it." However, after an analysis of the movements, he concludes "if you had turned it like that (direction opposite to the first rotation) it would still be red here

[6]Here and in the example that follows, I have reversed the order of the positions to make them correspond to the description of the apparatus given in section 1. The manuscript actually indicates I → II and I → IV, but this does not make sense—Translator.

(IV)." Finally, he goes on to shapes that presage the transmorphic. "If the square is in IV, the star will be in III. It's always behind; it always pushes the star; it can't be in front."

MAN (10 years, 4 months): For a situation as simple as inferring the object in position III from lc in position I, young subjects make the direct permutation I $\leftrightarrows$ III. MAN, however, devotes himself to multiple rotations of both cycles on his model. These are all rapid and correct, but they are performed without seeing that everything cancels out. Only after making quarter turns forward of both form and color, then a quarter turn forward of color, then a quarter turn backward of color, and then quarter turns backward of both form and color does he correctly deduce that 3a will be in position III without still needing to change the places of the elements themselves. But subsequently, he goes back to his step-by-step method, only discovering the equivalence of the results of rotations performed in both directions through experience. He proceeds similarly for impossible pairs and makes errors when he is queried about them. Thus, he states that it would be possible to have 2d in position III along with 3a in position IV, but later finds in the abstract the impossibilities of two simultaneous transitions from position I to position III and from position III to position IV, because I → III brings about III → I.

All problems, then, end up being solved through compositions of successions, directions, and amounts of rotation even though, as MIC declares "everything is shifted." Although it is true that such compositions lead eventually to the constitution of correct and invariant sequencing of shapes and colors in both directions, this sequencing is only discovered and handled step by step by displacing elements from one position to the following position. Such a method not only is limited by the fact that the transformations involved are linked to one another and have no "freedom," but it is costly in addition, as shown by the useless multiple rotations of the subjects just discussed as well as by TIE's five quarter turns instead of a single quarter turn from position IV to position I. In a word, intermorphic correspondences permit the formation of invariant connections, as in the case of the square that "is always behind the star" and "pushes" it according to MIC. They do not, however, attain the general organization characteristic of operatory structures with all of their simultaneous morphisms. As partially inferential compositions, they enjoy a certain degree of necessity, but this necessity is local, so to speak, because such compositions proceed step by step without reaching the closure of the systems seen at the following level. As for the nature of these intermorphic compositions, they depend, of course, on transformations (rotations), because they necessarily result from them. As morphisms, however, they consist in correspondences among correspondences. The fact that the square is behind the star, as MIC says, is already a correspondence insofar as it is a repeatable relationship. Combined with other correspondences of the same rank, it gives rise to regular successions that constitute other correspondences, but this time these are correspondences among partial correspondences that have now become components in a larger system. One can, therefore, characterize intermorphic compositions as the construction of correspondences of second degree.

4. TRANSMORPHIC CORRESPONDENCES

First, here follow some facts:

DOM (11 years, 3 months): From the first question (situation A), DOM says that if 1d is in position I, 3a will be found in position III because "the green (d) was there (I), it's two after and, because the square was there (3 in position III), it's two after".[7] For 3b in position I, 2a will be at position IV (correct) because it is "this one which was in front, and the color (a) in front of the blue (b)." He continues in similar fashion: "If the square is yellow, I move everything forward a notch. The colors, I will have 4d, la, 2b," and so on. He immediately gives reasons for impossible pairs and invents an example: 1 in position II and 4 in position IV "because they're not opposite each other, they're side by side (4,1 on the disk)." In order to show that all colors can be paired with all shapes and that all shapes can be paired with all colors, he immediately constructs a square with 16 boxes (Cartesian product) and continues to answer questions correctly without consulting his model.

LOU (11 years, 8 months): "You're forced to move a notch, which does the same thing (as in the other direction). If you do the opposite (other direction), you move all three. The color that comes after will always continue to be after (invariance of successions)." For the green square in position I replacing the red triangle, "the triangle has to be on the bottom (III); it's a red triangle." Or again, in order to prove the impossibility of the star in position IV with the triangle in position I, which he invents as an example, he says, "If you do that with the star (from position II to position IV), the triangle has to move here (from position I to position III)."

[7]Note that this is incorrect: 3b would be found in III. Whether this is the actual response or a mistake in both the manuscript and French edition is of no consequence, because the conclusion that Piaget draws from it, that is, that it represents reasoning in terms of a general system, remains unchanged—Translator.;fnt

CLA (12 years): CLA constructs a linear model rather than a copy of the circles and immediately solves the problem of the yellow triangle in position III. The red square will be in position I because, in the model "it's two places after the square." For the triangle in position I and the cross in position III (impossible), she says, "That doesn't work, the cross will be here (IV). I'm sure. If you make it turn in the other direction, it's the same. Whether you go one way or the other, you come back to the same point."

CRI (12 years, 1 month): CRI sees immediately whether a pair is possible or not through inferences starting from immobile states of the model. "Can you try?"—"I can (he takes hold of the disks). No, it comes back to the same place." The investigator asks him to invent some pairs, either possible or not. "The impossible ones are easier." He then indicates on the model neighboring relationships excluded by separations, and so forth.

The first general characteristic of these reactions is that the subject no longer reasons step by step in terms of immediate successors but in relational terms describing the sequences of the system in general. Moreover, he does this independently of absolute positions except when applying these relationships to elements or to their variable replacements. It is for this reason that expressions such as "it is two after" or "one in front" (DOM), "it is two places after the square" (CLA), and especially "The color that comes after will always continue to be after" (LOU) are invariant relationships that are part of a complete cyclic succession and no longer positions established step by step. Among other things, the explanation given for the conservation of this succession in relation to both directions of rotation results from such a system. As LOU says, a quarter turn in one direction equals three quarter turns in the other and leaves the relative positions unchanged (cf. also, CLA).

The second general property of transmorphic correspondences of this sort has to do with the generalization of their necessary character, insofar as they are deduced from transformations that henceforth constitute a closed structure (group of rotations). "You're forced to" or "has to" says LOU several times or "I'm sure" says CLA who, like other subjects, gives the reason that certain pairs are impossible instead of only establishing that fact after several tries (tries that CRI judges useless since the necessity of his deductions suffices).

The third correlative aspect of the transmorphism is the "freedom" of transformations and cotransformational correspondences. This freedom is defined by the double characteristic of "arbitrary" departure point and "univocal" arrival point, and it is opposed to the still "bound" status of the intermorphic procedures. Thus, the subject may start from no matter what position or element in order to end up with another single element whose position is determined by the general system without any longer needing for Ia to be in position I as it is in his model. Moreover, the model is no longer a static configuration but simply a tool for helping the subject remember the set of successions and amounts of rotation, invariant and independent of the direction of rotation, at the heart of modifications substituting one global object for another in a given position.

The invariance within subsets of substitutable positions allows such correspondences to be considered as morphisms conserving the structure. That was already the case with intermorphic correspondences, but there it was accomplished step by step without simultaneous visualization of the system or freely substitutable arrangements of the elements. With transmorphic correspondences, however, one may begin to speak of automorphisms and to consider the elements and their relationships, both free and obligatory, as consituting the beginning of an "elementary category" ("special category" in the terminology of Wittmann-MacLane or "precategory" in that of Henriques). Independent of all terminology, this difference in the mode of composition separating transmorphic from intermorphic correspondences is instructive. At the intermorphic level correspondences are only constructed to the second degree, and the components of such correspondences are based on the transformations that constitute their terms or contents. At the level of transmorphic correspondences, however, something peculiar happens. At that level, these correspondences are composed with one another by means of a logical calculus the instruments of which are nothing other than the generalized product of the transformations serving as content at the intermorphic level. In other words, the subject operates on morphisms and integrates them into a whole by means of a general operatory system that he has constructed with the help of their predecessors.

3 The Rotation of Cubes

Jean Piaget
with
A. Moreau

The experiment reported in this chapter again deals with rotation. In this case, however, the subject no longer just follows a circular path drawn on a piece of cardboard or imposed on him by disks. Here it is a matter of discovering rotatory laws by making rotational movements. In large part, the subject makes the movements himself. An approach of this sort provides more information about the relationship between rotations and transformations that can be used in unraveling the problem of compositions. It allows us to examine that question by going back even to the preliminary but essential question posed in chapter 1 of knowing whether the initial comparisons and correspondences that prepare the way for transformations are sufficient to generate them or whether, on the contrary, it is transformations that determine and stabilize correspondences pending their composition.

1. TECHNIQUE

The experiment employs different sorts of cubes. Some are completely blank; some have a cross on one side; some have a cross on one side and a solid circle on a contiguous side; some have little men with their arms crossed on one or several sides; some have parts of a drawing on each side and can, like a puzzle, be put together with other disks to form a picture.

The experiment is carried out in steps, the order of which is variable:

1. Starting with a blank cube sitting on a square (base) drawn with pencil on a sheet of paper, the experimenter asks for different ways in which the

cube can be turned (problem of nonfinalized rotations and of the existence of "virtual" actions).

2. The subject is given a cube with a cross on the side facing him. The experimenter asks him to show the different ways in which the cube can be turned so that the cross will no longer be visible (problem of finalized rotations).

3. The subject is asked to compare different positions for different cubes (problems of the status of "state," of the utilization of indices internal to the cube, and of the existence of an external reference system).

4. The subject is asked to compare different rotations of a cube with their opposites (problem of the status of the "transformation").

5. The subject is given a cube with a cross and asked to compare different combinations of rotations. For example, he is asked to compare a quarter turn forward (¼F) followed by a quarter turn to the left (¼L) with a quarter turn left (¼L) followed by a quarter turn forward (¼F) (problems of the prediction of end states, of the coordination of transformations, and of the existence of a system of transformations).

6. The subject is asked to predict end states for n quarter turns forward (n • ¼F) or n quarter turns to the left (n • ¼L) (problems of the status of transformation and of understanding cyclic order, i.e., of intertransformational morphisms and of intermorphic compositions).

7. The subject is asked to anticipate the number of pictures that could be constructed using four cubes covered with puzzle pieces and to construct six of them (problems of the construction of the cubic object insofar as the sides are concerned and of side-to-picture biunivocal correspondences).

8. The subject is asked to anticipate, describe, and generate the set of positions for a single cube (problems of the status of state, of the system of states, of the existence of an external reference system, of cotransformational morphisms, and of the transition to the quotient).

9. The subject is asked to represent states and transformations in terms of a matrix and to calculate a final state by combining matrices of rotation (problems of the transition to represented transformations, of cotransformational morphisms, and of transmorphic compositions).

2. INTRAMORPHIC CORRESPONDENCES

Let us call transformations due to the subject's actions *material transformations.* Although such transformations are a special case of the *operatory transformations* discussed in chapter 1, in reality they only consist of various actions and are preoperatory.[1] Also, let us call sides or the presence of indices including the tardy establishment of relationships to an external reference system *states*. Later on we distinguish states from "positions." That said, the intermorphic correspondences first seen (around 5 or 6 years of age) may be characterized in a negative way by the absence of correspondence between material transformations and distinct states. Positively, however, they may be characterized by a sort of generalized and abusive bijection between states that appear to resemble each other, between material transformations that seem disparate to us, and between states and transformations. See the following cases:

FRA (5 years, 5 months): FRA envisions a rotation to the left and another backward among the possibilities, but it is "the same thing because you move it like that and like that."—"But is it the same when the cube is like that?"—"Yes, because it's flat there and on the other side, too." For a given rotation, he predicts that the cross will go "there behind" and then finds that it is "on bottom," but it is still the same "because it is still a square." After this, he recognizes that, starting with the cross on bottom, it will change if it is turned: "One time there I won't see it, and one time I'll see it."—"And if I turn to this side or to that one, is it the same?"—"No."—"Why isn't it the same?"—"Because when you put it there you don't see it, and when you put it there you don't see it."—"Then?"—"It's the same." Finally, he appreciates differences relative to direction "because the cube moves there (¼L) and after there (¼F)." He counts four then five sides.

MEN (6 years, 2 months): MEN seems to see the differences in positions from the start. "You can do this side (¼B—backward) and the other (¼F)." She is shown the cube with the cross facing her. "If I turn it this way (¼F), where will the cross be? . . . Is it still going to be looking at you?"—"I think so."—"Are you sure?"—"Yes." The movement is made. "On bottom!"—"And now (sideward rotation)?"—"Toward me."—"It's going to be looking at you again?"—"Yes." The movement is made; the prediction was correct. "It's on the other side!"—"But is the cross still looking at you?"—"Yes."—"But it isn't looking at you the same way?"—"No! Yes, it's the same, but there it was in front and there behind (in fact, a quarter turn to the side)."—"And like that

[1]In the French text, Piaget introduces acronyms for the various kinds of transformations. Tfm, he says, refers to *transformations matérielles* that are a special case of the Tfo mentioned in chapter 1. The problem is that there is no reference to Tfo in chapter 1. I reason, therefore, that Tfo must refer to the *transformations opératoires* discussed at the end of the present chapter, chapter 3. Because notations of this sort are difficult for the reader, I have eliminated them altogether—Translator.

(toward her)?"—"Not in front . . . toward me." She tries. "It's on the bottom (unexpected)." The experimenter then tries different positions without the cross. "Here's a side that's all white." Several turns are made. "Is it the same white side looking at you each time?"—"No (not sure) . . . Yes."—"Are you sure?"—"Yes." A little circle is drawn on one of the blank sides and the block is turned. "No, it's changed." The cross is then put facing her and a quarter turn to the right is made. "Is it the same?"—"Yes."—"Why is it the same?"—"You can put it any way but not the same." She counts four sides, then says, "I forgot one."

CEL (6 years, 4 months): The cross is toward her. "If I turn it toward you (¼F), will it be looking at you or will it be someplace else?"—"It's going to be looking at me." The movement is made. "It's on the bottom."—"And if I turn it like that (¼R)?"—"It will go there." The movement is made. "It isn't there!"

RIU (6 years, 9 months): Similarly, RIU at first says that if the cube is turned toward him (¼F), the cross will be "Here (still facing him)."—"It will still be looking at you?"—"No, here (on the right side)." The movement is made. "It is on the bottom! (Surprised)." And so forth. He predicts that the cross will remain oriented in the direction of rotation.

To begin with, we see that transformations are not understood as rotations relative to the object's axes but only as movements in one direction. The construction of the object itself remains incomplete, because it has only four sides (or five with manipulation). Even when just four sides are considered, there is no rotation. Subjects never predict that the cross will be on bottom and are surprised when this is found. Lacking rotations, there can be no correspondence between transformations and their results. The only correspondence involved is that between the direction of a movement and the position of the index (the cross, etc.) which, supposedly, the movement brings about in linear fashion. Moreover, when the subject establishes the falsity of such predictions, his findings do not lead to correct correspondence but leave states and transformations undifferenitated.

It seems, therefore, as if intramorphic reactions (Level I-A) are only manifested by errors and lacunae. Despite that systematic deficiency, however, they are interesting because intramorphic subjects somehow manage to find correspondences that are "always true." Such correspondences may be indices of logical tautology, but in this instance they testify to an unexpected need for comparisons. They amount to isomorphisms, either among states, that are always "flat" and "square" (FRA) or "a side that's all white" even if a turn is made (MEN), or among transformations "you move it like that and like that" (FRA). In other words, it is not positions that are compared but the qualitative characteristics of the sides, whence MEN's remarkable statement that it is the same because "you can put it any way but not the same." It is precisely the characteristic of correspondences to seek out equivalences beneath differences. This indicates that the first correspondences no more contain transformations in advance than the negative findings following false predictions lead to them.

By contrast, at Level I-B (age 6½ to 7 years) subjects discover rotations around axes and begin to put transformations and states into correspondence by differentiating them from one another. Although this involves successful intramorphic correspondences, it does not yet lead to stable compositions when the result of two, three, or four partial rotations (quarter turns) combined in a single sequence must be predicted:

SAN (6 years, 6 months): Unlike the preceding subjects, SAN quickly discovers the possibility of turning the cube to the left, to the right, backward, and forward, but his predictions remain a mixture of errors and successes. For the cross toward him with rotation to the left, he begins like subjects at Level I-A by predicting that the cross will be on the left side. "You see the cross, it is looking at you; and if I do this (¼L), will it look there (left)?"—"No, toward me (correct)."—"And if I turn it toward you (¼F), where will the cross be?"—"Toward me . . . it is on the bottom?"—"Yes." The experimenter demonstrates. SAN, however, fails on four quarter turns forward starting with the cross facing him as well as on two quarter turns forward and four to the left. By contrast, after long reflection, he succeeds on a quarter turn forward followed by a quarter turn to the left, which is the beginning of composition. However, his success is not repeated on a second combination of two rotations.

CAR (6 years, 6 months): After turning the cube in all four directions, CAR immediately succeeds in predicting what will happen when you begin with the cross facing him and then make a quarter turn forward. "Unh . . . bottom."—"Let's see."—"Correct."—"And if it's looking at you, and I turn it to the left?"—"There, still there (correct)." Then he makes a mistake on the composition of ¼F × ¼L, but he finds the solution after manipulating the cube without the cross. The reverse order (noncommutative) is predicted to give a different, then (without trying) the same result. He fails on the composition of three quarter turns toward him, fails again on the same problem even after the result of the movements is established, and fails on the composition of five quarter turns forward. He succeeds on the cross facing him, a quarter turn forward, then one to the left, but when four quarter turns are involved, he hesitates. By contrast, if you make a quarter turn to the left or to the right, "It is the same, because you always see the cross." Like SAN, he counts six sides.

JER (7 years, 11 months): JER immediately predicts that if the cross is facing him and a quarter turn forward is made, "It will be on the bottom," but he falsely concludes that starting from the same position, it will remain on the bottom after a ¼F and ¼L. For the same sequence of rotations in reverse order, "I would have to try it. There's a way. You try to turn it like that and then toward there."—"And in your head?"—"Yes, in its head, but you don't have a cube in your head." (The movement is made.) "Oh! Jeepers!"—"And how many times so that the cross (facing him) will be looking at you again?"—"Three times."—"Sure?"—"Four . . . unh . . . three."—"Why?"—"One time on bottom, one time it's there (behind), three times it comes back to the top. Four times!" Similar failure initially on four times to the left. Etcetera. He predicts four sides and is surprised, using a cube with drawings on the sides, to find six.

From the beginning, these subjects are themselves capable of performing the four different rotations of the cube. The important new development here is that they no longer characterize the cube's states only in terms of their qualitative properties but come to conceive them as generated by rotations. This leads to correct correspondence between a state and a transformation. This is particularly evident in their immediate predictions that forward rotation will result in the state, "on the bottom." If, however, transformations play the decisive role in understanding this beginning of morphism, it is still true that the way for them is paved by putting the sides of the cube in correspondence with one another. Thus, the cross corresponds to the blank side opposite it, and so on. Such preliminary correspondences are a necessary but not sufficient condition for rotatory transformations.

By contrast, even if Level I-B subjects are able to connect a state with a transformation, they still do not succeed in predicting compositions. The only way they can handle several turns in order is to actually perform the rotations bit by bit and empirically establish the results. That being the case, can we say that the principle is understood and that all that is is lacking is representational ability (because, as JER says, "You don't have a cube in your head,")? It is one thing to walk through the steps of a succession by means of empirical trials and another thing to conceive the results of a succession as necessary. This is the state in which these beginnings of empirical composition remain at the intramorphic level.

3. THE INTERMORPHIC LEVEL

Intermorphisms are characterized by the beginning of the necessity just discussed. Let us begin with some cases that can be classified as Level II-A:

FRE (6 years, 4 months): With the cross facing him, FRE is asked, "How can you turn it so you don't see it anymore?" —"Like that (¼F).""—"Is there only one way?"—"That (2 × ¼F)."—"Where is it?"—"There (behind)."—"More?" He indicates ¼R, starting with the cross behind. "More!" He indicates ¼L. "How many ways?"—"Three (in the same direction; he demonstrates ¼, 2 × ¼, 3 × ¼)."—"A turn like that (left) and a turn like that (right), are they like each other?"—"A little bit. When you turn it, it's there or there (opposite sides)."—"And like that (forward and backward)?"—"No, because it's in front and behind."—"But are they like each other in some way?"—"Yes, a little like what we just did (left and right and, therefore, two symmetries)."—"And like that (forward and left)?"—"They're not like each other at all." When the experimenter asks about the composition of these two rotations, he makes a mistake, as he also does for the reverse order. He fails as well on six consecutive rotations despite his initial predictions and thinks that even an adult cannot make the calculation for 20 or more rotations. By contrast, establishing that the cross remains facing him after a turn to the left, he generalizes this result to "always."

LED (7 years, 6 months): LED predicts that the cross facing him will move "to the bottom" for ¼F and deduces soon afterward that it will be the same for the composition ¼L × ¼F. However, he continues to think, incorrectly, that it will be the same for these rotations in reverse order. By contrast, he sees the necessity of n rotations to the left giving "always the same," that is, the cross toward him. Likewise, he succeeds on 2 × ¼F: "It will be behind." But he thinks that five rotations will be needed to bring it back facing him: "Once there (facing him), the second on bottom, the third there (behind), the fourth there, and the fifth there,"thus counting the starting state and the end state twice through confusion of states and rotations.

SOL (8 years, 3 months): For the same reason, SOL believes that 4 × ¼F will bring the cross "on top" but generalizes the cross facing him for n rotations to the left: "And if you do it nine times?"—"It will always be the same." By contrast, he fails on compositions of rotations forward and to the side.

The following cases of Level II-B present more advanced compositions:

VAL (6 years, 4 months): VAL immediately indicates the cross on the bottom for ¼F, but at first supposes that it will be on top for ¼L. By constrast, once the elementary correspondences are fixed, she succeeds in composing ¼F × ¼L by predicting that the cross will be on the right and on the reverse order by predicting that the cross will be on the bottom. And she also succeeds for four turns forward (¼F). "And if I turn it four times to the left?"—"There (facing her)."—"And 25 times?"—"All the time there."—"Are you sure? . . . Are you?"—"Yes."—"How do you figure that?"—"Every time I do four, it always lands there."—"And nine times toward you (9 × ¼F)?"—"On the bottom."—"How (etc.)?"—"I made one, two, three, four (previously) and five, six, seven, eight, and nine!"—"And five, then."—"There (immediately indicates on bottom)."—"How (etc.)?"—"There were four there, and there's the fifth."

NOR (8 years; 7 months) NOR counts six sides: "Four around and two." He then immediately succeeds on the composition ¼F × ¼L, but for these rotations in reverse order, he predicts, "There, behind," instead of on the bottom. By contrast, for 4 × ¼F: "It will go back there (facing him) because there are four sides."—"And 13 times?"—"Well, on the bottom. Because 4 + 4 makes 8 and for 12 it's there (facing him) and 13 on the bottom."—"If you want to put the cross behind?"—"Two times forward, no three times, ah, no, two."—"Is there another way?"—"Yes, (he turns the cube to the left and then rotates it on its base)."

LAU (9 years, 5 months): LAU succeeds on ¼ × ¼L. "And if I do left first and then forward, will it be the same?"—"No, it'll be on the bottom."—"Can you say that they're alike?"—"Yes, but they're opposite." LAU understands immediately that six drawings can be made on a cube.

From this one sees that the order in which success with compositions is achieved is: (a) series of lateral rotations (n times to the left or right), (b) successions of forward and backward rotations, and (c) compositions of rotations in both of these directions with understanding of their noncommutativity. Lateral successions are, naturally enough, the easiest. Once it is established that a sideward rotation does not change the fact that the cross is facing the subject, all the child has to do is to hold on to this invariance. In both other cases, successions must be combined with inversions. In those situations, particularly, the results indicate clearly that intermorphic correspondences are based on intertransformational operations. That does not mean, however, that morphisms are absent. On the contrary, they derive necessarily from such operations, and the interplay of comparisons is then applied back to the transformations. Thus FRE sees an analogy between left-right and forward-backward symmetries despite the difference in the results of each (cf. LAU also).

We still need to analyze the kind of necessity that characterizes intermorphic connections, however. To begin with, it is clear that all that is involved are connections established bit by bit between successive actions. These actions are, of course, no longer actually carried out, as was necessary at Level I-B. Rather, they are imagined, at first with errors and then correctly (cf. LED), and inferential generalizations are drawn from them by calculation, as with VAL and NOR, etcetera. The calculations bear only on the six sides, however. They do not take account of external references systems in relation to which 24 distinct "positions" must be distinguished. This amounts to saying that intermorphic necessity remains local insofar as it is linked to compositions among correspondences or transformations of the same rank that have not been subordinated to a general system. Such subordination is characteristic of the higher degree of conceptualization observed at the following level.

4. THE TRANSMORPHIC LEVEL

Here are some examples:

PHI (10 years, 11 months): PHI finds four ways to turn the cube according to left-right and forward-backward relationships. "When you put the cube like this or like that (quarter turn backward and then another of the blank cube without the cross), can you say it's the same?"—"No, it's different. It's set another way; it's not the same side touching the paper." He makes, therefore, a spontaneous distinction between the face and the position. "And like that (pivoting the cube a quarter turn)?"—"No, it's different."—"Well then, if we call them positions, how many are there?"—"Four times four equals sixteen."—"How do you figure that?"—"You multiply the number of sides by itself.?"—"By itself?"—"Ah, there are six sides; six times six equals 36."—"Are there 36 or 16?"—"Thirty-six, you can turn it on each side, like that (he makes it pivot four times standing on one side), so you have four times and . . . ah! four times six equals 24."—"You think that's right?"—"For sure, there are 24." The cube with the cross is presented and he asked if $\frac{1}{4}F \times \frac{1}{4}L = \frac{1}{4}L \times \frac{1}{4}F$: "No, it's not the same direction." He demonstrates, making correct predictions. "And nine times toward you, where will the cross be?"—"Toward the ground."—"How's that?"—"There are four sides. If you turn it four times, it comes back the same way. Nine is four times two plus one more turn."—"And 24 toward you?"—"The cross will still be toward me."—"And 24 to the left?"—"The cross won't move no matter how many turns you make." With regard to cubes with drawings, including the situation where six drawings correspond to the six sides, he says, "There are six sides per cube, yes, that makes six drawings . . . but you have to change the order (of the four cubes to be assembled in order to make a drawing)." He succeeds at matrices.

ERI (12 years, 1 month): ERI gives the same responses as PHI. He succeeds on compositions forward and to the left using the cube with the little man and the flower: "He will be lying, stretched out, but on his side."—"And the flower?"—"There (on the bottom)."

POL (12 years, 0 months): POL succeeds on 15 pivots to the right. "How many ways can you put the cube?"—"Twenty-four, because there are six sides, and because you can make it turn four times, four times six equals 24."

The decisive fact in these reactions is the subordination of correspondences to a general system. Up to now, compositions were successful only in terms of intermorphic arrangements of components of the same rank. Henceforth, they will take on a new character by being subordinated to a system. For example, it seems as if PHI only responds like VAL or NOR at Level II on questions concerning compositions forward and to the left or the other way round. In fact, however, his answers now include an essential new element; that is, he specifies that the directions (¼F × ¼L and ¼L × ¼F) differentiate "positions." In effect, whoever says "general system" makes reference to properties of the system as a whole. In the particular case of the rotations of a cube, the character of total system is obvious. It consists in a transition from six sides, up to that point the only thing distinguished, to 24 positions stemming from a combinations of sides and directions.

This distinction of positions ("set another way" says PHI) is dependent on reference to external space: "It's not the same side touching the paper." Until this level (from age 10 years, 8 months on), only a single subject had used a relationship of that sort, and he did so only to redundantly specify the expression "on the bottom." He counted only six possible positions for the cube. What, therefore, permits the whole to be conceptualized as a transmorphism is that transformations are put into correspondence with the positions that result from them and these positions are determined by reference to external space. Transmorphisms go beyond what can be observed relative to the sides as well as relative to compositions arrived at by actually carrying out actions bit by bit or by imagining them step by step. It is the same for correspondences between positions and the six drawings on the cubes with pictures.

In addition, then, to the exhaustive character of the correspondences resulting from the transition from six sides to 24 positions, these new findings allow us to confer a "freedom" on correspondences. As usual, we define this by the two properties of arbitrary starting point and univocal endpoint determined by the transformation. These different acquisitions assure the exhaustivity, the freedom, the virtual simultaneity of steps of reasoning that depend on one another mutually, and the closure of the system (source of the automorphisms). They give one, then, the right to see in this transmorphism an elementary category. There is, moreover, another remarkable fact. If the elements of the whole linked together by morphisms have gone from six to 24 through the transformation of the instruments of comparison,[2] the six starting states have in return become, starting with the 24 terminal states, a quotient set based on their equivalence insofar as including four positions each.

Finally, the capacity of subjects to use the matrix calculus to which they are introduced constitutes an additional index of the nature of transmorphic correspondences. Because this calculus involves previous learning and not just spontaneous construction as was the case with the 24 positions, I do not insist on this however. But I do attempt to spell out the differences between transmorphic acquisitions and the preceding intermorphic correspondences. If one characterizes the transmorphic by a calculus operating on morphisms and comparable, all proportions guarded, to the calculus on functions of which Henriques speaks in his chapter, one might say that there is already a calculus at Level II-B in the reactions of VAL and NOR. In fact, all that is involved is an enumeration of rotations observed as quasi-discrete units. By contrast, in subjects of the transmorphic level, compositions involving 24 positions rather than six sides presuppose coordinations in terms of operatory structures that are external to the system. Moreover, they involve a calculus that has to be constructed (proof of this being its tardy character) and that encompasses more than simple enumeration. As usual, the transformations on which intermorphic compositions bear have passed from the rank of content (or terms) of correspondences to that of form by being generalized and completed and by bringing out the reasons for them, whence new compositional possibilities.

In conclusion, we again find the usual relationships between correspondences and transformations in the preceding facts. Putting the states and sides of a cube into correspondence consitutes a necessary preliminary preparing the way for transformations. At first, however, only relationships among contiguous sides are involved. At a second level, the fact that relationships among transformations become intertransformational goes hand in hand with the fact that relationships among morphisms also become intertransformational. At a third level, the discovery of the total structure leads to a composition of morphisms using a calculus drawn from this operatory system. Out of this comes the internal necessity of these

[2]Piaget introduces the undefined acronym Tfc at this point. The context and his previous references to Tfm (material transformations) and Tfo (operatory transformations) (cf. Footnote 1, this chapter) suggest that he means to refer to "transformations of the instruments of comparison" in an abbreviated way. Consistent with my previous reasoning on this point, I have suppressed the acronym and substituted the term implied—Translator.

coordinations which, as a system of simultaneous comparisons, replace the group with a category. Moreover, in addition to operatory transformations modifying their contents in successive steps, one sees, from the first to the third of these levels, a transformation of the instruments of comparison themselves. This is due to the fact that the differential characteristics of intra-, inter-, and transmorphic correspondences are particularly clear in the result obtained.

4 Compositions and Conservations of Lengths

Jean Piaget
with
I. Flückiger
and
M. Flückiger

In this chapter, the problem is to divide a total length L, presented as a fence around the edge of a field, into two complementary subsets. One subset is to be formed of boards,[1] BD, of identical dimensions for a given situation, and the other is formed of wires, W. The wires link the boards together according to the alternating sequence BD-W-BD-W-BD, a BD at each end. Subjects are asked whether the wires are equal and whether the whole length is covered. Three or six boards are used, but the pattern of construction is always the same.

However simple such questions may be, they appear worthy of study for at least three reasons. To begin with, the composition of correspondences is our general objective, and in this situation, it is solidary with a programmation rather than with isolated situations successively presented. In effect, placing boards at equal intervals and closing the intervals with wires requires, if the instruction is followed, placing a BD at each end of L and dividing, or let us say more simply "apportioning," this totality into BD and W sections. Correspondences enter from the fact that the distribution must be predicted from the start using an interplay of compensations. If the boards are longer, the wires will have to be shorter and vice versa.

The second interesting thing about these programmed compositions is that, even though they can proceed by inferential means and even though the relationship in play can be made explicit, they are so figurative that one

[1]Piaget speaks of solid fences (*barrières pleines*). Because there is no convenient term for this is English and because, in America, solid fences are usually made of boards and referred to as board fences, I have translated *barrières* as boards—Translator.

can easily predict and correct them by simply perceptual-motoric means. As you might expect, young subjects proceed in this manner. Even so, it is interesting to establish whether or not programmation is involved and, more particularly, to see to what extent their perceptual solutions involve taking consciousness of the structure in play. For example, will subjects discover that n boards correspond to only n − 1 wires or, in other words, that each wire corresponds to two rather than a single board? Can they perform the surjections or injections that make it possible to compare the total length of the wires, L_W, with the total length of the boards, L_{BD}, independently of how many of each there are?

Finally, the relationship of the boards and the wires gives rise to an interesting question of conservation. For a given length (L) in which there are two equal boards in variable positions, the length of the wires is L − 2 BD. Do the wires and boards together constitute a sum of constant length despite displacements of the boards? And what correspondences are involved in this conservation?

1. MATERIAL AND TECHNIQUE

The experimenter has two sheets of metal at his disposal. They are 50 cm in length, painted green, and have three rows drawn on them. A border is drawn 44 cm from one end. The extra space is needed when the child, despite the instruction, goes beyond the border and has to evaluate this overshooting. The boards, BD, are made of magnetized cardboard so that they can be moved but at the same time stay firmly in place. Three different kinds are used: (a) The smallest are designated S; (b) the medium size ones, designated M, are twice as long as these so that M = 2S and their length is such that when they are evenly distributed on L, the spaces between them are equal to M; (c) the big ones, designated B, are equal to 3S, so that B = 1½M = 3S. Either three or six boards are used. When three are used S = 4.4 cm, M = 8.8 cm, and B = 13.2 cm, and the corresponding spaces are s = 15.4 cm, m = 8.8 cm, and b = 2.2 cm. When series of six are used S = 2 cm, M = 4 cm, and B = 6 cm, and the corresponding spaces are s = 6.4 cm, m = 4 cm, and b = 1.6 cm. If, however, there is a simple relationship between the solid sections formed by the series of three or six, that is not the case for the intervals. Likewise, the board-to-interval relationship is complex except for M and m.

The subject is told that an integral enclosure must be constructed by putting a board at each end and the others in between so that the remaining space is apportioned into equal intervals. He also is told that he will have to connect the boards by "wires" which he must cut himself from long thin spaghetti. This leaves him free, if he desires, to begin by using the pieces of spaghetti as measuring devices. Generally, the experimenter proceeds in the order medium, then small, and finally big. Once the construction is finished, the experimenter asks whether the total length of the wires is the same as the total length of the boards when they are put together. In doing so, the experimenter may, on occasion, put the wires in a line. In much the same way, the experimenter establishes whether the subject has understood that n BD's correspond to only (n − 1) W's or that 2 BD's correspond to one W. The question of complementary substitution[2] and conservations is treated in section 5 (later) using a simplified technique.

2. THE INTRAMORPHIC LEVEL

The following subjects proceed in perceptual-motoric fashion, but by succesive paths without the programmation that the instructions presuppose:

RIT (4 years, 7 months): First, RIT places the 3 M's toward the center. Then, when it is suggested, she puts two of them at the ends and the last one in the middle, but with a larger space on the left than on the right. "Is there the same distance there as there (the m's)?"—"No."—"Can you make it the same?"—She reverses the inequality. For the three S's, she puts two on the ends without problems, then puts the third near the first, then corrects it. There is no problem with the three B's, but with six S's she puts two at the ends and then puts the other four together in the middle with very little space between them. "Can you put it so there is the same space between the boards?"—She separates the four boards in the middle slightly.—"More?"—"Yes." She separates them more on the right, then goes on to a nice symmetry, two close together in the center, and two near the ends. After that, she separates the two in the center and places the four in the middle at equal intervals that are not equivalent to the intervals between the first and second and the fifth and sixth which are closer. With 6 M's, one sees a beginning of programmation. The first is placed all the way to the right, the second not far from that, the third at the other end, the fourth next to the third but not at the same distance as the second from the first, and finally the

[2]"*Vicariance*" has been translated as "complementary substitution," following Piaget's definition with reference to class logic on page 109 of *Essai de Logique Opératoire* (Paris: Dunod, 1972): "[This expression means] that if, in an equation of the form $A_1 + A'_1 = B$, A_2 is substituted for A_1, then it is also necessary to substitute A'_2 for A'_1, A'_1 and A'_2 being the complementary classes of A_1 and A_2 respectively." (Cf. "substitution property" discussed by Birkhoff and Bartee, p. 47, *Modern Applied Algebra*. New York: McGraw-Hill, 1970)—Translator.

fifth in the middle. The intervals m are somewhat equal but there is no place for the sixth board, which she therefore places on top of the fifth. Finally, with six B's the program is fulfilled: The first is placed all the way to the right, the second all the way to the left, then the third, fourth, fifth, and sixth are put in place starting from the first so that she ends at the second board with almost equal intervals. The experimenter goes on to the placing of the wires. RIT evaluates the intervals between the B's of the conserved series carefully, but from beginning to end she chooses pieces of spaghetti that are too long and shortens them at both ends successively in order to adjust them to the neighboring boards instead of shortening them once only in function of the interval. The experimenter places the m's above the s's (recall that $m < s$ because $M > S$) and asks where the s's went. RIT thinks it was with the B's (the B's are larger than the M's), making, therefore, a direct correspondence between the sizes of the W's and the BD's, although in action and with the series in view, she correctly grants the inverse correspondence. After a demonstration, the experimenter asks, "If you pretend that all the m's are boxcars and make a train of them, would it be the same as a train made of the s's?"—"No."—"Would it be bigger or littler?"—"Bigger (again judging on the basis of the M's)."—"Are you sure?"—"No, medium (judgment on elements)."

SOP (5 years, 0 months): For the six M's, she begins by making a series of elements squeezed together, then with increasing intervals on one side. When reminded of the instruction to make the intervals equal, she almost corrects them. With six S's, she puts one all the way to the right and places the others irregularly, leaving the left extremity unoccupied. When reminded, she equalizes the intervals, but without putting an S at the left end, and she does not see that there is any other way than, "You have to take another one (7th!)." With six B's, she fills up the whole space including the ends with four of them and "doesn't know what you can do" with the two remaining. Then she pushes them together and puts in the fifth element that extends beyond the border, and so on. With three boards, her solutions are better, but the intervals are still unequal except with the three B's.

BOU (6 years, 1 month): With six S's, BOU respects the instruction to make the intervals equal, but he does so without making his construction conform to the total length or to the positions of the two extremities. The result is six S's massed on the right hand half of the metal sheet. These are well distributed, but the left side of the sheet remains empty. "Can you move them?"—"No."—"Then (the experimenter gives him six M's)?"—"Ah, if I could take that one (a B) to finish!" Then, "I'm trying to push them all over there (to the left). Ah, but that doesn't work; too many stay (on the right)."—"What can you do?"—"You have to say that the ones on the ends are stuck (as if it were not necessary to begin in this way!)." He completes the task, although with irregularities of the intervals, then corrects this to three pairs of boards close together (1-2, 3-4, 5-6), but again neglects the empty space on the left: "You'll need seven of them!" With six S's, he begins by putting three in the center and one at each end: "That's right?"—"Not yet, there's no place for this one (the sixth)." He finally succeeds. He judges the B's to be the biggest boards and the s's to be the biggest intervals, but he does not see the equality M = m. As for the spahetti wires, like RIT, he takes ones that are too long and cuts them at both ends.

Programmation is distinct from simple planning because it puts every action into correspondence with those that must follow it (precursivity) and not only with those that preceded it (recursivity). It seems clear, therefore, that the subjects just described begin without programmation and only succeed in approximately equalizing intervals by means of numerous after-the-fact corrections. This does not mean that they do not have plans, but their plans only aim at a general regularity to be constructed step by step. With SOP, the elements are initially squeezed together, then placed at increasing intervals (recursivity); with RIT, they are distributed according to a progressive symmetry; and even with BOU, although they are placed right off at equal intervals, this is accomplished bit by bit without predicting their distribution relative to the total length. That is not to say that such plans do not lead to correspondences. Except for very momentary exceptions, they all respect what we call, further on, morphisms of alternation, that is, an interval or a wire between each board and the following one. But lacking programmation of the distribution, this alternation constructed recursively favors the maintainance of an empty space at one end as if each board had to be followed by an interval. It should be noted in this regard that without the experimenter's insistence, these subjects never begin by putting a board at each end, which confirms the absence of precursivity.

This absence of precursivity is also evident in the frequent and surprising difficulty these children have in correcting mistakes by changing positions sufficiently. RIT who has succeeded in making the intervals equal with five M's does not want to change them further in order to put in the sixth. Likewise, SOP "doesn't know what you can do" with the two B's remaining. In order to remedy an empty space with the S's, she wants to use a seventh element. And one finds the same reactions with BOU. Equally noteworthy is the curious way these children have of cutting the wires at both ends, evaluating the interval being more complex than adjusting the ends of the wires where they come in contact with the boards. And the same may be said of subjects' failure to predict that the length of any wire will be the same for all the rest because all of the intervals are equal. These facts, added to the preceding, demonstrate the general lack of precursive correspondences. At this level, therefore, one cannot expect any more understanding of the correspondence between n BD's and (n-1) W's than one can expect a comparison between the total lengths L_{BD} and L_W. See in this regard RIT's responses which go so far as to substitute a direct correspondence between L_{BD} and L_W although in action she used the inverse correspondence.

3. INTERMORPHIC CORRESPONDENCES

Toward 7 or 8 years of age, programmation appears from the beginning. This does not mean immediate success, but rather an effort to coordinate distinct types of correspondences: (a) the alternation of the BD's and W's; (b) the correspondence of a BD with each end of L; and (c) isomorphism of the intervals. From this results the necessity of a plan of apportionment and, therefore, precursive correspondence between the placements successively chosen for the BD's and a final result respecting these correspondences. Clearly, therefore, this programmation implies intermorphic construction achieved in steps. Here are some examples:

SCA (7 years, 2 months): The experimenter gives him six M's. He begins by counting them, puts one at each end, puts in a third, thinks that the space is too large, and tries it with the same length of m and M by cutting a wire W = m. Helped in part by chance, ("You have to break a small piece and see if it goes between each board"), he knows how to exploit the result and makes a correct apportionment. Then he appropriately cuts the other W's, basing himself on this separation m. By contrast, when the experimenter aligns the m's and asks if the total length of the BD's will be equal to the length of the m's, he says, "Yes, that should be okay because the boards are the same as the wires." He is mistaken on the total lengths, therefore, because he fails to make the correspondence n BD → (n-1) W. He constructs his row of BD's, establishes the inequality, and only then concludes, "There're more boards." But this makes him begin to doubt that one could fence the whole field with six BD's and five W's. "No, you'll have to have another wire because one's missing."—"But you could before?"—"Yes (he rebuilds the fence and confirms $L_{BD} > L_W$)." The experimenter goes on to six S's, and SCA sees right away that the interval will be s > S "because there (M), it's bigger (M > P)." He puts S_5 and S_6 at the two extremes, then gropes around making spaces too small, then too large, so that he is only able to use four S's. Finally, he succeeds in finding the correct distribution and without problems cuts equal W's for all the intervals. As for the total lengths, he sees immediately that $L_S < L_W$, because "the wires are bigger."—"How much bigger?"—(He puts an s against an S)"That much." He has no difficulty seeing that the sum of six B's is greater than that of the b's. He cuts the W's "all the same size" but again believes that there are six of them.

CAT (7 years, 6 months): CAT does not have SCA's initial luck. For six M's, she begins with an attempt where the wires are too short. She ends up with L = 6 M + 6 W. She then removes the last wire, places an M at the end, and correctly adjusts the four other boards without wires. Once the wires are added, she thinks that, if the M's = m's, the sum of the M's and of the W's are equal. By contrast, for the S's and the s's (where the s's are much bigger), she responds correctly.

NIC (8 years, 10 months): NIC makes successive trials with alternating overcorrections. For six M's, she begins with W's, all equal, but a little bigger than M. M_6 is, therefore, too squeezed by M_5. From this, she goes on to W's of equal size, but half as large as the preceding ones. This leaves a large space. She returns to the longer W's and rediscovers the same problem: "The boards (M) are the same size, the wires are too, but you can't put them between M_5 and M_6." She then makes the fence without the spaghetti and, after adjustments, succeeds. For three M's, she measures the two m's with her fingers without problems. For the sum of the M's and of the W's, she says, "It's not the same because the wires are the same as the boards, and that would make too little (if one aligns them one under the other); it leaves an empty place (equal to the difference between W_5 and M_6)." For the sum of the S's and the s's, she says, "There are more posts than wires. It's not the same. You've bought the same length of wires (among themselves) and not the same number of posts (as wires)." Comparing the M's and the S's, one sees that M to S and m to s: "It's the opposite." And if one aligns the BD's and the W's in both cases, "It's not the same." In fact, NIC seems to understand quite well the first of the two situations, maintaining that if m = M, then 5m < 6M). For the second situation, however, she cannot decide whether fewer s's than S's but with s > S will give a greater total length or not, either being possible because there are more S's. She is, therefore, logically correct. Moreover, in advance of SCA and CAT, who only judge $L_S < L_s$ by perceptual means, she grants the correspondence n BD → (n-1) W in both cases.

SYL (8 years, 9 months): SYL begins with an m that is slightly too small so that M6 does not reach the end. She pushes it into place and readjusts the other boards. For six S's, she arrives at the correct distribution by placing them under the M's. She tries the same thing with the B's, but at first she does not put them close enough together. The W's are only subsequently put in place. For sums, she sees right away that an m is equal to an M and that there are five m's as opposed to six M's. With regard to the S's, "The wires (the s's) will be bigger. A piece of wire makes more than a piece of board." But "there will always be five wires and six posts." She establishes that the sum of the s's extends over almost all of the field and that the sum of the S's extends over a lesser part. "You didn't think about putting them closer together?"— (She takes an S and evaluates six S's, then an s and evaluates five s's; she then declares that these two lengths together "Must give that (the length of the field) . . . Yes, it's the right length."—"Then you can know the difference?"—"Yes, all of the wires (the s's) are longer than all of the small boards (the S's)."—"And with the medium boards?"—"All of the medium boards are longer." And all of the B's also. By contrast, she grants readily enough that one could have a fence where the sum of the BD's is equal to that of the W's, but does not see how to do it despite the little cardboard cutouts that one puts at her disposal.

NAT (9 years, 8 months): NAT sees right off that the sum of the M's exceeds that of the m's and that the sum of the B's exceeds that of the b's. With regard to the S's, "If you use the small ones (S's in the gaps s), you need two or even three to fill the empty space. So you need more wire (sum of the s's) if you want to use the small boards"—"Could you have a fence where the sum of the boards is equal to the sum of the wires?"—"Yes, you could."—"How?"—"I don't know."

LAU (9 years, 0 months): LAU is an example of subjects from 9 to 10 years of age who succeed naturally in making correct distributions when they proceed perceptually but who, when they wish to proceed by measurements, grope even more than the preceding subjects. This is because they fail to take correct measurements for transfer from one interval to another. Even after failing with a measurement that is too small, m_1, then with one that is too large, m_2, LAU hopes to equalize them, not by looking for an intermediary, but by taking the difference $m_2 - m_1$ away from m2. This leads, of course, to two m's that are both too small. Once he manages to find the correct distributions, total lengths are not a problem. In the case of the S's, LAU, like NAT, measures one s to be equal to around three S's and comes to correct conclusions.

FAI (9 years, 9 months): With the six S's, FAI uses an S lying sideways as measuring device. This leaves a large empty space in front of S_6 which was put in place in advance. He tries again with the S on its side plus a small additional space. Again, the space in front of S_6 is too large. He measures it with two fingers and wants to carry this width of two fingers over to every interval!

ISA (10 years, 0 months): ISA makes the same mistake. She wants to carry the too-large final space over to all the other intervals. Sums are evaluated without problems, and ISA is firm in her assurance that the sum of the BD's plus the sum of the W's will extend the whole length of the field (complementarity of the two subsets).

CRI (10 years 8 months): CRI also proceeds by making measurements and gropes around, going from measuring devices that are too short to ones that are too long and vice versa. She does not take account of their differences, however, and therefore cannot use them to counterbalance one another. For the sums of the s's and the S's, she compares the unequal intervals and chooses one of intermediate size: "It's a little like an average, it could do for everything." Problems of sums are immediately resolved, but even while affirming that the sum of the s's is greater than that of the S's, CRI claims that, "You can't know" by how much (because there are six S's in comparison to five s's and because $s > S$). "And if you put them end to end?"—"No."

In contrast to the subjects described in section 2, we find that all of the subjects here begin with a programmation that obligates them to compose the different sorts of correspondences with one another. This includes the correspondences between two BD's and the extremities of the field, between the BD's and the W's by alternation, between the equal lengths of the W's, and (except for SCA and CAT who do not consciously succeed on this one) between n BD's and (n-1) W's. Even when the child proceeds in terms of successive trials and errors by attempting several intervals in the array $BD_1 \rightarrow BD_6$, he does not lose sight of the fact that he must respect and conserve the precursive direction of the compositions, nor, therefore, does he lose sight of the goal to be attained. What is instructive from the intermorphic point of view is that the addition of new compositions slows up the resolution of problems. This is what happens when 9- to 10-year-old subjects disdain perceptual methods facilitating simultaneous consideration of the correspondences to be established and appeal to measurement. In effect, measurement includes an additional composition underlying transitivity. Instead of comparing a space d_1 with a space d_2 directly, measurement requires that d_2 correspond to d_1 only if d_1 is equal to the measuring device x and if x then is equal to d_2, whence $d_1 = d_2$ by mediation. Things become even more complicated if one has to compare the measuring devices among themselves in order to arrive at correct answers, whence the errors made by LAU, FAI, ISA, and CRI.

With respect to the correspondence $n\ BD \rightarrow (n\text{-}1)\ W$, because the wires are placed between the boards with the explicit goal of joining them to one another, it is probable that subject establishes correspondence between each W and a pair of BD's, hence $n\ W \rightarrow BD_a BD_b$, whence his rapid understanding. Regarding the total lengths of the BD's and W's, subjects imagine an intermorphic composition on their own. This composition involves the following: (a) surjection of the BD's in a continuous whole (materially or representationally); (b) surjection of the W's in an analogous continuum; and (c) isomorphism of the two or the injection of one into the other.[3] Isomorphism is not realized in our cases, but NAT and others believe that it is possible without knowing how to obtain it. The comparison of the sum of the S's with that of the s's poses a special problem because there are more S's than s's but they are smaller. Perceptually, the solution is simple, but logically the three solutions "greater than," "less than," and "equal to" are possible insofar as one does not make measurements. This is what makes NIC, who lacks a metric, hesitate. It is also the source of NAT's and LAU's measurements as well as of CRI's extreme reaction. Recall that despite her correct perceptual judgement, CRI claims that one cannot determine the difference between the two sums at issue, as if there were a logical contradiction between 6S > 5s and s > S.

It remains for us to point out ISA's interesting reaction assuring herself that the sum of the lengths of the BD's and W's will go the whole length of the field. This not only involves complementarity in terms of exhaustive surjection of the two subsets of the length L, but it also involves implicit utilization of complementary substitution. The latter has to do with the fact that the whole, L, is conserved whatever may be the distributions of 6M + 5m, 6S + 5s, or 6B + 5b. In section 5, we return to complementary substitutions of L with conservation of the sum of the W's when one or several BD's are displaced.

4. THE TRANSMORPHIC LEVEL

As already agreed, transmorphic compositions differ from intermorphic compositions in that they refer to a general structure that goes beyond coordinating correspondences of the same rank. With the problems presented here, the advent of the transmorphic level is marked by the use of numerical divisions and multiplications instead of merely spatial operations like the "dividing up" or "putting together" seen in the preceding levels. That does not mean that subjects give up perceptual solutions or measuring devices, but only that they add the method of calculation, which they generally prefer:

---

[3]Birkhoff and Bartee (*op cit,* pp. 10–11): "An injection is often called a *one-one* transformation of *S* into *T.*" "A surjection is thus a map of *S* onto *T.*" I have used the prepositions *into* and *onto* accordingly—Translator.

MAR (11 years, 10 months): For six M's, MAR begins with a somewhat irregular perceptual distribution, and then immediately goes on to calculation. She verifies by measurement the equality of the M's, multiplies four cm by six, then says, "You measure that (total length) and divide by the number remaining, here five spaces." Next, using a measuring device evaluated at a glance, she finds a remainder that she proposes to divide by five in order "to add this little piece, ⅕ to each spaghetti." By contrast, she forgets that there are five s's for six S's and begins by saying, "It's half of a medium board (M), so the space is double." Later, however, she subtracts six S's from L and divides the remaining space by five. Regarding total lengths, she thinks it would be impossible to construct a fence where L_W and L_{BD} are equal because there are always (n-l)W for nBD. She supposes, therefore, that identical total lengths must have the same number of objects.

COR (11 years, 3 months): COR begins with a measuring device that is too small and rejects the idea of trying a larger one. She proposes instead to divide the remainder by five. "Five millimeters (too much) are left, so you add a millimeter to each one." Same method for the S's. For a total length of the BD's equal to that of the W's, it is necessary to put the BD's "up to the middle of the field" and divide the other half by five: Each "piece of wire must be longer because there are more boards than wires."

DAN (12 years, 3 months): Same reactions. For equal sums, "You take the complete length, then you divide half of it by the number of posts" and the other "by five."

Without doubt, division is an operation that is learned rather than invented by the child. However, everyone knows that its spontaneous employment is limited and late because certain teaching lacks active understanding. Its appearance here at Level III is therefore meaningful because it indicates the completion of the system of precursive correspondences, which then takes on a new form. Instead of trying to apportion the whole into alternating BD's and W's directly using a method of successive approximations, the whole is right away divided into two subsystems, that is L_{BD} and the complementary length $L - L_{BD} = L_W$. This is done on the subject's initiative and not because of some additional question that is asked. Only then are the subsystems divided into six BD's and five W's, whose sizes are determined metrically at one stroke rather than being evaluated step by step. No comment is needed to see that transmorphic compositions of this sort differ from intermorphic compositions according to the usual criterion: They use operations to join correspondences to one another in function of a total system understood as such from the beginning. Even if the operations involved are related to schooling, using them in a particular problem only reinforces the spontaneous operations of partitioning, apportioning, and uniting with complementarities constituting components of the total system. In contrast, the programmation belonging to Level II, although analogous in principle, achieves nothing but step-by-step coordination.

5. COMPLEMENTARY SUBSTITUTION AND CONSERVATIONS OF THE SUM OF INTERVALS

At the end of section 3, we saw how the question of sums or or total lengths brings up the question of complementary substitutions. It seemed interesting, therefore, to examine this problem with a simplified technique that did not involve fences, and so forth. We therefore set cardboard blocks in various positions on two small strips a few centimeters in length with stops at either end, that is, |__________|. The experimenter simply moves the blocks and asks whether the sum of the spaces in between them is conserved or changed. Or he arranges immobile blocks, recognized to be equal in width, at different points along the strips and has the subject compare the spaces in between. The spaces are measured by means of pieces of colored paper the same width as the blocks which are, themselves, of different colors.

In what follows, we distinguish three groups of subjects according to whether they fail, succeed after failures, or immediately master the questions. The problem is for us to analyze the correspondences involved in conservations. Here are some cases from the first group:

DOM (6 years, 1 month): DOM is shown three blocks separated by unequal spaces and asked to compare this arrangement with one where two blocks are pushed together at one end of the strip and the third is set at the other end leaving a single space between. "The spaces," says DOM, "they aren't the same. That one there (big space) is bigger than the two pieces [of space]. The two spaces are smaller because it's cut up." Despite establishing the facts ("After all, you can close it"), she will not concede that the big space recurs when all three squares are pushed together at one end, leaving only a single space at the side: "No, a little piece is missing." New trials only change her mind a little. For three blocks set at equal distances from one another, she says, "All just right, perhaps." However, after moving the one in the middle so that the spaces in between are not equal: "That doesn't work because there you need a little piece and there a big one." The experimenter, therefore, only obtains from DOM erroneous perceptual evaluations that do not make use of experience.

XAN (6 years, 3 months): She begins with the same situation as DOM and contends that the empty spaces will not have the same length "because here there're two walls together and there there aren't". For two blocks quite close together and the third at the other end: "That won't work; it's too big." For three blocks at equal distance, she establishes that the spaces are equal. When the experimenter moves the middle block very slightly: "Too big."

STE (7 years, 0 months): STE gives the same reactions for three blocks. For a single block, he succeeds in recognizing the equality of the spaces when the block is at the left end on one strip and at the right end on the other: "Same size." When one of the blocks is pushed a bit toward the center: "No (spaces not equal), because here the stake (block) is in the middle."

Let us now turn to some cases where subjects fail initially but eventually discover the solution. It is interesting to see what motivates this discovery. The examples are as follows:

FOR (5 years, 10 months): For single blocks set at the left end of one strip and near the center of the other: "There, (first strip) there's more." He establishes that the space in the first situation is equal to the two spaces in the second. The block on the first strip is then put at the other end: "Can you take one of these papers that is already cut and close off the field?"—"No."—"None of them?"—"No."—"If you put these two (pieces matching the spaces on the second strip)?"—"No, you'd have to cut a piece."—"And that one there (piece matching the space on the first strip before the block was moved)?"—"Ah, that would work (he verifies this)." But for a single block a little to the left of center and another a little to the right: "No, you'd have to cut a piece; there isn't enough left (at the other end)." He establishes that the pieces cut for one strip nevertheless work for the second strip. The experimenter then puts blocks at either end of the first strip and two blocks pushed together at one end of the second strip. In this case, the single spaces, equal but placed differently on either strip, are judged to be equivalent: "They're the same."—"How do you know?"—"There, there're two (blocks) and there, there're two!" He then generalizes when the two blocks at the ends are brought together a little. "You have to cut it in three pieces."—"What do you do to see if it's really the same size . . . by moving the little walls?"—(He pushes them together.)—"And if you move them again?"—"It's always the same. You put the paper in what's left."

PAQ (6 years, 0 months): PAQ begins by failing with a single block at the left end on the first strip and at the right end on the second: "Here it's bigger." She fails even worse where one block is placed to the right on one strip and at the center on the other. She cuts papers for the block in the center and judges that the space for the block on the right is larger than the papers. She finds, however, that the spaces are equal through superposition: "Exactly right!" She then generalizes to the other positions and in each case predicts that the little wall plus the papers will extend the whole length of the field.

FAB (8 years, 1 month): Despite her age, FAB at first fails when three blocks are presented. She cuts three pieces for one of the strips and denies the equality when the blocks are distributed so that there are two spaces. Then, brusquely, she says, "That will work," and moves the blocks so that the three papers fit.

In cases where success is complete, both sorts of argument are found:

CAR (7 years, 6 months): CAR succeeds for the various positions of one block ("same length because the field is the same length") and for three: "Because there are three cardboards (blocks) and there also." The empty space, therefore, always equals the total field minus the blocks.

TOR (8 years, 2 months): Same success as CAR, but "because if you move the little walls, that will give you the same thing."

These interrogations bring up two distinct although solidary problems. One is the problem of complementary substitution in general. This consists in the fact that if the distribution of the elements of a whole (here the total length) is changed, the whole is conserved. PAQ and CAR say this explicitly, but not all subjects in the second and third groups do. The second problem has to do with conserving the sum of the intercalary spaces. These are the only things whose dimensions change with changes in distribution, because the blocks remain invariant and only change position. Conservation of the sum of the intercalary spaces is discovered or justified by two sorts of arguments. On the one hand, subjects may reason that the total length, T, composed of the spaces, S, and the blocks, B, remains constant ($S + B = T$) and that the length occupied by the blocks remains constant as well. This means that for the spaces one has the invariance $S = T - B$ (see FOR, PAQ, and CAR). On the other hand, variations of S result from displacements of its parts (solidary with the displacements of the B's). This means that what is gained by one is lost by another, according to a simple displacement of the difference (see FOR, FAB, and TOR). Transformations come into play in both cases, but they are accompanied by inter- or cotransformational correspondences. In cases where the first sort of argument applies, the correspondence involved is that between the direct operation $S + B = T$ and its inverse $S = T - B$; in cases where the second sort of argument applies, it is the correspondence between what is taken away at the beginning of a displacement and what is gained or added at the end (commutability).[4]

It is possible, then, to give a general formula for conservations that unite complementary substitutions with commutable displacements. Let A_1 be the part displaced when the object's form or distribution is changed and A'_1 be the part that remains in position. Let us designate by a the starting state of A_1 and by b the endstate, so that: $aA_1 \rightarrow bA_1$ = its displacement. On the other hand, let us designate by u the union of A_1 and A'_1 at a certain point of contact or neighboring of A'_1 (in situation aA_1) and by w the union of A_1 and A'_1 at another point. If the process is repeated several times (with A_2 and A'_2, A_3 and A'_3 defined in the same manner), one then has:

$$(aA_1 \text{ u } A'_1 = A'_1 \text{ w } bA_1) \Leftrightarrow (aA_2 \text{ u } A'_2 = A'_2 \text{ w } bA_2) \Leftrightarrow (aA_3 \text{ u } A'_3 \ldots), \text{ etc.} = B \quad (1)$$

We see, therefore, that each parenthesis contains the expression of a commutability, whereas the union of one parenthesis with the following by the equivalence, $\Leftrightarrow$, manifests a complementary substitution (A_1, A'_1, modified to become A_2, A'_2, etc.) with conservation of the whole, B. With regard to our subjects' two forms of arguments, we can say that their solidarity is concretized in the interpretion of the unions, u and w. Those subjects who center on the common characteristic of union are oriented toward the first argument, that is, complementary substitution, and those who center on the difference of points of contact are oriented toward the displacement and its commutability.

The interest of this simplified technique is that when subjects no longer have to construct a fence with regular and equal intervals or to maintain certain numerical relationships among the intervals and the boards, they arrive at the correspondences of commutability or complementary substitution directly and can, moreover, bring them into intermorphic correspondence by simple deduction leading from one to the other. By contrast, with the fence technique, the necessity of a composition is implicated as early as the programmation, whence the notable jump between the inter- and the intramorphic.

[4]For commutability, also see chapter 5, section 2.;fnt

5 The Composition of Differences

Jean Piaget
with
E. Marti
and
E. Mayer

Several previous studies[1] have examined the situation where young subjects are presented with two equal collections, A and B, and then n elements are transferred from A to B. What has been shown is that after the transfer young children expect the difference between the two collections to be of magnitude n rather than 2n. It is as if they forget that the n elements added to B are, in fact, the same elements taken away from A. However elementary, this commutability only tardily imposes itself with necessity on the subject.

In the present study, this problem is reversed by using a long string attached to a post and bent around another (see Fig. 5.1) to yield two unequal segments, A and B, of difference m. The problem set for the subject is how to make the string segments equal. Success depends, of course, on the realization that what is added to B is also subtracted from A. The solution m/2 indicates that the subject is not content just to add m to B. Rather, he puts the increase in B into correspondence with the decrease in A without forgetting the subtraction involved and without forgetting to conserve the sum A + B. Because the equivalence $\Delta(-A) = \Delta(+B)$ is a form of commutability and because the conservation of the whole A + B remains true even when m is varied (complementary substitution), the

[1]For "commutability," see *Experiments in Contradiction* (Volume XXXII of *Études d'Épistémologie génétique,* 1974), Chapter XI, 1, pp. 188–189, as well as the article by B. Inhelder, A. Sinclair, A. Blanchet, and J. Piaget, "Relations entre les conservations d'ensembles d'éléments discrets et celles de quantités continues," *Année psychologique,* 1975, *75,* pp. 23–60.

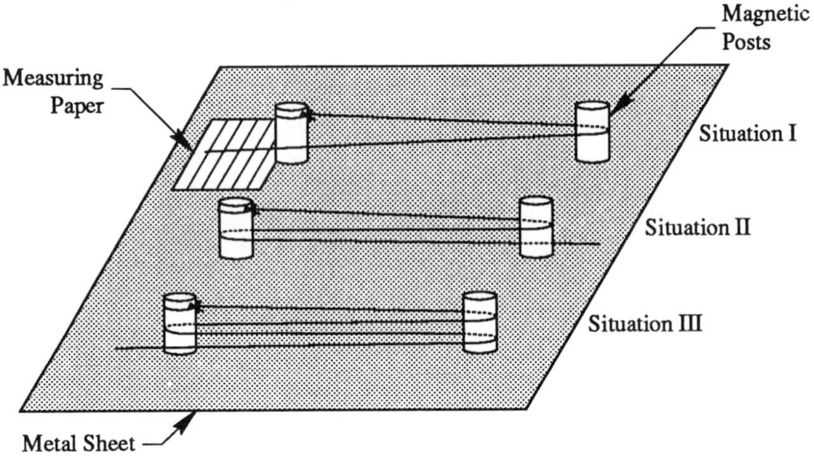

FIG. 5.1. Post and string apparatus.

morphisms in play are of a very general nature.[2] This is even the more the case when one asks the subject not only to find m/2 for A and B, but to make the generalizations m/3 for A, B, C and m/4 for A, B, C, and D. In addition to all this, an easier test is sometimes used. This consists in asking subjects to equalize the segments between A and B or between A and BC or A and BCD. It is also interesting to examine the interstructural correspondence between these two situations of the posts and the roads.

1. EQUIPMENT AND TECHNIQUE

Posts. The interrogation includes three parts. The first part is done using a metal sheet 26 cm by 37 cm and six cylindrical magnets 2 cm in height. In all situations, the magnets, serving as posts, are placed in pairs 20 cm apart (see Fig. 5.1). In Situation 1, a string tied to the post on the left (Post 1), circles around the post on the right (Post 2), and extends 8 cm back past the first post. Thus, the string covers the distance between the posts twice. In Situation 2, things are identical to Situation 1 except that the string is longer, and after returning to Post 1, it winds around that post and goes back to Post 2, extending 8 cm beyond it. In this situation, the string traverses the distance between the posts three times. Finally, in Situation 3, an even longer string is wound around the posts as in Situation 2, makes yet another turn, and extends back past the first post by 8 cm thus covering the distance

[2]The relationship of these morphisms to those of section 5 of the preceding chapter is obvious.

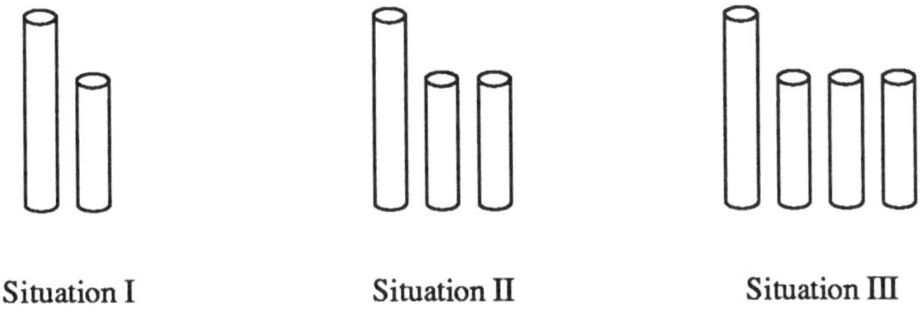

FIG. 5.2. Clay "road" apparatus.

between the posts four times in all. In each situation, the end of the string extending past the final post lies on a piece of measuring paper, m, of the same length, marked in off in six units. The situations are shown in Fig. 5.1.

In each of the situations, the child must get rid of (make a "loop", close . . .) the tail of string by moving one of the posts. He is asked to anticipate the amount of movement necessary using the units on the measuring paper under the tail. The action is then carried out without the subject seeing. The subject then assesses the result and makes new predictions, e.g., about how to correct an error.

Roads. In a second part of the experiment, the equipment consists of elongated pieces of modeling clay of different lengths called "roads." In Situation 1, one long road (A) and one short road (B) are presented. In Situation 2, there is a long road (A) and two short ones (B and C). In Situation 3, there is a long road and three short ones (see Fig. 5.2).

The child's goal is to make the roads equal in each situations. The experimenter keeps the small road or roads in his hand. The child tries to correctly anticipate the number and length of the piece or pieces of clay he will need to make the roads equal.

Combined. In the third part of the experiment, the child is asked questions concerning comparisons between the two previous parts and concerning the possible utilization of the "road game" as a model applying to the "post game." It should be noted that the order of the first two parts of the experiment was reversed for half of the subjects, making comparisons independent of the factor of succession.

2. THE ABSENCE OF COMMUTABILITY

There are two reasons why the problem of commutability[3] must be carefully examined from the point of view of correspondences. First, there are

[3]See Footnote 1, this chapter.

diverse forms of commutability that call upon different morphisms. Second, it is necessary to establish whether understanding the various forms of commutability requires intermorphic compositions or whether intramorphic correspondences are sufficient. With regard to the first reason, one can distinguish simple or double commutabilities according to whether they bear on a single object or on two, the variations of one of which depend on those of the other. In the first case, commutability consists in understanding that, when an object like a stick is moved, the space gained at its point of arrival is equal to the space lost at its point of departure. In other words, commutability consists in understanding that the length of the stick is conserved rather than believing, as young subjects do in many situations, that the stick has lengthened. In its elementary form, double commutability consists in understanding that when two objects whose dimensions or quantities are interdependent are displaced in the same direction, the increase in one will be equal to the decrease in the other, hence conservation of the whole. This was just seen in the case of the intervals in section 5 of the preceding chapter. Because conservation was far from being immediate in that situation, we theorized that an intermorphic composition was necessary in order to achieve it.

Another form of double commutativity to be considered is that of double bidirectional commutabilities. For example, in the configuration $^{A}|\_{B}$ the lengthening of B is equal to the shortening of A. Even though this dependence is understood precociously, however, A + B is not conserved initially (as we have seen with respect to functions[4]). Likewise, in the present experiment with the posts with strings looped in continuous fashion, a double bidirectional commutability is also involved. This is due to the fact that the lengthening of sector B of the string, necessary to diminish the distance m, causally entrains an equal shortening of sector A. This is the source of the errors and gropings encountered in young subjects for whom inverse functions remain problematic for a long time.

Although the situation presented in this experiment is complex, it has advantages nonetheless. This is because analyzing the difficulties encountered here help us better understand the even more serious difficulties encountered later in the experiment with roads involving double bidirectional commutabilities without loops but with discontinuous breaks. Let us begin, therefore, with some examples of the initial level in the experiment with posts:

CRI (5 years, 4 months): Situation 1: "You pull that (Post 1) and that makes the same length."—(She tries [pulls six units] and reverses the inequality.)—"Did you pull too much or not enough?"—"Not enough

[4]Volume XXIII of *Études d'Épistémologie génétique,* Chapter 4.

(she points to the piece that has become too long and pulls it [again six units], then establishes the new irregularity). "They're not the same size. One's smaller; the other is bigger."—"What can you do?"—"You pull here."—"Do you think so?"—"I can't. It would do the same thing as that (reversed inequality)."—"Then, what can you do? Pull more, pull less?"—"I don't know."—(The experimenter pulls by one unit instead of by six, as CRI has done up to that point.)—"That makes it smaller."—(The experimenter continues up to three units, making the strings equal.) "Can you explain it?"—"There were six and now three."—"And with Post 2 how many would you have to pull?"—"Six! (she tries) It's not the same size. (she pulls again by six units in the other direction, then tries three and reaches equality)."—"And before, to make this loop with the other post, how many did you pull it?"—"Six."

SAN (6 years, 4 months): SAN began with the roads which made things a bit easier. In Situation 1, he wants to displace Post 1 by m: "This whole piece?"—"Yes."—"(Tries) That doesn't work."—(The experimenter puts things back in their original positions.)—"Up to there (again indicates m)."—"Do you need to move it more or less than before?"—"Less (shows 5, then 2, then 3)." The experimenter goes on to Post 2 which SAN wants to displace five units. After trying: "Not enough." He finally arrives at three units but does not understand why it is the same difference with both Post 1 and Post 2. In Situation 2, he notices that there are two loops and begins by predicting success by moving Post 1 by three units because that was successful in Situation 1. At the same time, however, he chooses an arbitrary distance for Post 2, forgetting what had surprised him in Situation 1.

JOS (6 years, 10 months): In Situation 1, JOS understands that he has to get rid of the tail, m, for which he is given a paper of equal length. To do this, he chooses to move Post 2 away from Post 1 by the length of m. A, therefore, becomes too short by m. "You have to push it less." But he moves Post 1 forward again by m. He starts again slowly and stops at 3. In Situation 2 (A,B,C), however, he comes back to the difference m, that is, six units.

These reactions are very clear. Segment A goes beyond segment B by m, so the subject generally only seeks to lengthen B by pulling on its short end (Post 1), or more rarely (JOS), to shorten A by pulling on Post 2. In both cases, however, what is changed (segment A or B) is only considered at the forward end of its movement. In other words, only the projected and then attained point of arrival is considered, as if it were a matter of a fixed rubber band whose point of arrival can be changed without changing the point of attachment. There is, therefore, a complete absence of commutability in the sense of a correspondence between the space gained at the point of arrival and the equivalent space lost at the start. In this particular case, however, what complicates the problem is that A and B are not two independent straight lines, in which case the subject would quickly understand that by advancing B by a distance of m he transfers the same distance to its starting point. Faced with a string looped around a post, the child constantly reverses the inequality but does not understand why. The reason, of course, is that in this situation the commutability is not only double but also bidirectional and inverted such that every modification of A brings about a modification of B and vice versa according to the inverse function $(+ B) \leftrightarrows (- A)$. This change of direction remains misunderstood and causes difficulty. Even when the aforementioned subjects arrive at the correct solution (displacement of three units for $m = 6$), they do not grasp the reason for it and do not generalize it when using the other post.

Nevertheless, one sees that even in these cases certain valid correspondences are used. These, however, are empirical and purely intramorphic. Examples would be CRI's prediction of the same but reversed inequality or momentary generalizations of the displacement of three rather than m units. But the general failure of CRI, SAN, and JOS to understand the relationships in play shows that solution of the problem requires intermorphic compositions. At this level, the absence of these is still such that the inverse variations of $+ B$ and $- A$ are not yet understood even to be bijective.

3. INTERMORPHIC COMPOSITIONS

The conquest of the intermorphic is accomplished in several steps. Here are some examples of the first step (Level II-A) where the intramorphic is still dominant:

PIE (7 years, 6 months): In Situation 1, PIE wants to move Post 1 forward by m as well as move Post 2 backward by the same amount. After trying this: "You have to put them a little closer."—"Up to where?"—"Up to there, that's half."—"And if you move it two squares?"—"There (½)."—"Why half of it?"—"Because I saw that it was wrong before." In Situation 2, she predicts: "Still half of it."—"Some other way?"—"You might put the post there (4 instead of 3); the little tail will come to there (correct)." In Situation 3, she predicts: "Three squares (half), that way they will all be just alike (meaning equalization of A, B, C, and D)." She tries out her hypothesis about Situation 2: "You'll have to put it on square 2 (correct)."—"Why?"—"Because the string (ABC) is bigger than the other (AB in Situation 1)."—"And there (in Situation 3)?"—"On three, halfway."—"Why?"—

"Because the string always changes. (Tries.) Here! (Close to the first square)."—"Less than there (Situation 2). How do you explain that?"—"I don't know."—"Where are there the most turns?"—"Here (Situation 3)."—"And where do you have to move the posts the most?"—"Here (Situation 1)."—"If you had more turns, would you move the post more or not so many squares?"—"More."—"If you made five turns?"—"Three squares. If you put it on two, there would be a tail sticking out."

PAT (7 years, 8 months): In Situation 1, PAT begins with a displacement of m, then sees that it has gone too far in the opposite direction: "How did that happen?"—"I don't know. When you pull the string, it moves."—"Then where do you have to put the post?"—"There (correct)."—"By how many (units)?"—"Three."—"Right. And with another turn (Situation 2)?"—"There (3 units; she tries). No, there (2 units)."—"Why?"—"The string is longer; it goes past it (for 3 units)."—"And like that (Situation 3)?"—"Four, it's longer."—"And here (between 1 and 2)?"—"Less."—"There (Situation 2), you moved it two and here (Situation 1) three. Why?"—"It's shorter."—"Here (Situation 2)?"—"You have made more turns."—"Then should you move it more or less in three (Situation 3)?"—"More."

NAT (7 years, 5 months): NAT begins prudently without anticipations: "You always have to look when you do it (moves the post)." In this way, she succeeds in establishing a movement of three units for Situation 1, but she then predicts m for Situation 2. For Situations 2 and 3, she even supposes that it must be moved by more than m: "Because it's a long string and you'll have to turn it (more) to make a turn."

LAU (7 years, 4 months): LAU begins with the same prudence in Situation 1, finds the solution of three units, but subsequently predicts m. After verification of three, he goes on to try out his idea in Situation 2: "You have to move it six, but with the other (Situation 1) you have to move it three . . . the string is longer."

KAR (8 years, 1 month): After predicting m, KAR gives the same reaction as NAT. By contrast, after trials for Situations 2 and 3, she correctly concludes that: "Each time it will be a little bit smaller," but "you can't know why."

GER (9 years, 4 months): GER gives the same reactions for Situations 2 and 3. He predicts six, "No, less (5 then 1 unit) because if I start to pull that (B), that (A) starts to move, too" and "because when you move it, it pulls and the string comes back." Then, after establishing three units for Situation 1, he predicts four will be necessary in Situation 2 because if "the string is longer, it stays longer, the end that's moving." Thus, GER is at the threshold of Level II-B, but with his formula "the string comes back" he still hangs on to the idea that in Situations 2 and 3, larger displacements are necessary.

The interest of these reactions is that, although remaining at the intramorphic level, they indicate what is lacking in order to attain the intermorphic level. Moreover, they prepare the way for that level even though they do not reach it. Their general progress over Level I is the discovery of the correspondence between the difference m in Situation 1 and the displacement of the post by m/2 in order to cancel out that difference. But this only constitutes an intramorphic correspondence linking two terms and not two elementary correspondences together, and it only proceeds by empirical trials without understanding the reasons for the results. And yet, the subject, having begun by a displacement, m, and not by m/2 (except in cases of prudence where the child wishes to try things out before pronouncing himself), now begins to search for reasons to explain the failure with m. Thus, PAT says, "When you pull the string, it moves," and, in particular, "if I start to pull that (B), that (A) starts to move, too" (GER). In other words, what the subject is in the process of discovering is a connection between two simple commutabilities. One of these insures that if B is pulled by pulling Post 1, what is gained at the point of arrival corresponds to something that "moves" at the other end. Likewise, seeing A being displaced in the direction opposite to segment B, he concludes that "that starts to move, too" and that there is, therefore, correspondence between the space left by A in m and "something that moves" in A beside Post 2. This is another simple equally intramorphic commutability. The intermorphic consists, therefore, in connecting these two symmetrical inverse correspondences and in understanding that the two commutabilities are really only one, but one that is bidirectional and in opposite directions. GER (at the threshold of Level II-B) is close to realizing this when he says, "when you move it (B), it pulls and the string comes back." The problem, however, is that even though these subjects discover that a link exists between these two commutabilities, they still do not understand the fact that one determines the other according to a quantitative symmetry such that every displacement of B in one direction brings about an exactly equivalent displacement of A in the other direction.

Another interplay of correspondences preparing the way for intermorphic correspondences is the interplay that joins the observable fact, "more turns," and the greater length of string in Situations 2 and 3: "it's a long string and you'll have to turn it (more) to make a turn" (NAT) and "you have made more turns" (PAT). But this elementary intramorphic relationship is not composed with the one that was seen in Situation 1 except to extensionally and illusorily generalize the displacement m/2 of the post in Situation 2 and 3. On the contrary, all of these subjects come to a sort of erroneous intermorphism leading from the "longer string" to the false need for a larger displacement (up to > m with NAT). Only KAR using direct trials sees that "each time it will be a little bit smaller," at the same time specifying that "you can't know why."

By contrast, in the majority of these subjects (PIE, etc.), the reactions closest to the intermorphic are those that lead to predicting the same result if one displaces either post. This equality of the lengthening of B on the left or on the right is not obvious (see NAT) and will be questioned by older subjects.

The second step in the conquest of intermorphic compositions is to establish correspondences integrating the positions of segments A and B in Situation 1 into a whole. This step, therefore, succeeds in establishing double bidirectional commutability but not for Situations 2 and 3, which it handles only by trial and error:

CES (7 years, 10 months): CES immediately predicts m/2 for Situation 1: "What is it?"—"Square three."—"Why three when the paper is six squares?"—"If you move the post to six, the string (A) will pull back to there (1)."—"And if you move this post (Post 2)?"—"Also three (he compares the right and left sides using his hand)."—"How did you know?"—"The size there and there."—"But why half?"—"To make the loop. If you put six, one would be long and the other short." Situation 2: "Also three (this is tried out). You could move it two (he verifies this)."—"And with the other post?"—"By three . . . by six." He goes as far as proposing ten, then four, and then establishes that two is correct. For Situation 3, he begins by proposing three: "It goes up to there and the string pulls back to there."—"And for (Situation) 2?"—"By two."—"Why?"—"Because the string is longer."—"And here (Situation 3), is it longer or shorter?"—"Longer."—"Then?"—"By three (tries). That's wrong; by two or by one."—"Why?"—"There (Situation 1) I did three, it pulled back a lot; here (Situation 2) two, it pulled back less; and (Situation 3) one, still less and it works fine."

MAN (8 years, 4 months): Situation 1: "In the middle . . . if you move it the whole way (m), it will be longer (B > A)." But he proposes three for Situations 2 and 3 and only finds the correct answer by trying out two and one without being able to explain it, except to say that "the length of the rope" has changed.

JOE (9 years, 1 month): In Situation 1, JOE indicates half of m: "If you pull that much (the whole distance), the end of the string (A) is going to come back in the other direction. It's going to do the opposite. One to the right; the other to the left."—"And with Post 2?"—"The same thing on the other side." But for Situation 2 he predicts a displacement of m. For Situation 3: "You could do the same thing, but it'd be silly.

It's better to do something different." Upon trying: "Ah! I understand. The longer it is, the less far it comes (he shows this in Situations 3, 2, and 1)."

These reactions are doubly instructive from the point of view of the intermorphic and of its relationship to the transmorphic. The intermorphic consists in composing correspondences of correspondences with each other, and the transmorphic, in addition to doing that, involves an operatory synthesis of higher rank. Here, the intermorphic is marked by the understanding of a necessary quantitative dependence between the advance of B and the retreat of A, because the first pulls the second if Post 1 is moved. Whereas subjects of the preceding group only had an inkling of some connection, and that only because empirical trials disconfirmed their prediction of m, these subjects anticipate a quantified function. Cancellation of the difference, m, implies the displacement m/2 of B in one direction and of m/2 of A in the other, therefore "half and half" as one subject says. Because both of these displacements along with their simple commutativities are included, their integration into a single whole becomes a double commutativity, bidirectional and in opposite directions, and constitutes an intermorphic composition.

That being the case, a new problem arises. Why, if the subject understands that the shortening of either A or B makes the other lengthen, does he not grasp by simple generalization that with three lengths the shortening of one will ipso facto make the two others lengthen simultaneously because they are attached to the same post? And why does he not understand that with four lengths, modifying one brings about modifications of the others in the opposite direction? Not only do these subjects not understand, but either they do not take account of the numbers or their reasoning goes in a completely different direction. Like subjects PIE and GER (Level II-A), they initially think that either they can stick with m/2 or that they must choose a movement greater than m/2 because, as CES says, "the string is longer." (It should be remarked that this expression was made without any allusion to the number of turns.) It is only with empirical trials that they discover the law, "The longer it is, the less far it comes," and so forth, but this law remains a simple empirical impression without providing the least explanation.

The big difference between Situations 1, 2, and 3 is that in Situation 1, the shortening of A and the lengthening of B go hand in hand with an advance of one and of a pulling back of the other. This is easy to establish by comparing their movements without leaving their internal reference system. By contrast, in Situations 2 and 3 where the string makes several turns around the same posts, two sorts of movements must be distinguished. On the one hand, each segment of the string is displaced in the direction opposite to the direction of the preceding one, because they are wrapped around the posts. On the other hand, moving one of the posts only shortens the longest segment, A, and simultaneously lengthens B and C ("it pulls both ropes at the same time," MAN will say during the following step, section 4) or B, C, and D. Moreover, it does so independently of their relative movements which are difficult to follow in detail. One must, therefore, make reference to a total multivariational system, although in Situation 1 this reduces to a pair of variations. This lengthening of two or three segments in opposition to the shortening of a single segment obliges one to substitute a more complex composition for intermorphic correspondences by symmetrical equivalences (m/2 against m/2) of Situation 1. In this complex composition the initial overlap, m, is divided by the number of elements displaced (m/3 or m/4), and this is done without the possibility of being based on the simple empirical finding of two movements in opposite directions as in Situation 1.

4. TRANSMORPHIC COMPOSITIONS

The complexity of Situations 1 and 2 is mastered only at what I call Level III-B, around 14 or 15 years of age. Recall, in this respect, that intermorphic correspondences were not attained immediately but that the way for their composition ατ Level II-B was prepared by a Level II-A. Similarly, with transmorphic compositions we observe the existence of a Level III-A where certain developments appear that will lead to the transmorphic by dissociating the two pairs of distinct relationships, "advance-retreat" and "lengthening-shortening." Moreover, this beginning understanding leads to the interesting consequence that the equivalence of moving either Post 1 or Post 2 is thrown into question, as if there were regression on this point although, in fact, it is a sign of progress:

JEA (9 years, 3 months): JEA predicts m/2 in Situation 1, "because if you pull (Post 1) clear to the end (the whole distance m), it will make the string short (A)."But he believes that a displacement of m will be needed with Post 2. With respect to Situation 2, "It's not the same. There are two turns and there (Situation 1), there is only one" (he speaks, therefore, of turns and no longer only of lengths), therefore "it changes" but he can do nothing but predict a change.

SOP (10 year, 7 months): SOP likewise predicts a displacement of m for Post 2 in contrast to a displacement of m/2 with Post 1, "because that will make the string (A) go forward by six (units)." In Situation 2: "There are more turns. When you make a lot of turns, that makes more." After trials establishing the contrary: "Let's say two."—"And there (Situation 3)?"—"There (Situation 1), you had to move it a half, there (Situation 2) a third, then there (Situation 3) it must be a quarter. One turn, one half; two, a third; and three, a quarter."

MAN (11 years, 7 months): In Situation 1, MAN says three with Post 1 but six with Post 2, "because there will be another piece of string that will come." He indicates the general direction of A and B forward, then he corrects his prediction of six to three by indicating the partial rotation of the longer string around Post 2. In Situation 2: "You have made two turns," but even so he predicts m/2 (for first one and then the other post). Upon establishing that a movement of two units is correct, he finds the reason this is so: "because it pulls both ropes at the same time. It pulls more." He then explains that for Situation 1, m is "double (twice as much as the displacement to be made), and there (Situation 2), triple."—"And there (Situation 3)?"—"Quadruple."—"Then by how much?"—"By two."—"Like there?"—"No, by one . . . by one and a half." But he still believes that by modifying the total length of the string, it will change.

LOU (11 years, 0 months): After at first believing in the inequality of the actions of the posts, LOU recognizes that with Post 2, one also has m/2, "because it lets go of the string and it takes it in on the other side." Situation 2: "Three (tries—very surprised)."—"Then?"—"By zero . . . no, but less than three. Two or one, that would surprise me."—"Then?"—"By two."—"And with Post 2?"—"Also by two, because there are three turns."—"And here (Situation 3)?"—"By one."—"Why?"—"One less like I did before."

ROL (12 years, 2 months): Situation 2: "It's the same as that (Situation 1) except that there is one more turn (tries by moving three units). It's too much, it must be one and a half. It must be half (of the three units moved in Situation 1), because there is one more turn."—"Why?"—"It makes it move more because it's longer . . . no, it's because it's wrapped around the posts."—"And here (Situation 3)?"—"There, it's a fourth . . . the string is still wrapped around the post. It takes more room."—"Then?"—"Then . . . "—"And like that (five turns)?"—"Still less. One centimeter."

ERI (12 years, 3 months): After multiple trials and error, ERI arrives at m/2 for Situation 1, m/3 for Situation 2, and m/4 for Situation 3, "because the string has been wrapped more times around the posts."

First, with respect to Post 2 in Situation 1, one sees the distinction between "lengthening-shortening" and "advance-retreat" appear. In contrast to the case of Post 1 where it is established that A pulls back when B goes forward, the two segments appear to both advance when one pulls on Post 2: "There will be another piece of string that will come," as MAN says before discovering the partial rotation around Post 2, whence the equivalence of his action with that of A.

This distinction is, therefore, the source of an apparent regression for the question of the two posts in Situation 1. More important, however, it leads these subjects to the essential discovery in Situation 2 that, as MAN says, "It pulls both ropes at the same time," independently of their relative directions which are opposite to one another. In other words, as the majority of subjects express it, if there are more turns, "it makes more movement." This means that the shortening of the longest segment no longer corresponds to a single lengthening as in Situation 1 (two segments in all), but to two in Situation 2 and to three in Situation 3, whence the more or less laborious arrival at the correct responses m/3 for Situation 2 and m/4 for Situation 3. There is, therefore, progressive transition to the transmorphic, the level attained right off by the following subjects:

COR (14 years, 11 months): Situation 1: "If there're six (units for m), the string is divided into two parts, it's therefore m/2."—"And with Post 2?"—"The same."—"And here (Situation 2)?"—"One third of what's left over, because it goes back and forth three times."—"And there (Situation 3)?"—"A quarter."

VIN (15 years, 11 months): Situation 1: "By three. It's going to pull back one half here and go forward the other."—"And if I move Post 2?"—"Same thing. There it'll shorten by three (the long section) and lengthen here by three." Situation 2: "By two . . . it pulls twice as much as here (Situation 1). Here you divide six by two and there by three."—"And there (Situation 3)?"—"You divide by four."—"Here (Situation 1), it's as if you only pulled once and there (Situation 2) twice."

PHI (16 years, 1 month): PHI begins by trial and error in Situation 2 but in Situation 3 rapidly concludes: "I divide six by four because that makes four turns . . . that turns four times, it's the whole rope that moves, so it's divided by four."

It seems, therefore, in view of the trial-and-error approach of subjects 11 to 12 years old and the belated character of immediate solutions (14- to 15-year-olds), that the general structure of Situations 2 and 3 differs substantially from that of Situation 1. The two essential novelties are: (a) that two of the three segments (or three of four) are equal from the start and must conserve this equality when they are lengthened in order to equalize them with the longest segment, which must be shortened; and (b) that by displacing a post, one lengthens all of the segments by the same length in the direction of this displacement, independently of their relative directions relative to one another. If we call x the length of the equal segments and m the difference between them and the free segment (which will be of length x + m), it is a matter of dividing m among n segments (among three for Situation 2). In that case, the segments B and C, equal to each other, will take on the value $x + m/3$. With regard to the free segment, A (= x + m), it gains m/3 on the side where it is pulled by displacement of the post, but on the other side, it loses m/3 because it is not held back; moreover, it loses the two lengths of m/3 gained by B and C. Therefore, it loses from the free end $3(m/3) = m$, which cancels the overlap m, whereas having gained m/3 on the side of the post that moves, it becomes equal to B and C, all three taking on the same length, $x + m/3$.

One sees, therefore, the differences relative to Situation 1 where there is simple compensation between two unequal segments, A and B, and where, therefore, there is also double inverse commutability. By contrast, in Situations 2 and 3, there is multicommutability. Because, however, all of the movements cannot be followed perceptually, lengthenings and shortenings are not calculated as a function of advances and retreats (except partially for the free segment A), but as a function of the relationship between m and the number of the segments. There is, moreover, bijection between the increases in each segment on one side and the elimination of the m/3's on the side of the initial difference m. This calculation presupposes, therefore, reasoning in terms of a general system with n variables and no longer only in terms of intermorphic compositions among variations of the two terms of a pair as in Situation 1. Thus, one finds that the transmorphic character of this composition is quite different than that of intermorphic compositions. In transmorphic compositions, correspondences are composed by means of operatory calculations which themselves depend on a general multivariational system. The closure and automorphisms of this system are based on conservation of the whole (total length of the string) across transformations and allow one to see in the system an elementary category as well. Added to this are comparisons, which we come back to later, between this problem of the posts and the question of roads to be made equal. When the interrogation began with the latter, subjects were several times inspired to find the solution of dividing the difference, m, by the number of segments of the string, despite the difference between the discontinuity of the roads and the continuity of the string.

5. THE QUESTION OF ROADS AND COMPARISON OF THE TWO PROBLEMS

It is interesting to compare the preceding problem to an analogous one where it is also a matter of equalizing two to four lengths, but this time discontinuous segments whose parts must be displaced by transfers rather than by pulling. This question is easier, of course, but it nevertheless gives rise to a succession of instructive correspondences. Here are some examples of a first level:

CRI (5 years,4 months): Situation 1: "I would like you to give me a piece so they are both the same length."—(She indicates the lower part of A equal to B, breaks it, adds it to B and pushes it a little to try to equalize the pieces.) "Its much too big (A < < 2B)."—"(The experimenter goes back to the beginning.) Try to find a piece so that . . . and so on."—(She again takes a piece equal to B but cut from the top of A.)—"Why there?"—"So they're the same length." Subsequently, CRI cuts a piece corresponding to the difference A − B, which undoes the inequality, then succeeds in cutting it almost in half. "Can you be sure?"—"I don't know. Maybe here (goes back to one piece: B)[5]." In Situation 2, she starts off the same way, that is, −B, then cuts what remains of A in two and, by trial and error, arrives at two equal roads, and what is left over produces a third road of equal length. "Is it like the other game (posts)?"—"It's straight, and that is too. You also make a line."

DAM (6 years, 3 months): DAM also cuts a part equal to B from the bottom of A, then seeing that it does not work, cuts a part equal to B from the top of A. "Will you have the same thing?"—"No, I don't think so"; but he starts over again three times. Then he wants to cut off the part of A that exceeds B and divide it. He cuts a piece that is too big, cuts it in two, and does not succeed. In Situation 2, he settles on two large and one small roads: "I don't have enough clay."

SAN (6 years, 4 months): SAN exhibits the same reaction with a part equal to B cut from the bottom of A. He does the same thing in Situation 2, but he is more successful at cutting the part of A that exceeds B in two. In Situation 3, he cuts the difference A − B in three pieces that he adds to what remains of A and to B and C. Whence three large roads that are more equal and a small road, D. After this, he takes away three small pieces from the top of A and ends up with five roads.

JOS (6 years, 10 months): JOS gives the same reactions in Situation 1: A part equal to B is taken away from the bottom and then the top of A. But between these two efforts he comes close to cutting the A − B segment in half without exploiting this mixture of luck and learning.

The common characteristic of these reactions and those of the same subjects on the problem of the posts is that in order to equalize two elements, they only think about making the smaller larger or about making

[5]The meaning of Piaget's clarification, that is, (*revient à un bout: B*), is unclear—Translator.

the larger smaller without trying to predict the effects that the modification imposed on one will have on the other. In the case of the posts, they displaced the distance m (= A − B in the case of the roads) without seeing that doing so simply reversed the inequality. In the present case, Situation 1, they at first only attempt to double the length of B by taking something off the bottom or top of A without wondering what, in that case, happens to A's length and finding to their surprise that a great inequality exists. When in the course of subsequent trials and error they momentarily fall upon the correct solution (DAM and JOS), they do not understand why and go on to others without exploiting it. In Situations 2 and 3, the attempts are better but only for the simple reason that more pieces are taken away from A, which fosters equality. In a word, these subjects very much put the project of increasing the size of the small elements into correspondence with the obligation to take x away from A, but they do not succeed in the double correspondence based on commutability that would permit them to attain the equivalence B + x = A − x. With regard to the comparison between the problem of the roads and that of the posts, it remains purely figurative: "It's straight, and that is too. You also make a line" (CRI), and so forth.

By contrast, from Level II-A on, the solution is found, as it was with the posts in Situation 1. Here, however, it is discovered for Situations 2 and 3 as well:

PIE (7 years, 6 months): PIE does the road experiment before the post experiment. Situation 1: He takes only half of the distance A − B, "because I saw, I did a big one (took away the entire distance) and I have taken half of it." Situation 2: "I want to cut here and here (correct), then that will make a piece for here (B), one for here (C) and then that (what is left for A)."—"Are these three pieces just alike?"—"Yes, they have to be, because otherwise they aren't the same length." Situation 3: "I do here and here four times."—"You make four parts, and there are three little roads?"—"Yes, but that one there (A), it needs some too (a quarter of the initial difference)." After interrogation concerning the posts, the experimenter asks for a comparison of that experiment with the roads. He indicates Situation I and says that "You cut it in two so they will be the same, and here also in two."—"And there (Situation 3)?"—"Here (posts) you will almost cut it in two." In contrast to his original responses with the posts, he now, under the influence of the roads, correctly reconstitutes the equalities of the strings in Situations 2 and 3.

LAU (7 years, 6 months): In Situation 1, LAU moves half of the difference from A to B, and in Situation 2, only takes two parts away from A. "Why don't you cut it right at the end?"—"Because the two little roads would be longer than what's left." Situation 3: four quarters, one of which is for A. Comparison with the posts: "They have to be the same length."

CES (7 years, 10 months): CES succeeded immediately with the posts in Situation 1, but a residual of the preceding level remains for the roads. However, he succeeds by trial and error in Situation 2 and immediately generalizes to Situation 3: "How many parts (do you have to make)?"—"Three. No, that's wrong (before seeing the result). Four! (He cuts them and succeeds)."

MAN (8 years, 4 months): In Situation 1, MAN says immediately, "You have to cut it in the middle" but curiously he begins by a transition using all of A − B before finding "half of the part that's too long."

PAT (7 years, 8 months): Situation 1: She cuts off the difference, then divides it in halves. Situation 2: She immediately divides the difference into three pieces and places them on A, B, and C. Situation 3: "Four, like that."

We see, then, that if around 7 or 8 years of age some groping or even some residuals of Level 1 are still seen, in the majority of cases the solution is immediate or rapid, as it also is with the problem of the posts in Situation 1. But the interest here is that, as already seen, Situations 2 and 3 seem easier to master than Situation 1 (cf. CES), whereas with the posts they were quite a bit more difficult. The reason for this is simple: The bijection between the m/n, that is, the relationship of the differential segment to the number of elements, to be taken away from A and their final annexation to the n elements is applied, in the case of the posts, to a pluridirectional multicommutability. This involves translating the advances and retreats of the elements into a bijective interplay of lengthenings and shortenings, whence the difficulty of the abstraction required. In the case of the roads, by contrast, the subtractions and annexations modifying the lengths are effected by discontinuous actions of the subject and no longer by the circumvolutions of a single string, the details of whose movement are not simultaneously perceptible.

It no less remains that the same problem is involved, which subjects of Level III see quite clearly:

ROL (12 years, 2 months): "It's exactly the same. The roads (in Situation 1), you have to share half, and there (posts) you have to move (he remembers what he did: three units), afterward (Situation 3), you cut a third and so on . . . It was with the third (Situation 3) that I saw that it was the same thing."

EMA (13 years, 0 months): "If you look at it carefully (posts), it's thanks to the roads you make (that you succeed)." Effectively, in order to understand Situation 3, he had reproduced the situation with the roads by means of a string: "I cut four times (meaning cut the excess length of A into four pieces), and I put each of them on one of the strings (at the other end)," which is a direct image of the bijection of the m/4's taken away at the beginning and the m/4's added at the end, as in the case of the roads.

VIN (15 years, 11 months): "You always divide—and there, too—the length of what's left over . . . of the ends that are too long."

PHI (16 years, 1 month): "Here (posts) it turns twice, three times; four times; there, there are two, three, four roads. You have to make the same calculations." In Situation 2, "I made thirds (posts) and here (roads) you again have to change the dividing, it's also divided by three."

This correspondence of structure with structure is thus engaged in the direction of functors and is added to what we have said in section 4 with respect to the kinship between the transmorphic correspondences observed and elementary categorial organizations.

6 The Sections of a Parallelepiped and a Cube

Jean Piaget
with
H. Kilcher
and
J. P. Bronckart

The sections of a solid are doubly instructive from the point of view of the composition of correspondences. On the one hand, the role of transformations is reduced to a minimum. This is because, unlike the successive displacements or divisions, and so forth, examined in the preceding chapters, sectioning solids does not involve composing successive sections among themselves. In terms of transforming action, one section is similar to another. The only thing that differentiates them is the composition between the line one starts with and the path one travels according to variations of position and direction. To be sure, sections are transformations, but transformations that require a set of morphic comparisons for their compositions to be understood. On the other hand, because a section comes from cutting through a solid and thereby generating a plane form that is not necessarily equivalent to any of the external faces, the interplay of correspondences will be fundamental in defining these new surfaces. One can even maintain in this regard that the solid to be sectioned constitutes a tridimensional space in miniature that is comparable to external space in general, and that it includes its own internal visual figures that the sections will actualize. In that case, just as the psychogenetic evolution of geometric notions passes through three phases,[1] intra-, inter-, and transfigural (algebrization), so the psychogenetic evolution of "subfigural" notions having to do with sections and their visible sides must must pass though phases of intra-, inter-, and transsubfigural correspondences. At least that is so insofar as the subject sticks to what is observable, devotes himself to

[1]Moreover in parallel with the history of scientific geometry itself.

inferences by taking account of the three dimensions, or goes on from there to a general structure whose deductive compositions are systematic. Thus, it is immediately clear what forms the usual three levels of compositions among correspondences will take. Either they will remain intramorphic, that is, prior to compositions, they will become intermorphic, that is, involve composition among correspondences of the same rank, or they will achieve the transmorphic, that is, achieve a higher degree of freedom.

More specifically, a section is a surface (in our case, a plane) produced by transecting a solid with a line, x, drawn on one side of the solid and travelling through it along another line, y, at some angle to x. The surface s being a function of these two lines, s = f(xy), the problem is to analyze the correspondences that subjects establish between the variations of x and y and those of the form of s. We start at a level where young subjects only consider x and have to discover y (see Fig. 6.1).

1. EQUIPMENT AND TECHNIQUE

To begin, the experimenter presents the child with different solids made of modeling clay (parallelepiped, rectangular solid, cubes, spheres, ovoids, and cylinders) and different surfaces made of heavy paper (rectangles, squares, and circles). The purpose of doing this is to see whether subjects spontaneously classify the objects into solids and surfaces and to determine what criteria they use. All of the material is presented in conglomerate with

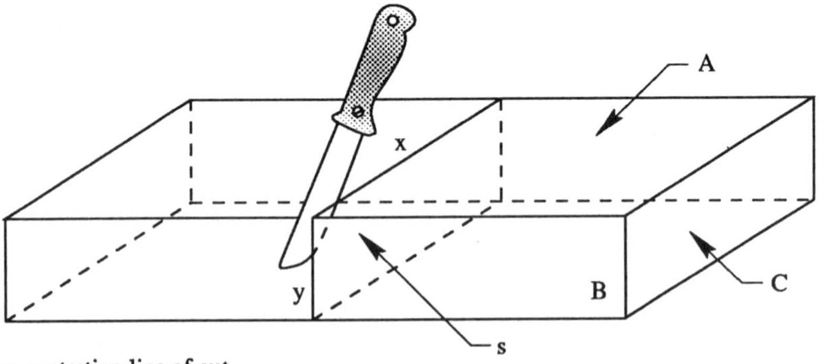

x = starting line of cut
y = path of cut
s = surface of cut
A = upper & lower surfaces
B = long lateral surfaces
C = ends

FIG. 6.1. Parallepiped sections apparatus.

a simple request for classification and description. Then the experimenter proceeds to a comparison of the group of surfaces and the group of solids: "Are they the same?"; "Why?" In particular, the experimenter prompts a comparison between the squares and the rectangles.

Only after this is done, does one go on to the sections. The subject is asked to place the knife on the parallelepiped (Situation 1) at the place where he would like to make a cut and to do this gently enough so that he marks the clay. The knife imprint, therefore, traces a straight line on the solid. That done, the subject is asked to anticipate the form that the new surface created by the cut will have. When it seems that the instruction has not been understood, the experimenter presents a reference situation in the form of a breadroll that one can slice or cut lengthwise and asks the subject to draw the form that will appear with the sectioning. He then stresses that all subsequent questions will have to do with internal surfaces of this sort:

1. The subject is asked to make the section, to find and explain the result both in terms of the type of form (qualitative plane) and in terms of its size (quantitative plane).
2. The subject is asked what section will have to be made to obtain some rectangular surface different from the one obtained.
3. The subject is asked what to do in order to obtain a form other than a rectangle, for example, a square.
4. The subject is asked what are the different forms that one can obtain by sectioning a parallelepiped rectangle.

The same technique is used for sectioning the cube (Situation 2). The experimenter then requests a comparison of the results of sectioning in Situations 1 and 2:

5. The child is asked how to obtain a parallelogram by sectioning the parallelepiped along a line at a right angle to its external form.
6. The subject is told that he can obtain other forms of triangular, trapezoidal types, and so on, and is asked what he might do to find them.

In what follows, we only speak of the sections of the parallelepiped and the cube. The other solids only served for counterproofs and the analysis of their sections was done long ago.[2]

[2]J. Piaget and B. Inhelder, *La Représentation de l'Espace chez l'Enfant.* Paris: Presses Universitaires de France, 1947.

2. ELEMENTARY CORRESPONDENCES

From 6 to 7 years of age, the form of the surface of the section is still only predicted as a function of the line x and of the upper surface of the solid, as if the solid had no thickness and reduced to that surface (A). There is, therefore, no need to consider the reactions of younger children:

ALA (6 years, 5 months): ALA wants to cut the top side, A, of the parallelepiped along the longer median: "It will be a little bit a rectangle because that makes it the same (as in A), only it's not like up there. That will be littler (he indicates the two halves of A on either sides of the cutting line x)." For the transverse cut: "It will be a square."—"But when you open it?"—"Ah, no, a rectangle. No, because here (the top half), it has to be a square for sure, then that has to be a square."—"Why?"—"Because you cut it there and that makes a square here (in A) and everywhere! (The cut is made.) No, a rectangle because the top (A) is bigger than there (height of the solid)." For the next cut, he draws a triangle and proposes a section cutting off a corner of A. The cube with a median section will give a rectangle because A is split in two. Upon trying, he finds that a square is obtained. "How would you have been able to tell that?"—"I look at the edge (of the section), and first I looked all around the edge that we cut (meaning the edge of A)." He proposes a diagonal section and then concludes: "You're going to have a square and, to be honest, a triangle."

ORA (7 years, 0 months): "What is it?"—"A rectangle, it's stretched out."—"If you cut into this rectangle, and we open it, and we look at the form inside?"—"(He makes a transverse cut.) It will be a square."—"How do you know that?"—"Half of the length is a square."—"But inside?"—"Always a square. You'll see."—"Can you draw it?"—(He draws a square.)—"Where is it?"—"There (half of A)."—"But that part there (the cut)?"—"Also a square."—"How do you know that?"—"Because it's half of the rectangle."—"Can you make another form?"—"Yes, a triangle. I cut two lines catty-corner (corner) and that becomes a triangle."—"Where is it?"—"There (on A)."—"And inside?"—"It's a rectangle, but the whole thing is a triangle . . . there, inside, there is a rectangle." Subsequently, however, with regard to the diagonal of the cube: "You already see a triangle, so inside it will be a triangle. (He makes the cut)."—"Well then, a little surprise?"—"Inside it's a rectangle because it's stretched out a little more."

DAN (7 years, 9 months): DAN is sure that, contrary to a cube (which he calls a block), "a square is not as long as a rectangle" and you cannot "put anything inside" by drawing on the surface. These details obtained, as was done with every child, the experimenter asks him to predict the shape of the surface one will see by cutting through the parallelepiped. DAN proposes that the cut be made transversely and predicts that a square will be found, A being divided in two by the line x. The cut is made. "You predicted a square, and it's a rectangle."—"I was not talking about what was inside (he is well aware that the contrary is true)."—"Why did we find a rectangle?"—"Because that (the uncut parallelepiped) is a rectangle, and it always stays a rectangle, and I don't see why you have (would have) a square at one end." Next, the line of the cut, x, being diagonal, "It will be a triangle (and) it won't be a rectangle any more."—"But it's still the same rectangle as when you made a straight cut?"—"It's really the same thing, but I made a mistake (because) it was a triangle inside." For the cube: "It will always be square; inside it will still be the form of a square. Oh! You're not sure inside (he indicates the diagonal), it will be like a triangle (and he draws it)."

CEA (8 years, 0 months): With respect to the diagonal, CEA again says: "It will be a little triangle."—"And inside?"—"It will give the same form as on the outside."

These reactions testify to the extremely pregnant[3] character of a topological system of notions that one might be tempted to consider as prior to and determining of all correspondences. In reality, however, it is a matter of concepts constructed in close collaboration with a very general interplay of spatial correspondences, and it is these correspondences' incompleteness and lack of composition that accounts for both the properties and limitations of these subjects's initial ideas. Let us first try to describe these beginning notions. Then we analyze their interdependencies with correspondences according to the hypothesis that correspondences, as systems of comparisons, guide conceptualization.

The essential thing about these ideas is that they substitute the still preoperatory concept of enclosures (enveloppements)[4] for the concepts of

---

[3]Piaget's use of the term "*prégnant*" here and elsewhere in this work refers to the "Principle of *Prägnanz*" familiar from Gestalt psychology. In a note in the English version of Wertheimer's *Productive Thinking* (New York: Harper & Brothers, 1959, p. 239), the editor writes: "The principle of *Prägnanz,* first formulated by Wertheimer with reference to perception, asserts that the organization of the field tends to be as simple and clear as the given conditions allow." Piaget also has used this principle to explain the stabilization of conscious states and to account for cognitive repression. Throughout this translation, the term *pregnant* is used in this technical sense—Translator.

[4]Piaget and Inhelder used the terms "*enveloppe,*" "*envelopper,*" "*enveloppement,*" and so forth, at least as early as 1947 (Piaget & Inhelder, op cit, p. 129) and said of them: "The relationship 'between' is a special case of the relationships of '*enveloppement.*' These relationships, therefore, just as do the relationships of neighborhood, separation, and order, constitute elementary spatial intuitions." They go on to explain that the position of one point "between" two others is an *enveloppement* in one dimension; the internal or external position of a point relative to a closed figure constitutes an *enveloppement* in two dimensions; and the internal or external position of a point relative to a closed solid constitutes an *enveloppement*

surface and solid continuous in two or three dimensions. In other words, they present two characteristics: (a) The whole includes more than the sum of the parts, and (b) of special interest in this case, there is still undifferentiation between extension and intension.

We have known for a long time about the enclosure aspect of these preoperatory surfaces characterized by their perimeter. ALA again illustrates this when he says, "I look at the edge, and first I looked all around the edge that we cut." As for the solid, it is an enclosure made of surfaces in the preceding sense, but these surfaces are not composed with one another through an interplay of dimensions and coordinates. For that reason, solids essentially are reduced to their upper surface. "They're the same," says ALA of a cube and a drawing of a square. At the same time, solids are provided with an interior permitting one to "put something inside," thus constituting a new whole. If, however, one wishes to spell out what these subjects call the "whole" (cf. ORA for whom "the whole" is opposed to "there inside") and, even more, what they mean by "inside," one finds himself caught in a web of contradictions that would be inexplicable except for the second fundamental characteristic of preoperatory enclosures, that is, undifferentiation between extension and intension. For example, 7 elements drawn from a collection of 30 make "more" than 7 drawn from a collection of 10. Or more relevant to sections, a point imaginable on a square figure will itself be a square, whereas on a circle it will be round.[5] From such a perspective, it becomes clear that the notion of "inside" can have two meanings that the subject struggles in vain to bring together. It expresses a sort of global inclusion such that, in extension, it is a matter of part of what is enclosed, whereas in intension, it shares the qualitative characteristics of what does the enclosing, which is to say, of the upper surface, A. That is why ORA, having marked a triangle on A says that "inside" there will be a rectangle, because A is rectangular, but that "the whole thing is a triangle" because one has provided it with such a figure. That is also why afterward for the cube he returns to unified extension and intension by saying "You already see a triangle, so inside it will be a triangle."

If, with all this in mind, we go back to the question of correspondences, we become aware that in continuous materials they manifest a very

---

in three dimensions. Further, they indicate that relationships of *enveloppement* or *enlacement* are "intuitive results of the action of surrounding". In the English translation of that work (*The Child's Conception of Space,* New York: W. W. Norton, 1956) *envelopper* was translated *surrounding.* In discussions of topology in English (see Courant & Robbins: *What is Mathematics?,* London: Oxford University Press, 1941) the terms *envelop, surround, enclose, interlace* are all used without, apparently, any of them being a specific or privileged technical term. Because in English the various forms needed seem more natural for *enclose* than for *surround,* I have translated *envelopper* as *to enclose*—Translator.

[5]J. Piaget and B. Inhelder, op cit, p. 153.

understandable lack of composition that in good part accounts for the preceding notions. Insofar as the construction of the enclosure itself is concerned, it is clear that it is solidary with a surjection. Everything observable on a surface or within a solid corresponds to a single enclosing that encompasses it in a single general figure. By contrast, when the subject tries to use the correspondence reciprocal to this surjection and what we call "multijection" to go from the totality back to the elements, he has trouble. This maneuver is relatively easy when collections of discrete objects are involved (but only "relatively," as we well know from the study of inclusion). But with continuous materials, he runs into the systematic difficulty that the elements are intimately adjoined and quasiuncuttable. Where imagining the result of sectioning is at issue, the only thing he can do is put that result into correspondence with the characteristics of the enclosure. That correspondence will, however, remain intensive because, in extension, localization in a continuous environment runs into the difficulties that we just saw. The only way, then, to overcome this essentially intramorphic level will be to organize the sides of the solid according to three dimensions. This allows a direction to be assigned to line y and the surface s of the section to be constructed as a function of x and y connected by new correspondences.

3. THE INTERMORPHIC LEVEL

The problem is, therefore, for the subject to free himself from the pregnance accorded up to this point to the upper face, A, of the solid and to construct within the solid's interior a tridimesional system corresponding to the coordinates of external space. It will facilitate analysis if we first note that these two sorts of constructions, interfigural for space in general and "intersubfigural" for the dimensions of the solid, begin at the same age of 9 to 10 years. But it remains for us to understand what correspondences or morphisms help effect this change in perspective. Up to this point, we have only been familiar with its operatory and transformational aspects.

Recall that in the introductory part of the experiment the subject is presented with different solids and surfaces in an attempt to have him find a dichotomy answering to this distinction without suggestions of any sort. The first fact to emphasize is that he finds nothing of the kind at Level I ("they're the same," said ALA of a square and a cube). At 8 years of age, the subjects studied here still do not spontaneously oppose surfaces to solids but do refer to the third dimension when they compare two solids with distinct thicknesses:

MAR (8 years, 4 months): Limits herself to distinguishing small and large.

CRA (8 years, 0 months): Distinguishes "the flat and the tall" and says of a solid that it is "thinner" than another.

PAC (8 years, 6 months): Speaks immediately of "thick" versus "thin," but does so with respect to two different solids.

By contrast, from 9 to 10 years of age comparison centers on the opposition between surface and solid:

PAC (9 years, 9 months): Says that the surface is "a lot thinner" and, even more important, recognizes that the sides of the parallelepiped are surfaces: "Yes, all of the faces are rectangles."—"How many?"—"(He counts) Six!"

GER (9 years, 11 months): Refers to the thickness: "It's thin."

FRED (10 years, 10 months): Refers to the height: Cubes are "squares with more height" and there are six of them because "there're several sides (and) you can turn them any direction, and it always makes a square."

EVA (10 years, 2 months) and **ALEX (10 years, 3 months):** Also invoke the height. The second says of the square that it is "completely the same (as a cube) but not as thick, not thick sides."

ROB (10 years, 11 months): Finally uses the terms solid and surface to indicate that the first "is fuller" than the second, whereas MIC (11 years, 11 months), referring to himself as a solid, says that he "takes more room" than she does ("in the air,"specifies EVA), which is complementary double reference to his internal and to his external space.

The new fact that becomes apparent around age 9 or 10 years is that subjects take consciousness of three dimensions. Naturally, this occurs in various actions well before these ages, but it does not occur in thought as the surprising reactions of Level I (up to and including 8 years of age) show. But let us recall that it is only at these same ages of 9 to 10 years that subjects succeed in constructing not only coordinates in general but even verticals and horizontals when it is a matter of predicting, for example, the surface line of water in an inclined beaker or the position of a plumbline relative to a crooked wall. The correspondences permitting the transition from the preceding level to this intermorphic level must therefore be common to the structuration of external space and to the internal dimensional organization of solids without being limited to the latter.

That said, these correspondences seem to be of two necessarily conjoint types. One type teases out the commonality or, in other words, the parallelism of direction between two or n straight lines. Although, very precocious, this first form of correspondence stays within the interior of a plane. The second type of correspondence leads to orthogonality based on symmetry, because the perpendicular to a straight line is the only line generating two equal angles. Equally precocious, this correspondence also ends up not leaving the plane. By contrast, when compositions between parallelism and orthogonality are increased, the third dimension sooner or later results. This is because if parallelism and orthogonality suffice to characterize a plane, they still can be generalized to relationships among planes, which may in turn be parallel or orthogonal (or whatever one wishes, but relative to these norms). Now the strange fact apparent in the reactions of Level I is that side A of the solid is privileged by being "higher" in itself, as if the "top" position were not relative to the subject's own position. It is sufficient, therefore, to "turn [the solid] in any direction," as FRED pertinently says, in order for the right angle between a median cut through A and the plane of A to become the right angle between a vertical side and the base or, in other words, in order for the horizontal side to become vertical ("vertical squares," as FRED also said with respect to cubes).

The essential novelty that the intermorphic compositions of Level II generate with respect to anticipation of results is that internal surfaces are put into correspondence with the visible, including the vertical, sides of the solid. But this progress is not accomplished in one fell swoop. Initially, one sees cases intermediary between Levels I and II where subjects still predict an internal triangle for an oblique section but subsequently understand why that is not the case:

PAU (8 years, 6 months): For the transverse median, PAU still predicts that two squares will result from the division of A, but he is not sure what will be found on the inside ("I don't know") except that, "It will make four corners." Seeing the rectangle, he explains that "it's changed there" in parallel with the vertical side. For the diagonal: "There will be two triangles because three corners make a triangle." However, while drawing what he expects, he changes his mind: "It will be a rectangle because in this direction it is stretched out and in the other direction, too," which results, therefore, from correspondence with the two vertical sides of the solid.

GER (9 years, 11 months): GER also predicts a square for the transverse section, but she revises that opinion when the experimenter asks her what they will see on the inside. Now she predicts a rectangle, "Because if you cut it, it makes the same width as there (surface visible at the side). It will, therefore, be exactly the same (as the lateral side)." By contrast, for the diagonal, it will be a triangle (which she draws). Upon seeing the rectangle, she explains it by pointing to one of the visible parallel sides (the longest). For the cube, she correctly predicts a rectangle when a diagonal section is made.

And here are some frank cases:

PAC (9 years, 9 months): PAC predicts a rectangle for the transverse section, but at first he bases his prediction on the total length. Then, the cut made, he corrects his error by saying, "It's similar to this edge (side A opposite A)[6] no, that one (small vertical side)." For the long diagonal, he predicts a rectangle, but leaning. After sectioning, he establishes that it is longer than with the longitudinal median. For the cube, the median will give a square but the diagonal: "Unnh . . . Ah, no, again a rectangle because it is longer." By contrast, he does not see any means by which to obtain a square section with the parallelepiped.

FRE (10 years, 0 months): FRE begins with the diagonal: "A triangle."—"And on the inside?"—"It will always be a rectangle because it will always be stretched out and then . . . vertically, it will have the same height as the rectangle (vertical sides)." For the transverse median: "A square."—"Inside?"—"It will still be a rectangle." He shows its height in parallel with the visible vertical side. "Could you have a square on the inside?"—"No, it's impossible. You would have to put the form (visible in A) vertically." For the cube, he only predicts squares, even for the diagonal. Seeing the rectangle, he explains it "because you have cut cross ways."

LYN (10 years, 2 months): LYN also predicts only rectangles for the first solid, longer with the diagonal and of a width corresponding to the visible vertical sides. Then, showing progress in generalization of these spontaneous sections, she sets in motion a series of intermediary sections between the transverse median and the diagonal, saying that the rectangle "will always be bigger (meaning longer) because you make a bigger slant (lines x)." But she does not see that it is the same for the cube. After trying: "Can you cut it so there will be another rectangle?"—"Like that (line x close to and parallel to one side) . . . Ah, no, it will make a square." She then thinks that by sectioning across a corner one will succeed: "You have to cut it on the angle." From this fact, she accepts that with the first solid, one could perhaps make a squared section and prepares to "cut on the angle" again, but doubt overtakes her: "You can't have a square."—"Are you sure?"—"Yes, you would have to calculate it out." She then points to the height and proposes an oblique section of the same length but, lacking measurement, only imperfectly succeeds.

---

[6]"*Côté A face à A.*" It is unclear what Piaget means; perhaps PAC is comparing the cut surface to one part of the front side of the divided parallelepiped (side B) whose top and bottom edges are also edges of the upper and lower surfaces A—Translator.

XAN (10 years, 3 months): Curiously, XAN begins with a section that goes obliquely from top to bottom. The line y crossing through the solid is, therefore, not parallel to any visible side. He predicts: "A rectangle like that (inclined)," but without for all that granting that its size will be greater than the size of a vertical section that is not inclined. "It'll be the same. (Tries) No, that makes it bigger," and he proposes increasingly inclined cuts, this time predicting the result: "I went farther when I cut, so it'll be bigger." In order to have a thinner rectangle, like LYN he cuts one of the corners. "Do you think that you can make a square with one cut?"—"No, it'll make rectangles. That makes a triangle."—"Inside?"—"No, a rectangle. I could make a square by not cutting so far, more on the edge and a little cut." With the cube, he sees right off that the diagonal will give "a little rectangle."

The great progress these subjects have made over those of Level I is obvious. To begin with, the solid has, in general, become an operatory enclosure where the act of enclosing is limited to joining what is enclosed into a whole. This whole, equal to the sum of its parts, is organized in such a way that the extension of its elements is differentiated from their intensive properties. The correspondences between parallelism and orthogonality will, from now on, be applied to the planes themselves and no longer only to lines in the plane. This leads to the tridimensional structure that allows the surfaces of a section to be predicted in function of their depth and no longer only in function of straight lines drawn on the upper surface. Henceforth, predictions will be based on systematically putting the different visible surfaces of the solid into correspondence.

These improvements are still subject to strong limitations, however. To begin with, sections along line y generally remain vertical. They are, therefore, confused with the height of the solid. Only XAN spontaneously imagines an oblique section and even begins in that way, but without predicting all of its consequences; LYN does the same when the experimenter suggests that she produce a square. As for the construction of a section of a parallelepiped with a square surface, all of the subjects just quoted believe that it would be impossible, or at least they begin by supposing that it would be. LYN and XAN subsequently discover the principle by which one might be produced. Apart from these two exceptions, the sections obtained are all reduced to rectangles, although of different sizes and varied forms, that are anticipated fairly well. Or they are all reduced to squares by means of a cube (ordinarily with prediction of a rectangle if x is one of the diagonals). Without doubt, putting the surfaces of a section into correspondence with the visible sides of a solid constitutes great progress in relation to Level I. At the same time, Level II is characterized by a significant lack of compositional freedom. In part, this is because the visible sides exert a limiting constraint, as if parallelism and orthogonality, norms that must be respected for a tridimensional system of references to be organized, exclude intermediary combinations of oblique directions and, especially, directions that do not join the upper and lower surfaces of the solid according to its height. Nevertheless, it remains clear that the compositions of Level II are already of an intermorphic nature, because each successful anticipation of the sections presupposes several simultaneous placings in correspondence.

4. IN THE DIRECTION OF THE TRANSMORPHIC

Transmorphic compositions are solidary with a general system within which all possible combinations are exploited in the form of deducible intrinsic variations. We have not found subjects 16 to 17 years of age (or adults who are not mathematicians) who succeed on these questions concerning the sections of solids. In effect, such sections can result not only in squares and rectangles (obtained at Level II but also in parallelograms (x and y not parallel to the sides), trapezoids, triangles, pentagons, and hexagons (section passing through three, five, and six sides). If the subjects that we place at Level III are freed from the parallelism between the direction y of the section and the vertical sides of the solid, they begin by imposing, as a restrictive condition, a parallelism between x and one of the sides of the parallelepiped. Then they are freed from this and come to imagine the surface of the section as capable of rotation within the solid. However, they remain subject to another significant restriction, that is, the respect for orthogonality that CLA (13 years, 5 months) expresses thus: "There're always right angles." Apart from this, the two instruments for establishing correspondences that were the source of great progress in the transition from Level I to Level II cause limitations when they are generalized as abusively necessary conditions. It is all the more interesting, therefore, in trying to understand the nature of transmorphic compositions and their differences with intermorphic compositions to analyze examples showing the difficulties of substituting "free" compositions for those that are initially "linked" by the steps of discovery, that is, that proceed step by step without the subject being able to decide immediately the degree of generality or necessity of the connections observed:

YVO (11 years, 9 months): YVO begins by a series of rectangular sections whose dimensions he evaluates quite well. "Could you find other forms?"—"(Marks x across a corner) That'd give a triangle. I don't cut straight down toward the bottom any more but at a slant. (He puts the knife back in the vertical position)."—"What does it change?"—"Do you see any other forms?"—"I think I can make a square. You have to measure (he does it after trial and error)."—"Again? A little more complicated form?"—"Some parallelograms? . . . that'd surprise me; you'd have to cut twice. (He then draws an oblique x on the upper surface and follows an inclined y on the vertical side). You go both on a slant and on a slant."—"And another parallelogram?"—"Maybe, you'd have to calculate it pretty carefully."—"And still another form?"—"I don't think you can make a trapezoid. You'd have to make two cuts. No, it must be possible."—"How?"—"I don't see how."

CLA (13 years, 5 months): CLA sections the solid into various rectangles. In order to find new forms, "You have to cut on a slant," which he does all along the length, predicting correctly that "it'll always be a rectangle but in a different position." He doubts that he can find parallelograms because "there're always right angles." Suggestions are needed for him to free himself from this idea.

VER (13 years, 7 months): VER exhibits the same reactions as CLA. Then, after all of the slanting cuts which produce rectangles, he is led to the idea of cutting a corner obliquely: "Of course, there, a triangle!" That leads to a square by equalizations that he indicates in advance.

CAT (14 years, 10 months): CAT begins with perpendicular cuts, then goes on to a single oblique and only finds rectangles: "However you cut, you always have right angles; you can't change the angles." She then comes, through very cautious trials, to two obliques: "That will give . . . I'm going to see (she cuts clear to the end) a trapezoid! Ah, yes, it's because you don't cut straight there and there (obliques)."—"And a parallelogram?"—"I'll try; logically, yes!"

CRI (16 years, 6 months): CRI exhibits the same limitations initially, but when the experimenter assures him that one can find other forms, he discovers the possibility of the two obliques: "You cut by two opposing angles. I didn't start a whole side, but from an angle . . . You don't cut parallel to a side."

Even though these subjects do not reach transmorphic systems, they do clearly show us the method that leads to them through deduction or qualitative calculation of all of the realizable intrinsic variations. On the one hand, the method is to extend the field of correspondences to new variables, but on the other, it is to exclude their limiting character and assure that one goes beyond them. As far back as the first level, we see in the choice of the line of the cut, x, a transition from medians to nonmedians but diagonal, then to nondiagonal nonmedians. At Level II, the novelty is the parallelism with the visible sides of the solid, but with the restriction, except in rare attempts, that the section remain vertical. Then generalization of a vertical oblique begins. However, the subjects just cited demonstrate how difficult it is not to believe that this oblique is not unique and to go on to two obliques. As for the number of sides that cross the line of the section, the transition from two (or four) to three is realized by these subjects who discover the possibility of the triangle, but none of them succeed with five or six which would assure the pentagon or hexagon.

In sum, the principal difference between the transmorphic and the intermorphic is due to the freedom of compositions among correspondences. However, as this freedom is only conquered by deductive means, subjects of Level III attain it only very partially on this difficult problem. Even so, they offer excellent instruction concerning the characteristics of transmorphic organization.

7 Correspondences of Kinships

Jean Piaget
with
Ch. Brulhart
and
E. Marbach

The preceding chapters all have been concerned with morphisms inherent in operatory structures of a geometric nature. They involved situations where the subject had to transform figures or objects in order to solve various kinds of problems. Spatial problems were particularly indicated for the type of analysis at issue because of the multiple intermediaries that they exhibit between observable figurative entitites and deductive compositions. In the three chapters to follow, we address a more specifically logical domain by focusing on the construction of reciprocities and symmetries that generate an especially interesting kind of morphism.

Let us begin with definitions. When speaking of operations, we use the qualifier, *inverse,* insofar as they involve cancellations or negations. By contrast, *reciprocities* (represented by arrows) refer to relationships or correspondences that, without negation of their terms, involve a reversal (*renversement*[1]) of direction. An example might be the relationship of father to son. (If there are several sons, there would, of course, be multijection, but we are concerned specifically with the reciprocal of surjection.) As for symmetries, they will be reciprocities by bijection, but with, in addition, equivalence of terms such that A = B where A is the brother of B.

[1]I once translated "*renversabilité*" as "empirical reversibility" (see Footnote 2, p. 95, *The Equilibration of Cognitive Structures*). In that context, the term referred to nondeductive anticipation of a return to the starting point of a physical transformation rather than logical reciprocation. Here, it refers to kinship reciprocities that are, in fact, a form of logical reversibility in Piaget's concrete operational groupings. For that reason, I have not retained the distinction introduced previously—Translator.

That said, let us begin with kinships, all of which are reciprocities. These can either be asymmetrical, as in the uncle-nephew relationship, the terms and arrows of which do not have the same meaning although the relationship remains the same; or they may be symmetrical, as in the case of two brothers. Symmetrical or not, such reciprocities are completely general as far as kinship is concerned, and that is so however distant the reciprocities between arbitrary individuals may be. After all, barring possible polygeny of the human species, we must all have a common ancestor even if that means going back to Adam.

One of us has already addressed the problem of kinship reciprocities. (That, alas, was more than 50 years ago.) Questioning 4- and 5-year-old children, I obtained dialogues of the following form: "Do you have a brother?"—"*Yes, he's called Raoul.*"—"And does Raoul have a brother?"—"*Ah! No, there are only two of us in the family.*" Since those far-gone days, I have always believed that analyzing elementary kinship systems might be interesting. The techniques I have tried have involved distinguishing figures in terms of height or color or using nesting books (*cahiers emboîtés*) or tree-diagrams. Unfortunately, all of them have proved inadequate in one way or another or have merely displaced the problems. It was only while studying morphisms that the more natural idea of employing little dolls, identical in appearance but linked by means of differentiated arrows, occurred to us. Whence, at last, the present experiment which fills in a half-century-old lacuna!

In fact, kinships constitute the most complex of the "groupings," and that in three forms. They do so first in the form of counivocal multiplications of classes; they do so second in the form of the same operations bearing on relations. As such, they are isomorphs of complete classifications (systems of inclusions) or of their translation into relations (trees), but with two differences. One difference is that in kinships the classes or relations of a set of elements cannot be changed in the way that certain classifications seen in the history of zoology were replaced by new classifications. The other is that the classes and relationships involved in kinships include every distinctive denomination. In other words, even though there is no term that designates the relationship between two species of animals of the same genus, the sons of the same father are brothers. Similarly, even though no term defines the relationship between species a belonging to genus A and species b belonging to genus B related to A, the son of the father's brother is a "first cousin," and so forth. The point is that these designations are relative and transferable among distinct families. They include, moreover, the possibility of complementary substitutions within a single whole which constitutes a third form of grouping. Such changes in "point of view" permit one to start from relationships between an individual, X, and those of his near or distant relatives P(X), and to calculate what the relationships between the individual, Y, a member of P(X) and his own relatives P(Y) of which X is a part. If X and Y are of the same rank (for example, C and D are first-cousin sons of A and B who are brothers), such a complementary substitution of points of view will reduce to a simple symmetry: E, son of C, will be the "second cousin" (*cousin issu de germain*) of F, son of D, and vice versa, as C will be the first cousin once removed (*l'oncle à la mode de Bretagne*) of F just as D will be the same for E, and so on. By contrast, if X and Y are not of the same rank (e.g., uncle and nephew) and if, in particular, they are more distantly related, calculation of their relationships still will be possible and will conserve the equality $X + P(X) = Y + P(Y)$ through complementary substitution. In this situation, however, they will become increasingly complex[2] because they involve multiplication of asymmetrical reciprocities.

From the point of view of morphisms, surjections and their reciprocals, that is, multijections (one to several), are what is essential. It is, however, necessary to add a fundamental correspondence that we call "cosurjection." Cosurjections link terms belonging to the same surjection (and, therefore, terms of the same rank). An example would be the correspondence between brothers. It might be useful to indicate that at higher levels, in addition to these simple or symmetrical cosurjections, we will need to introduce the notion of "asymmetrical co-surjections" for terms of unequal rank. The reason for this is that the reciprocity of such terms with one another is asymmetrical in relation to the longitudinal or vertical axis of the tree. That, for example, is the case between cousins of distant degree who are not of the same generation. (The terms "uncle" and "nephew" then cease to apply; the expression "cousin once, twice, thrice removed, etc." [l'oncle à la mode de Bretagne] does not extend beyond short distances). But let us for the moment stay with symmetrical forms. From the point of view of the logic of relations, an antisymmetric relationship composed with its converse gives a symmetrical relationship. Likewise, we say that a surjection composed with its reciprocal, a multijection, generates a cosurjection. However, in contradistinction to an isomorphism the latter is still not transitive even if it is symmetrical. Instead, it is "allotransitive";[3] for example, the cousin of my cousin can be my cousin, my brother, or myself. As for isomorphisms, they naturally come into play when it is a matter of recognizing the same structure in two different families independently of the kinships that link the families to one another. In other words, it is a matter of recognizing the same structure in two different families independently of their position in

[2]See Jean Piaget, *Essai de Logique Opératoire*. Paris: Dunod, 1972, pp. 150–163.

[3]Piaget uses the term "aliotransitive." Insofar as I can determine, this term does not appear in French dictionaries, the prefix alio- is not used in French, and there is no cognate in English. Apparently, what Piaget wanted to mark was the fact that cosurjections can take on several forms. I conclude, therefore, that he intended the prefix allo- as in *allotrophy* or *allomorph*—Translator.

the tree that includes them both. Finally, complementary substitutions of points of view with conservation of the totalities involved leads to automorphisms and, therefore, to one of the characteristics of categories.

1. TECHNIQUE

The equipment consists of wooden dolls of very rudimentary form (a ball on a pedestal representing head and body). All are similar and the same size, and so forth. They are arranged in different patterns and numbers (starting with two) depending on the question, but their relationships are always determined in univocal fashion. This is done through the use of arrows cut out of heavy paper. On each arrow a relationship such as "is the father of," "is the brother of," "is the aunt of," and so on, is written in clear and complete terms. This indicates the relationship between the dolls linked by the arrow. The experimenter puts certain of these arrows in place between dolls without mentioning the reciprocals; the subject puts others in place by choosing from among 16 relationships involving three generations marked on arrows placed at his disposal.

The experimenter begins by having the child represent his own family. He then asks the child to add other arrows in addition to those he used spontaneously until all possibilities have been exhausted. What one is especially interested in are reciprocals which, in general, are neglected by small children. After this is done, the experimenter goes on to compositions of relationships. Two or more relationships might be given between A and B and between B and C and the child asked to find the relationship between A and C (e.g., who is the father of the father or the cousin of the nephew?). Or a composition might be given and the child asked to find its components (e.g., who is the uncle?).

Another question consists of having the child compare two equivalent structures presented in more or less different spatial dispositions (Figs. 7.1 to 7.4) while being able to change an arrow to its reciprocal or to replace two arrows by their combination (like "grandson" in Fig. 7.4).

When this part is completed, the subject is presented with a piece of cardboard to which blank arrows arranged in different ways are glued. He is instructed as follows: The same thing must be written on all the arrows; there are both men and women dolls; all of the arrows that can be used for this relationship have been put in place. The subject must find what relationship is compatible with each of the arrangements and indicate whether the dolls are men or women (Figs. 7.5 and 7.6).

It is often instructive to have the child try to express the relationships uncle, nephew, cousin, grandfather, and so forth, using only component relationships like father, son, and brother. Naturally, it is also necessary to establish whether the subject understands the subordination of all of the

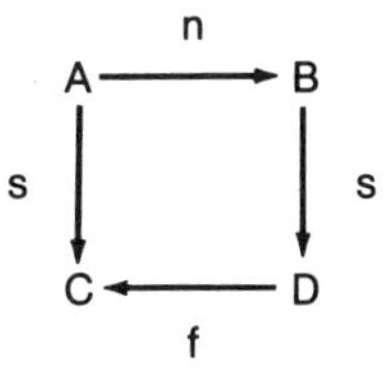

FIG. 7.1.
Structure 1.

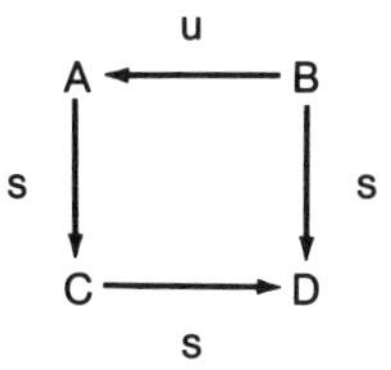

FIG. 7.2.
Structure 2.

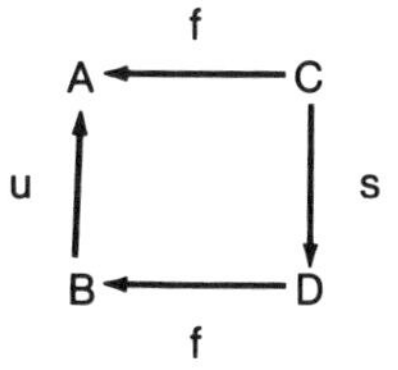

FIG. 7.3.
Structure 3.

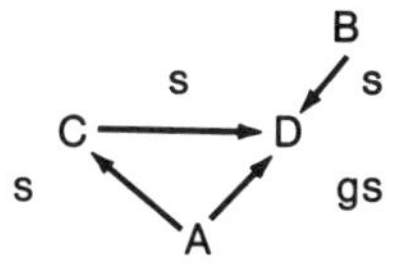

FIG. 7.4.
Structure 4.

$A \xrightarrow{f} B$ = "A is the father of B"
$C \xleftarrow{s} D$ = "D is the son of C"
f = father; s = son; gs = grandson; u = uncle; n = nephew

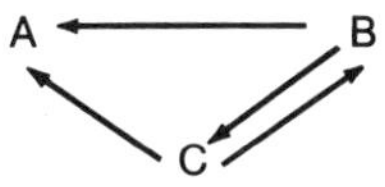

FIG. 7.5. Structure 5.

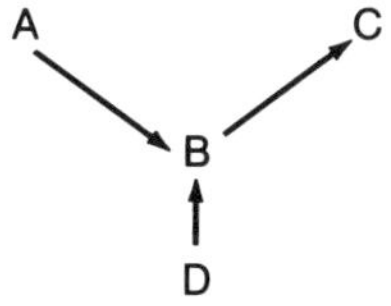

FIG. 7.6. Structure 6.

relationships in a family to the nearest common ancestors. To do this, it is useful to ask the subject to construct a tree or to complete a partial tree that he has been able to make some use of and to see to what extent he employs it as a reference.

With regard to complementary substitutions of points of view, questions can be posed with respect to each of the preceding situations. These begin with simple reciprocities or symmetries and ascending and descending arrows. For children of higher levels, the experimenter presents two sets of three persons with the arrows in place (different from one set to another) and asks the subject to add two new individuals, 7 and 8. He also asks the subject to choose relationships between 7 and 8, between 7 and one of the persons in set 1-3, and between 8 and one of the persons in set 4-6. The subject must calculate, therefore, all of the relationships involved from one point of view or another.

Finally, it should be remarked that, except in the case of the subject's own family, all of the questions bear on nonmarital relationships and are, therefore, based on simple paternal filiations.

2. LEVEL I-A: BEGINNING OF INTRAMORPHIC CORRESPONDENCES

First we should distinguish carefully between simple relationships like A is B's uncle and the correspondences that make such relationships repeatable;

that is, C is to D as A is to B (even by elementary transposition without reflection on the implicit "correlate"). Second, in the present study we should differentiate intramorphic and intermorphic correspondences. At the first two levels, intramorphic correspondences are elaborated bit by bit insofar as the subject's own family is concerned without being generalized to little sets of three arbitrary individuals, A, B, and C, to whom one assigns two relationships. At level II-B, generalization of this sort leads to intermorphic correspondences.

Here, then, are some examples of Level I-A where one finds the beginning of intramorphic correspondences. These are not yet stablized, however, as is seen by the fact that certain kinships are not conceived as relationships but as absolute predicates. For example, the subject's grandfather is at the same time the grandfather of all of the other members of the family including the subject's parents because the grandfather is "the" grandfather by intrinsic property!

RIC (4 years, 11 months): RIC has a brother, but his brother does not have a brother, and his mother has a father who is his grandfather, Grandpa, but further on: "Is your grandpa your mother's father?"—"No."—"And does your father have a father?"—"No."—"And does he have a mother?"—"Yes."—"Who?"—"Grandpa's mother (meaning wife)."—"And does your brother have a grandpa, too?"—"No."—"Only you?"—"Yes . . . ah, no. He has a grandpa, too (he indicates this with the dolls and arrows)."

BER (5 years, 9 months): BER allows that his father and mother are also the father and mother of his two brothers, but asked whether his parents have brothers, he responds that his father's brother, "He's François (his own brother); he's 12," and that his mother has two brothers, "Yes, me and my brother Olivier."—"But your mom, does she have a brother or a sister?"—"No, she only has boys."—"Did your grandpa have a child?"—"No."—"Is your father your grandpa's son?"—"Yes."—"Then he had a child?"—"Yes, Daddy, when he was young." He denies that his uncle is his father's or his mother's brother, but admits that he is his cousin's father, and he then recognizes that his uncle is his father's brother: "Yes, when they were both little children." Although he has just asserted that his grandfather has no child other than his father, he now allows that, "He's the father of two children."—"Still talking about Lucien, is he your brother's uncle, too?"—"No."—"Who's your brother's uncle?"—"My father is."—"Does your cousin have any cousins?"—"Yes, Alex and Philippe (his brothers)."—"And who are they for you?"—"My cousins."

ALA (6 years, 9 months): The father of ALA's mother, "He's my Dad, the Dad to Mom."—"Did you know your grandpa and your grandmother?"—"Yes."—"Did they have children when they were young?"—"Yes."—"Did you know them?"—"No."—"Who is your father's mother?"—"My mom."—"Isn't your grandfather your father's or your mother's father?"—"Yes, both of them."—"Your father's?"—"Yes, a little."—"And your mother's?"—"Ah yes."—"And do you have brothers and sisters?"—"Yes, a boy and a girl, Georges and Nicole."—"Does Georges have a brother?"—"No."—"And you, are you George's brother?"—"A little, not too much."—"What is necessary to be someone's brother a lot?"—"You have to love him."—"Does your sister have a brother?"—"Yes, Georges."—"And you, are you Nicole's brother?"—"A little, not too much."—"And Georges's?"—"Not very much either."

XYT (6 years, 5 months): "My grandpa is also my dad's and my mom's grandpa."

To begin with the analysis in terms of operations, it is clear that these facts bear witness to a lack of differentiation between the structure of classes (to be "a" brother) and the structure of relations (to be "the" brother of X). In addition, they testify to a lack of differentiation between the extension of these classes ("we are n brothers") and their intension (X is a brother). From such an undifferentiated point of view, it is not absurd to say with BER that his parents have brothers who are their children because they have children who are brothers. Nor is it ridiculous to maintain with XYT that his grandfather is his parents' grandfather as well as his own, because he is a grandfather in everybody's eyes (and perhaps called "Grandpa" by everyone). Likewise for BER, if his cousin has brothers who are also his (BER's) cousins, they remain cousins for their brother insofar as they possess this quality in intension. This role of intension undifferentiated from extension is evident with ALA whose fraternal feelings appear weak and who distinguishes the degrees of "a lot" and "a little" brother according to this affective criterion. Likewise, BER links his older brother, François, to his father and the two younger brothers including himself to his mother.

From the point of view of relations, then, the great difficulty is to distinguish the meaning of the relation "to have" a father, a cousin, and so on, from "to be" X's brother, etcetera. This relationship, initially foreign to the structure of filiations, begins with the undifferentiated meaning of a cobelonging to one's own family. There is, however, an important restriction. If the fact of being X's father is compatible with being X's brother, husband, or uncle (BER grants that his father is also his brother's father and then comes round to making him his brother's uncle!), it is never compatible with being X's son. Starting from this almost general lack of differentiation, the relationship "to have" is then oriented in what follows in the direction of filiation (starting from the ancestors) and cofiliation. ALA gives an interesting indication of this when he begins by responding, "Yes, of both of them,"when he is asked whether his grandfather is his father's or his mother's father. Subsequently, he attenuates this affirmation by saying "a little" with respect to his father and "ah yes" with respect to his mother, thus recognizing implicitly the true relationship in the second case. It is, therefore, this orientation in the direction of filiations that allows the transition from relationships to correspondences in the form of a very modest beginning of intramorphic surjections and cosurjections. Thus, RIC, after having denied that his brother has a grandfather, revises his opinion and indicates that RIC's grandfather is the same grandfather as his own. BER, after having, recognized that his uncle is his cousins's father, deduces from that that he is his father's brother. We have just recalled ALA's reaction to his mother's father. Certainly, these are only sketches, but they help us understand how the stabilization of a relationship generalized to several pairs of individuals engenders a correspondence, whereas the undifferentiated relationships with which children start know no regularity.

3. LEVEL I-B: INTRAMORPHIC CORRESPONDENCES

From age 6 to 7 years on the average or in certain cases age 8 years onward, one sees differentiation between relational and classificatory aspects sufficient for kinships to give rise to stable correspondences and compositions. But these still present a certain number of difficulties and, what is important, remain correspondences and compositions within the subject's own family without generalization to models proposed in the abstract:

JOA (6 years, 9 months): JOA gives a precise picture of his family with formula such as, "To the child, he (the father's father) is a grandfather,"but when he tries an arbitrary model he comes round to giving two fathers to the same person. "Do you have an uncle?"—"Yes, Armand."—"Who is Armand's father?"—"I don't know."—"Does he have a brother?"—"Yes, but I don't know who it is." By contrast, a moment afterward: "Who is your father's brother?"—"My uncles and aunts."—"Who is the father of your uncles and the aunts?"—"It's Grandpa and Grandma."—"Do you have any cousins?"—"Yes."—"Who is your cousin's father?"—"It's Grandpa and Grandma's son."—"They have one, then?"—"Yes, it's the same as me."—"If you had a brother, would he have a brother, too?"—"No."—"You wouldn't be your brother's brother?"—"Yes."—"Do your cousins have cousins?"—"No."—"Do you understand [what it means] 'to be the son of'?"—

"No."—"Your grandfather's sons?"—"They're my father, my uncles, and my aunts."

VIR (6 years, 9 months): "Your mother's father?"—"He's my grandpa."—"And your aunt?"—"It's hard to say. Perhaps my dad or my mom's mom, (no), it's my mom's sister."—"Did she have children?"—"Yes, a girl (etc.); they're my boy cousins and my girl cousins."—"And your uncle, who's he?"—"It's hard to say. Perhaps the husband of my mom or dad's sister."—"Do your boy cousins and your girl cousins have a grandfather?"—"Yes, my cousin from Geneva has the same as me. My cousin (who lives elsewhere) has the same, too."—"Everybody has a grandfather?"—"Yes, I think so, but you don't have to."—"Does your sister have a sister?"—"No . . . but of course, me!"—"And does your cousin have a cousin?"—"I don't know; anyway I don't know her."—"And you?"—"Ah yes."—"And your cousin's aunt?"—"I don't know if she has one."—"Your mother, is she your cousin's aunt?"—"But of course, certainly." Later, however, the experimenter asks: "Who is your cousin's aunt?"—"It all depends. The one in France, I don't know. The one in Geneva, my cousin's mother is my mother's sister's daughter's mother."—"Then?"—"Ah! It's my mother."—"And your aunt's father?"—"It must be easy but . . . "—"Your father's sister's father?"—"My grandfather."

YVE (7 years, 10 months): YVE says that his grandfather's sons are his father and his uncle. "And your brother's uncle is your uncle?"—"No."—"And what's your uncle Émile to your father, his cousin or his brother?"—" . . . "—"His brother?"—"No."—"Your mother's brother?"—"No, that's my uncle Loulou."—"Who are Loulou's father and mother?"—"Grandpa and Grandma."—"Is your grandfather André's grandfather, too?"—"No, that's somebody else."—"What's your father's father?"—"I don't understand."—"And your uncle's son?"—"I don't understand."—"Your uncle Émile's son?"—"It's Marc."—"And Marc?"—"My cousin."

DEN (7 years, 6 months): DEN gives the same reactions for her family, except for her grandfather who is the husband of her aunt. "Father and husband, it's the same thing?"—"Yes, the husband, for the children he's called 'Dad'." However, as soon as the experimenter goes on to an abstract schema[4], she is lost. For A, the father of B, and C, the brother of B, she concludes that A is the mother of C, and so forth.

[4]The distinction between *schème* and schéma has been preserved following Piaget's discussion of the issue in the English translation of *The Mechanisms of Perception* (New York: Basic Books, 1969, p. ix). In the "Author's Preface," Piaget pointed out that *schème* corresponds to an operative instrument of generalization whereas *schéma* corresponds to a figurative or topographical diagram. This distinction has not been preserved in most translations—Translator.

SAN (7 years, 3 months): SAN grants that her cousin's father is her uncle, but her father is not, for all that, her cousin's uncle: "I don't know. I'm not sure."

INO (7 years, 3 months): INO describes his family by placing the arrows correctly. "My father's father is Grandpa. He's Mom's father, almost everybody's father (hesitates). He's not the same person, not exactly the same. He's only Mom's; I have two grandfathers."—"Does that one have several children?"—"Three. My mother, my uncle, another . . . my aunt."—"Your aunt and your mother, what are they to each other?"—"They're two daughters."—"You, for example, do you have the same father as your sister?"—"Sure. If you don't have the same father, you're not brother and sister."—"Then, your aunt?"—"She is my mother's sister."—"Do you have cousins?"—"Yes."—"Who's children are they?"—"My aunt's. Wait. No. Yes, yes."—"You, what are you for your cousin?"—"Mom's son."—"And your mother, for your cousin?"—"She's his aunt. I finally understood."—"And does he have a cousin?"—"Sure, me."—"And if you had a brother, who would be your brother's brother?"—"I haven't understood."—(The experimenter repeats the question.)—"My cousin, perhaps."—"Who's your father's brother?"—"It's me. No, I have to think. A cousin, perhaps, sure. Ah, no, he's an uncle."—"Do you know what a nephew is?"—"It's two cousins. You can say cousins and nephews. No, it's Dad and Mom who say nephews. For me, they're cousins."—"And the nephew's uncle?"—"It's really my uncle."—"You're sure?"—"No, another person."—"Isn't it your father?"—"No, I have never heard that said; I have never seen that."—"Could one of your mother's brothers be littler than you?"—"Yes, he would be my uncle even if he is very little." However, after this excellent deduction, he reverses the relationship: "No, I can't be the uncle of my nephew, he would be as big as me, he would be my uncle, too."

FAB (7 years, 6 months): FAB gives good responses for her own family by using correct double arrows for immediate relationships. She also composes "uncle" with her father's brother. However, for an abstract schema where A is B's brother and B is C's uncle, she cannot find the relationship between A and C. She is close to it when she says that A is C's son but recognizes that an uncle's brother is not his son. She gets out of this by saying that, "C is A's pal," then she supposes that A is "C's father."—"Are you sure?"—"No."—"Then?"—"He's C's big brother." She has the same difficulties with A is the father of B and B is the father of C. She gives no response: "If C were you?"—"It's my grandfather."—"And if C is no matter who and A is B's father and B is C's father?"—"You have to say who C is, otherwise you don't know what arrow to use."—"(C) it's anything (any name)?"—"He's A's brother!"

MIR (8 years, 6 months): MIR gives correct compositions for her own family, but does not know the term nephew that she subsequently comes to understand quite well. By contrast, for the schema "A, B's father, and B, C's father," she gives the interpretation that, "It's a father and his two children." When the experimenter then reads what is written on the arrows: "I don't understand; there are not three dads!" It is only by translating the relationships between A, B, and C into terms of her own family that she succeeds: "Ah, it's Grandfather." The others schemas give rise to the same mistakes because, among other things, "B is C's son" is at first read as "C is B's son." But, while interrogating her in a purely verbal way ("who is the father's father, who is X's father, who is the father's brother, the uncle's son, the brother's father, the father's son?, etc.) all of her responses are correct except for "the son's son": "I don't know." The reason for these successes seems twofold. On the one hand, she translates everything into personal terms: "It's my father, my brother" . . . and so on, and even "my nephew." On the other hand, these verbal expressions imply an orientation (the x of y), whereas those of the arrows can be involuntarily reversed if one does not pay enough attention to them (cf. the aforementioned confusion between father and son). In the test where four terms are presented with their arrows but in part permuted and where it is a matter of discerning their equivalence, MIR cannot make a decision.

It is useful to consider the numerous cases of Level I-B because they illustrate so vividly the distinctness of intra- and intermorphic correspondences. In effect, the first only consist in recording correspondences internal to a system through reading observables, whereas the second involve compositions, notably when two or more systems are compared. Let us begin with these comparisons and, therefore, with the absence of intermorphism at this level. It is striking to see how lost these subjects are from the moment that one replaces their own relatives with first names by arbitrary individuals, A, B, and C related by arrows with inscriptions representing exactly the same correspondences that have just been mastered in terms of the child's family. Thus JOA does not "understand" the expression "the son of" but immediately indicates who his grandfather's sons are when the experimenter refers to his grandfather. Neither does YVE "understand" the expression "the uncle's son," but immediately designates Marc as "Uncle Émile's son." For the schema "A, B's father, and B, C's brother," DEN concludes that A is C's mother. FAB gets just as tangled up and insists, "You have to say who C is (meaning that C must be given the name of one of her family members), otherwise you don't know what arrow to use." When C is given an arbitrary label, FAB does not understand clearly. MIR understands the verbal expressions of kinships that she can assimilate to her family, but she does not master the schemas presented in terms of A, B, and C and inverts the directions of the arrows. Is it then simply because these models are "abstract" even though the arrows are furnished with inscriptions in clear and complete terms which the experimenter reads to the child? In fact, the difference is something else; that is, these schemas require compositions (C composed by means of relationships between A and B and between B and C). By contrast, the same correspondences, more or less easily stated with regard to the child's own family, depend only slightly on compositions at this point. In that form, they remain the product of knowledge acquired thanks to daily contacts and a common vocabulary which the child has learned.

In effect, intramorphic correspondences of this sort remain lacunary and point specifically to mistakes in composition. The easiest correspondences to establish are those that follow the order of filiations. That, after all, seems normal from the point of view of structures because filiations are the source of transformations. But even when at age 6 years, 9 months, JOA says, "For the child, he (the father's father) is a grandfather," and VIR says, "He's my grandpa," nothing proves that composition is involved. It is simply a matter of relationships among persons familiar to the child. The hesitations with regard to the uncle's father (JOA) and aunt's father (VIR) before generalizations are made support this point. Even then, VIR does not believe you "have to" have a grandfather. Even MIR, who masters all of the other verbal expressions of kinship at age 8 years, 6 months, cannot start with "the father's father" and invert it to "the son's son." Generally, however, there is surjection with respect to grandparents who are also the grandparents of brothers and cousins as well as the subject's grandparents and who, finally, are the parents of uncles and aunts as much as of the child's mother and father.

By contrast, collateral correspondences (cosurjections) are clearly more difficult to construct. The relationship of brother is still not immediately reciprocal (JOA, etc.). INO, one of the most advanced subjects, even says that if he had a brother, his brother's brother would perhaps be his cousin. The relationship of being cousins is more clearly difficult. YVE does not "understand" what "the uncle's son"means, and it is necessary to specify names for him to recognize his cousin. INO hesitates between uncle and cousin for the father's brother. JOA does not know who his uncle's brother is, although he says subsequently that his father's brothers are his uncles. YVE's uncle Émile is neither his father's nor his mother's brother, and moreover, YVE contests that his brother's uncle is also his uncle. VIR, after having affirmed that her mother is "certainly" her cousin's aunt, immediately forgets. To the question, "Who is your cousin's aunt?", she responds with a beautiful semitautological composition, "My cousin's mother is my mother's sister's daughter's mother." For SAN, her cousin's father is her uncle, but that in no way implies that her own father is her cousin's uncle. INO also hesitates between uncle and cousin in order to qualify his father's brother, and so forth.

4. LEVEL II: INTERMORPHIC CORRESPONDENCES

In a general way, intermorphic correspondences are distinguished from intramorphic correspondences by their recourse to deductive and necessary compositions rather than recourse to the empirical and incomplete generalizations of the previous level. This progress initially is manifested in two closely connected ways. First, one sees a capacity to create new correspondences starting from two, then three, correspondences among three, then four, arbitrary individuals, A, B, C, and D. Second, the correspondences within the subject's family are completely constituted. Later, there follows recognition of isomorphism between identical systems even when the relationships are presented differently; there follows the possibility of constructing a coherent system from terms A, B, and C and blank arrows; there follows the more or less successful reduction of all correspondences to one or two types only; and, in the case of symmetries, there follows reciprocity of points of view:

NAT (9 years, 10 months): NAT still gropes in the case of different groups of A, B, and C, but he eventually succeeds in every case: A, father of B, and B, father of C, gives A, grandfather of C; A, brother of B, and B, father of C, ends with uncle. A son of B, and B uncle of C: "It doesn't work because I'm not my uncle's son,"then, referring to his family, "Ah, no, it's A's cousin,"[5] and so on.

SOL (9 years, 6 months): For two reciprocal blank arrows between A and B and for one from A to C and one from B to C: "It could be two girls (A and B) and a boy (their brother, C)." For A → B → C and D → B, she imagines A and D to be the sons of B and B to be the brother of a father, C. A and D would then be cousins of C's daughter who would be herself: ("But I'm outside the game"). Coming back to the situation given, she makes C B's brother. For two families, Family I (A father of

[5]Because Piaget states that NAT succeeds in every case and because the task is to calculate the relationship between A and C, I have had to change the relationship given in this third case from $A \overset{b}{\leftrightarrow} B \overset{u}{\rightarrow} C$ to $A \overset{s}{\rightarrow} B \overset{u}{\rightarrow} C$. As given, the relationship between A and C could be $A \overset{f}{\rightarrow} C$ or $A \overset{u}{\rightarrow} C$, and NAT's answer would be wrong—Translator.

B, B uncle of C, and A grandfather of C) and Family II (A uncle of C who is the grandson of B, and A son of B) she at first only sees the relationship of uncle as being similar, then she completes the arrow "grandson" with its reciprocal "grandfather" as well as "father"by son: "There is absolutely no difference now. Before . . . it was not the same word."

PAU (9 years, 10 months): For A father of B and brother of C, PAU says right off that between B and C there is a relationship of uncle in one direction and nephew in the other. "Who is the father's brother's nephew?"—"It could be me, one of my brothers, or the son of another of father's brothers," thus, by allotransitive composition. In order to reduce the correspondences to "father and son," he says of the uncle: "He is the father's son, but that can also be my father."—"And the cousin?"—"There is my father, you have to go up and down: father, grandfather, and another father who has a son."

SCA (10 years, 6 months): At first SCA says that an uncle is not necessarily someone's brother but then revises his opinion. "Do all nephews have a grandfather?"—"It has to be; it's obligatory. The nephew's father is the grandfather's son."—"And does everyone have one?"—"Yes." For three blank arrows joining A, B, and C to D, he supposes three uncles or three sons.

ANT (10 years, 9 months): ANT succeeds in placing part of the arrows among four persons such that A is B's uncle and C's grandfather. He then puts "grandpa" between C and D. "And from A to D?"—"It's the grandfather. Ah, no, the great great grandfather," but he does not find the relationship between B and D and says of it that "there is no relationship." The reductions to father and son give: "Uncle is the son of my father's father."—"And the nephew?"[6]—"(He repeats what he just said) Ah, no. You have to go down. It's the son of my father's son other than me."—"Or another way?"—"My father's son's son who is not my son." The cousin of his cousin is "my cousin or myself."—"That's all?"—"Or still another cousin to infinity."—"Or?"—"Or my brother."

STE (10 years, 5 months): STE easily succeeds in compositions with three terms, A, B, and C, misses with four, but succeeds with a fifth where only brothers, uncles, and nephews come into play. For blank arrows ordered A → B → C and E → D → B, she sets aside brother relationships because they require reciprocity. She also sets aside father relationships because B would have two of them, but she retains

[6]ANT responds as if the question had been, "And your nephew?" Because of the way French speakers mark possessives, it is not clear whether this was the question or whether ANT's response is due to assimilation to his personal situation—Translator.

relationships of son. For two families, Family I (A father of B, and B uncle of C, the relationship between A and C remaining to be found) and Family II (B son of A, and C grandson of A), STE finds the third relationship and concludes that "It's the same, but in II, they (the arrows) are in the other direction."

DEN (10 years, 6 months): DEN succeeds in placing all of the arrows in a tree where A is the father of B and C, B is the father of D and E, and C is the father of F by introducing relationships of uncles and cousins in addition to grandsons.

The remarkable difference between these reactions and intramorphic correspondences is evident, and our first question concerns the reasons for it. One might suppose that it is due to supplementary information that the subject has acquired about his own family. This information then could be generalized by creating isomorphisms between it and arbitrary family arrangements among A, B, and C, and so forth. What is striking, however, insofar as the subject's relatives are concerned, is that the information that the subject furnishes has a constructive as well as an empirical character. This is particularly noticeable with respect to the allotransitivity of cosurjections, which is hardly something one uses every day. Although subjects of the preceding level still had difficulty in calling themselves their brothers's brother and even more difficulty in calling themselves their cousins's cousin, we now see PAU at age 9 years, 10 months give the range of possibilities for his uncle's nephews and ANT at age 10 years, 9 months give it for his cousin's cousins. This conquest or extension of cosurjections in collateral dimensions testifies to a new perspective. Certainly this is in part suggested by the child's own family, but it is immediately conceived as a general structure. The perspective in question, then, is the hierarchical inclusion of generations starting from the closest common ancestor. For ANT, this is the great-great-grandfather, but it is usually the grandfather. Recall that VIR does not believe that the grandfather's existence is required whereas SCA (10 years, 6 months) declares of the grandfather's role as founder, "it must be," even if he has since died. In other words, there is evidence of a series of relationships and correspondences that have become necessary because they are deductively based on a system of transformations in the form of filiations materially engendered by the successors of a common ancestor. It is this backing up of correspondences with a constructive structure making them composable that simultaneously explains progress in understanding relationships among one's own relatives and in generalizing them to arbitrary families. In both cases, progress consists in reasoning on the set of possible correspondences and no longer in reasoning on factual relationships between the subject and his family members. This transition from limited reality to unlimited possibility (which, in the case of being cousins, ANT calls "another cousin to infinity") naturally implies the preliminary condition of decentralization[7] in relation to one's own point of view. This begins with a reciprocity making every arrow correspond to an equivalent relationship in the opposite direction, for example, making nephew correspond to uncle, and so on. In opposition to the reactions of the preceding level, it is precisely this process, at work in the subjects just cited, that will finally lead to complementary substitution and to general coordination of points of view. It is this process that will permit solution of previously unsovable problems such as the composition of relationships among individuals A, B, and C, and so forth, or the concretization of the content of the arrows, or the equating of families with different arrangements of the arrows.

5. LEVEL III: TOWARD TRANSMORPHIC CORRESPONDENCES

In principle, intermorphic correspondences should suffice for any particular composition, but they still must be subordinated to a general tree structure. Moreover, the subject must understand that this tree structure coordinates not only some but all correspondences. Recall in this respect that ANT, presented with a complex structure, deduces some of its correspondences but says with respect to two distant terms, "there is no relationship" (and insists, "No, I say there isn't any"). This reaction indicates precisely that this general system is lacking. This is because, in fact, three sorts of morphisms come into play. The first is surjection, for example, when A and B, and so on, present the same relationship with a common ancestor X. The second is symmetrical cosurjection having to do with relationships between A and B, etcetera. And the third is what we call "asymmetrical surjections" as in the case of uncle, where an uncle and his nephew are issued from the same ancestor, Y, who is the father of one and the grandfather of the other without direct filiation between the uncle and the nephew. This amounts to saying that the collateral relationship is not, in this case, horizontal but oblique and that there is no longer symmetrical cosurjection between its terms. It is, therefore, the correspondences of uncles, nephews, and cousins of the nth degree that render relationships more and more complex, although always possible in univocal fashion. Added to this is the fundamental fact that this univocality of arrival points is combined with a multiplicity of possible trajectories ending at the same point. If A is the uncle of B, he is not only the brother of B's father but also

[7]For whatever reasons, Piaget speaks of *décentralisation* rather than *décentration*—Translator.

the father of B's first cousin (and by lengthening the arrows across generations, he is the son of B's grandfather or the grandfather of B's second-degree nephew,[8] etc.). The different paths leading from one term to another are easy to establish between first-degree uncles and nephews, but they grow more and more complex as the distance separating individuals within the tree increases. Abstracting out kinships by marriage, their common form is

$$x \downarrow g \leftarrow^{c} \rightarrow y = x \leftarrow^{c'} \rightarrow \downarrow g' y \qquad (1)$$

(where g and g′ = generations and c or c′ = horizontal distances) and calculations naturally can be effected on them. Transmorphic morphisms are morphisms that can be calculated in function of a general structure that controls and implies them all. They are opposed to particular intermorphic compositions among neighboring elements. The adjunction of asymmetrical surjections and cosurjections to symmetrical surjections and cosurjections and their compositions by different but convergent itineraries must, therefore, be considered characteristic of a transmorphic level. It is, nevertheless, a matter of course that because this structure is undefined with respect to the degrees n of relationship, subjects from age 12 to 15 years only postulate it and limit themselves to certain restricted substructures. Still, these achieve a certain degree of generality. Here are three examples, the first of which remains intermediary between Levels II and III:

CHA (12 years, 1 month): For blank double arrows between A and B and blank single arrows from A to C, from B to C, from A to D, from A to E, from B to D and from B to E: "A and B are brothers; C, D, and E girls (sisters)." For A and B linked to C and C to D: "A and B aunts of C and C (aunt) of D. The same for uncle."—"And sons?"—"No, he would have two fathers. Yes, that would work."—"For father?"—"No."—"For grandfather?"—"Yes." The experimenter presents Family I with three brothers 1, 2, and 3 and Family II where 4 and 5 are sons of 6 and where 6 is 7's son. The subject is requested to add two more persons in order to make one big family of the two presented. He adds 8, brother of 2, and 9, father of 6. He then indicates all of the correspondences in play. It is clear, however, that no "indirect surjection" yet comes into play, which makes things easier even though Family I remains in a triangle and Family II in the form of an arrow without fusion into a tree.

[8]I am not sure this designation is used in English. The relationships described are accurate. Usually, English speakers would say second cousin, first cousin once removed, or german cousin once removed—Translator.

VER (14 years, 2 months): For the same Families I and II, VER adds 8, father of brothers 1, 2, and 3, and 9, nephew of 8 and cousin of a member of Family II. She then indicates all relationships correctly including cousins, uncles, and grandsons. The experimenter asks her to replace the arrows with other arrows signifying only "father of" while conserving the kinships indicated. This requires putting them into a tree structure. She does this without difficulty and without modifying the spatial distributions but then finds that a father is lacking which she adds as 10, establishing its correct relationships.

REN (15 years, 6 months): REN gives the same reactions starting with Families I and II. She links them by 9, nephew of a member of Family II and grandson of 8 who is uncle of a member of Family I. A more complicated total system results whose reciprocities she correctly details, including uncles and grand-uncles as well as an arrow of which she says: "It's not a relationship that I am familiar with. It's his father's cousin (second cousin; [*l'oncle à la mode de Bretagne*]." For the translation of this system into correspondences of the form "father of," she adds two more individuals, 10 and 11, without modifying spatial positions. Everything is correct. She says of this, "You can arrange them in other ways, as you need to, in stories," but without feeling any need to do so.

One finds, therefore, that if CHA made the task easier by only adding a brother and a father, VER and especially REN have no fear of complications and introduce terms that will lead to "asymmetrical surjections." This makes every sort of composition possible including what REN calls a relationship that she is "not familiar with," that is, a relationship whose name she does not know. In these cases, subjects indeed attain a general structure as such, and it is all the clearer as they do not even feel any need for a figurative representation in the form of a tree with "stories" (as REN says).

In conclusion, in order to interpret the successive levels of correspondences distinguished in this chapter, we must insist, first of all, on the great difference that separates these facts from those of chapters 1 to 6. In those studies, subjects were invited to manipulate objects and thus to draw morphisms from transformations effected by or in front of them. By contrast, in the present study no transformation comes into play (except those, given in advance, that constitute the production of generations). The result is that the morphisms constructed by the subject only consist in combining relationships that are already given and, so to speak, observable (in their own families) or deducible starting from morphisms uniting fictitious individuals A, B, and C. Despite this great difference in experimental context, in the present situation one again finds the habitual succession of intra-, inter-, and transmorphic correspondences. The first only apply to observable individuals in one's own family; the second are composed using nonobservable individuals; and the third are calculated in generalizable forms as a function of a general structure with free and arbitrary compositions. But, if there is interest in finding the same process of construction, there is no less interest in establishing the retardations and décalages of these steps in relation to the results obtained in the preceding chapters. However easy intramorphic correspondences bearing on one's own family may appear, they are astonishingly misunderstood at the preoperatory level and barely mastered with the beginning of concrete operations. As for the intermorphic forms, they are only attained around 9 or 10 years of age. The reason for this is, no doubt, because transformations are absent except in the form of purely logical construction. These décalages seem, therefore, to confirm the subordination of morphisms to transformational structures.

We still need to specify that at the transmorphic level morphisms of kinship constitute a category. As Wittman has shown with the approbation of McLane himself, "groupings" can be put in the form of "special categories." As we have shown in our work on concrete operations, the kinship grouping is the richest of all of the groupings and its compositions are the most varied in their detail. Taken together, these facts suggest that the genesis of the kinship grouping, the steps of which we have just retraced, is representative of the psychological formation of "special" categories.

8 A Special Case of Inferential Symmetry: Reading a Road Map Upside Down

Jean Piaget
with
Annette Karmiloff-Smith

Symmetry constitutes an apparently complex correspondence. On the one hand, it is a variety of isomorphism; on the other, it involves a reversal of directions or of order starting from some point or axis such that the symmetrical of ABC but oriented toward the right or toward the top will still be ABC but ordered toward the left or toward the bottom. This reversal can present problems when it has to be constructed (especially in the situation studied in this chapter). From the figurative point of view, however, it corresponds to a perceptual "good form," so that figural symmetries play a very precocious and general role in young children. This is the case not only in their spontaneous drawings but also when one asks them to put some little unequal sticks "in good order." In this instance, instead of seriating them, they arrange them symmetrically. Similarly, in order to balance a scale, they resort to spatial symmetries well before they dream of equalizing weights, and so forth.

By contrast, in this chapter we propose to study a problem of symmetry where the reversal has to be constructed. In this particular case, it is a matter of reading a roadmap upside down. A fortuitous observation by a colleague indicates that such a question can be posed spontaneously to children. She was driving with a boy about 4 years old in an unfamiliar area on the edge of a large city. To find her way, she referred to a detailed map, and each time she did so, she explained to the child the correspondence between the map and the streets, squares, or buildings. When they began their return, the boy immediately asked a question the sense of which was, "Do we have a map for coming back? And how will we do it if we don't have one?" These questions make obvious the relationship between reversal having to do with symmetry that is not simply figural and operatory reversibility.

1. EQUIPMENT AND TECHNIQUE

First, the experimenter presents the child with a small map representing his district (about half countryside), his school, his house, and so on, and checks how well he understands it. He then goes on to the experimental map, 15 cm by 24 cm, representing the road leading from a forest to a beach, with a number of very irregular hairpin curves, six of which are very sinuous or angular in detail. The road also has seven bifurcations between the route to be followed and dead ends, and there are reference points distributed irregularly at the side of or not far from the road. After this second map has been introduced, the experimenter presents a large roll of wrapping paper (0.75 m by 4 m) on which is drawn the "real road"; he unrolls about 30 cm for the child and furnishes a small car that the child must drive from the forest to the beach. The real road is unrolled very slowly and the part traveled is rolled up so that decisions about the bifurcations must be made before the subject has established what side the cul-de-sac is on. The child constantly has to establish correspondence between the real road and the map. He therefore finds himself in a situation analogous to a driver who sees his whole route simultaneously only on the map and not as he effects real action. Some bifurcations go from left to right, others from top to bottom; for some the choice is facilitated by indices (river, trees, house); for others symmetry is the only instrument available for solving problems. For all bifurcations, however, the child needs to consult the map if he wishes to be sure not to make mistakes. When there are no bifurcations, or in other words for simple curves, he does not need a map. Each bifurcation is marked on the map by a small dot of distinct color which helps the child understand the protocol and may represent a form of spatial notation for the subject insofar as the order of bifurcations is concerned. The real road is not marked with colored dots.

The essential fact is that the map is presented in the direction opposite to that of the real road and is glued to the table. The subject can neither turn the map nor turn the real road. He can get up and consult the map in place but must then return to his place in order to drive the car. In other words, it is a matter of "turning the map in his head" (to use one child's terms), of localizing the spot where he is (bijection between map and real road), and of inverting the direction of the curves (top-bottom; left-right). Three young subjects 5 years of age were presented with the map rightside up. Their reactions exhibit certain interesting features relative to problems of correspondences before reversal is required.

2. THE INTRAMORPHIC LEVEL

This elementary level includes, first of all, reactions of subjects (Level I-A) who do not even succeed in simple bijection between a point on the real road and the corresponding point on the map when the map is rightside up. Such reactions are limited to correspondence between the two starting points and the two points of arrival. At Level I-B, bijections between intermediatry points are acquired, but not the reversal of direction. Here, then, are some examples of Level I-A:

SOP (5 years; 4 months): With the map right-side up, SOP correctly turns to the points of bifurcation situated near the beach, but only looking at the map in distracted fashion or without bothering about it. "Where are you on the map?"—(She indicates the whole trajectory.) At an intermediary point she makes a mistake in direction, then corrects herself but without looking at the map. "And there (middle point), where are you on the map?"—"(She leaves the forest and follows the map to a completely different point) There!" The experimenter shows her where she is, reexplaining the meaning of the map, but up to the end she continues to not consult it.

MOR (5 years, 7 months): With the map upside down, MOR muddles along the real road by trial and error. She, of course, makes mistakes when the experimenter asks her to indicate where she is on the map. When the map is placed right side up, she looks at it more but takes off on a dead end because she does not know how to use it: "Ah! I paid very close attention." When the experimenter asks her to show on the map where she is on the real road, she points to large curves without bothering with the colored dots.

And a case from Level I-B:

OLI (6 years, 10 months): Map rightside up: "If you make a mistake toward the place where you want to go, you look at the map and correct it." With the map upside down: "Here (map) the beach is at the top and there it's at the bottom." Near Point 7: "Where are you?"—"(Very long wait while looking at the map.) Here. (Correct, but he turns the wrong way.)"—"Why to that side?"—"To go to the beach (has top and bottom confused)." Near Point 3: "Where are you?"—(After a long wait, he heads in the right direction.)—"Why there?"—"Because here it's more curved than there . . . Ah! no (he changes sides and takes off into a dead end)." Point 4: "Where are you?"—"There." However, he again takes off in the wrong direction: "There, it's like a triangle, there it's curved, there it's straight, there it turns more, so there (wrong)." Point 6: "I am here (correct)." He readies himself for a turn in the wrong direction but pivots his hand (first attempt at inversion) and chooses the other direction. "Why?"—"Because there the [real] road is straighter, there a little more curved." And so forth.

The reactions of Level I-A require no comment. With OLI (Level I-B), one sees that although formulating the principle of reversal and for a short time seeking to apply it through a pivoting of his hand, he succeeds only with difficulty in localizing where he is on the map at various points during his trip. Of particular interest is the fact that, in order to direct himself subsequently, he only examines the curves and patterns of the road and pays no attention to whether it is going toward the top or the bottom. His decisions are, therefore, a function of what he actually sees on the map, but he acts as if the map were not upside down so that he takes off on the dead end every time.

3. INTERMORPHIC CORRESPONDENCES

When there is both bijection between the points of the map and those of the real road and inversion of positions, and, therefore, correspondence by symmetry, we can consider a coordination to be intermorphic. This is due to the fact that real composition is involved, because the two bijections are not the same as is the case when one isomorphism is only the prolongation of another. The best proof that a composition must be effected (in opposition to figural symmetries that are directly perceived) is that intermorphic correspondence is not attained in one fell swoop. It does not proceed from the single fact that the subject remembers that the map is "upside down" but must be conquered step by step. At Level II-A, in effect the subject succeeds with inversions only in local successive fashion. This explains why he has to reconstitute the turn around with each new bifurcation. Moreover, instead of operating in the abstract, he makes movements like pivoting his hands, his head, or sometimes his entire body:

GER (6 years, 9 months): GER begins by making two mistakes of direction and concludes: "The map is completely wrong."—"No, it's right."—"(He turns his hand around several times.) No, it's right. It's toward the trees. The map is upside down, I forgot." At the following reference point, he immediately makes the inversion and, as the experimenter suggests the wrong trajectory to him, he refuses because, "The big sheet (real road, not the map) is upside down!" At the next bifurcation, he hesitates for a long time, turns his hand and still makes a mistake: "Ah! I was forgetting what side the house was on."

CAM (7 years, 11 months): With each bifurcation, CAM turns, twists, or pivots her head or her whole body, making the widest movements possible. All of this, however, does not impede her from beginning with errors as well as with correct inversions. Starting with Point 5, by contrast, she succeeds on everything. On the other hand, when the experimenter asks her after the fact what she did when she saw the house, etcetera, she responds: "When you see the house, it's on the same side you have to turn to."—"Not the opposite?"—"No . . . Yes, yes!"

BUL (7 years, 3 months): BUL begins without inverting: At Point 2, she heads toward the dead end, "Because it's the same as on the map."—"How's that?"—"Because here (to the left), it's closed and there it's open. (tries it) I took the wrong road. You think that it (left) is here (left on the map), but it's there (right)." She subsequently succeeds at Point 3 by basing herself on the topographical index of the forest which it is necessary to approach. She does the same with the house at Point 5. At Point 4, she bases herself on "a big hump, like on the map." But in the end she only proceeds in terms of symmetries by turning her hand: "It doesn't stay on the same side; it turns (she pivots on her chair)."

These reactions remain intermediary between the intra- and the intermorphic. They are instructive with respect to the difficulties presented by inverted bijections when symmetries have to be constructed as is required here by a road to be traveled in steps. GER initially forgets that the map is turned around (he calls it "completely wrong") then revises his opinion and declares that it is his own trajectory that is "upside down." He, however, is an exception. Except for GER, these subjects do not lose sight of the need for inversion. Still, however, only an action scheme is involved without consciousness being taken of the general program. After successes at Points 5 and 8, CAM goes so far as to say that she has turn to "the same side" as on the map. The restrictive character of this action scheme is, therefore, indicated in three ways. First, it is not used when references to topographical indices (the forest with BUL, etc.) or to "humps" and special configurations of the road suffice and the scheme is not needed. Next, the adjustment of action brings up a new problem with each bifurcation, because solutions remain local successive, and without generality. This is why subjects keep making so many errors. And finally, inversions remain so far from conceptual generalization that the subject needs to mimic them by material gestures, by turning his hands, his head, or his entire body, so that inversion of bijection, is conceptualized in terms of material actions without further need of symbolization:

NAT (7 years; 4 months): After an initial error: "Ah! I made a mistake. I didn't look good enough at whether it went left or right."—(At Point 2) "Why are you looking at the map?"—"Because I see on the map whether I need to turn here or there (she turns to the correct side) . . . You have to turn right there (map), so left here (road)." At Point 6: "Wait. There it's harder. Before, there was a house; it was easier. But (without that) you have to look closer at what's happening on the map and then do it in the other direction here."—"Why?"—"I already told you that everything is upside down."

MUD (8 years; 10 months): MUD succeeds at Point 1. At Point 2: "Wait . . . to the left."—"But on the map, the road to the left is blocked?"—"Yes, but it's like that (he turns his hand). You have to think that you look at it with your head upside down." At Point 4, he refers to the topographical index of the trees, but at Point 5, he says: "It's always the opposite. Then here."—"The opposite?"—"Yes, right is left and left is right because the map has the forest on top, the beach on the bottom and here (his road) everything's opposite."

KAP (9 years, 6 months): KAP makes a mistake at Point 1: "I forgot that the map was turned." At Point 2, he refers to the river, but from Point 4 onward: "If you turn the map, you have to go to the other side."

CYR (10 years, 0 months): CYR still makes mistakes and sometimes resorts to reference points, but concludes: "I turned the map the other way in may head. That's what I should have done before," remarking, on the other hand, "It would be easier if you let me turn the map (materially), but I understand we're trying to see it the other way round."

Thus, one sees that these subjects continue to make certain mistakes and to use topographical reference points when that appears simpler. Nevertheless, they clearly formulate the generality of the inversion, the composing of which is a matter of bijection. In such cases, one may therefore speak of intermorphic correspondences in the sense that we assign that term in every chapter.

Let us again cite a precocious intermediary case whose initial error puts it at Level II-B but whose detachment from topographical indices puts us on the road to the next level:

NEL (8 years, 10 months): NEL makes a mistake at Point I: "Yikes! Oh no, I got it. Every time, you have to do the opposite."—"The opposite?"—"Yeah, if you turn there on the map, then on the real road, you turn here." For each of the following points (Points 2 through 8), he consults the map and says, "I do the opposite." The experimenter than asks him whether, at Point 2, it would not help him to look at the river and, at Point 3, to look at the trees, and so on. He answers: "You don't have to. That makes it harder. You only have to tell yourself to do the opposite at every step."

4. TOWARD TRANSMORPHISM

Subjects of Level III no longer make mistakes, even initially, and no longer resort to topographical indices. Nor do they any longer use anything but correspondences by symmetries. Were we to stick to these two reactions alone, we would only see in them the conclusion of intermorphic connecting. But there is an added novelty which in a general way presages the advent of transmorphic structures. This is the generalization of the necessary character that morphisms present henceforth. This characteristic arises from the fact that at the transmorphic level morphisms are deductively subordinated to a general transformation constituted by the reversal of the map. See the following cases:

PIE (11 years, 9 months): At the end of her choices, all successful, PIE concludes that, "When it's like that (↑↓), it's a little more complicated (than ⇄), but it always has to be the opposite."

BAL (11 years, 5 months): "If you turn the map, it's clear that what's on the right goes to the left."

MIC (12 years, 3 months): "Everything is the opposite, so you have to make as if the map were the right way round." It results that he expresses in his reading of the map the language that he uses to designate the real road. At Point 5, he turns correctly but says: "I turn right on the map and right on the road."-"But on the map it's left."—"Yes, but be careful. I'm going down on the map (in thought, because in reality he indicates the map road in the opposite direction to the real road), then, in fact, the right [correct] road is on my right."

ROL (14 years, 11 months): Likewise, ROL says at one point: "On the left (correct) because when I go down (!) on the map, that comes over to my left."

ALA(14 years, 6 months): "It's exactly the opposite every time. You can't make a mistake, but it's a little harder when it goes like that (↑↓)."

In opposition to the successive composition of intermorphic symmetries, two sorts of facts seem to indicate mastery, at this level, of the entire structure of turning around in a single take. The first is the statement of global necessity. "Has to be," "clear," "exactly" are terms that indicate the subordination of every particular inversion to the general reversal. The second, more curious, is a species of conceptual preinversion permitting MIC and ROB to translate directly what they see on the map into the language of what it is necessary to do on the road, for the very good reason that both the map and the road "go down" from the forest to the beach even though the direction of this going down is reversed from one case to the other. These reactions, therefore indeed, are oriented in the direction of transmorphisms, which we have said are compositions imposing themselves with logical necessity in function of a general structure. And this is so even if in this particular case, they do not go beyond the content of intermorphic correspondences in novelty.

5. TURNING PAGES

In order to evaluate the evolution of symmetries, it appeared useful to us to examine the more elementary situation of simple page turning. Subjects were presented with three forms red, blue, or gray in color glued to a piece of transparent plastic that could be turned like the page of a book, either in the left-right direction (Situation A) or from top to bottom (Situation B—see Fig. 8.1). In Situation A, the order of the Colors R and B was modified as well as the shapes of Forms 1 and 3. In Situation B, the order of the colors remained the same but the shapes of Forms 2 and 3 are inverted. Even though this test is naturally easier than that of the road map, it is interesting to find the same law of evolution in the reactions observed.

At Level I-A with the map, there was not yet bijection between reference points along the road to be traveled and those of the map, except for the extreme positions of departure and arrival. For page turning, however, Level I-A corresponds to an initial phase where the subject does not even reproduce the three figures involved in a rectilinear series, and moreover does not invert these figures correctly:

SOP (5 years, 5 months—see section 2 earlier) In Situation A, SOP gives a drawing where 1 is found above 2 and 3, the latter conserving the order 2 → 3 without inversion to 3 → 2. With respect to the detail of the forms, one finds a mixture of simple translations and partial rotations which seem due to chance.

ANA (5 years, 9 months): In Situation B, ANA places Form 1 beneath the other two, all three being reproduced as they are without reversal. After trying her idea, a new attempt ends in alignment, but vertical (1 at the top and 3 at the bottom). In Situation A, the linear order is achieved but without inversion of the colors or rotation of any of the three forms.

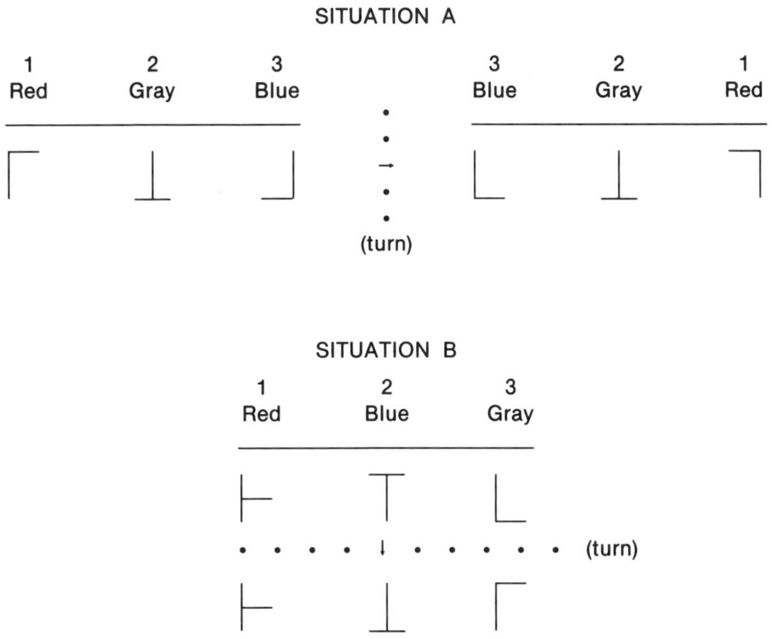

FIG. 8.1. Page Turning Apparatus.

At Level I-B, there is bijection between the forms of the models and those of the subject's drawing, in the sense that the linear order is conserved with its successions 1, 2, 3. In Situation A, however, the succession is not reversed into 3, 2, 1 and none of the figures is turned around, as if only simple translation were involved:

MOR (5 years, 8 months): In Situation A, MOR gives a drawing 1, 2, 3 without reversing either the order of the colors or forms and without reversing the forms themselves. The experimenter then has him establish the result of turning the pages by doing so in front of him, then putting the turned page back in place, and asking for a new drawing. This is identical with the first, that is, without inversion either local or global. In Situation B, the same reactions are found but this time with corrections after trials.

CLA(6 years, 5 months): CLA only gives translations conserving the order 1, 2, 3. Despite a lengthy trial in Situation A, he makes the same drawing again without any inversion. It is the same in Situation B.

Thus one sees that, as at Level I-B for the map (section 2), symmetry still is not understood and is reduced to simple bijection without reversal.

Between these reactions and Level II-B where inversion is successful, one can bring together a certain number of interesting intermediary cases as a Level II-A. From the start or soon afterward, subjects at this level understand that turning pages involves rotations, but they only succeed in effecting them correctly after various trials and errors and sometimes only with the help of slow pivots of the hand, as was seen with the road map. Some do not yet invert the order of the colored figures but try to reverse them in some way. For example, they may imagine rotation relative to a horizontal rather than a vertical axis in Situation A, although that rotation only occurs in Situation B. Others attain global inversion before inversion of each individual form and so on. See the following examples:

GER (6 years, 9 months): In Situation A, GER conserves the order 1, 2, 3 without reversing it to 3, 2, 1. For 1, he changes ┌ to └ (rotation of 180° along the horizontal axis), and he does not leave 2 (⊥) unchanged as he should, but turns it upside down to ⊤ (same rotation). After turning the page, he makes the same drawing again for Forms 1 and 2, but correctly turns 3 around (initially changed to ┌ by a double horizontal and vertical rotation). By contrast, Situation B gives place to success after corrections made subsequent to pivoting his hand.

CAM (7 years, 11 months): After having drawn 1 on the left in Situation A, CAM stops and says: "It's wrong, because if you close (meaning if you turn the page) . . . " and she correctly inverts 1, 2, 3 into 3, 2, 1 but conserves each figure as it is, as if it were only a matter of translations. By contrast, in Situation B, she succeeds in making the rotations.

BUL (7 years, 3 months): BUL begins without any inversion, then, upon trying, exclaims: "No! It's backward because it's been turned. The blue one (3) is at the beginning and the red at the end." In addition, she applies herself to reversing the forms, but by trial and error and with numerous pivots of the hand. The result is correct. In Situation B, there is initially an error for Form 3, then success with the second general attempt (without trying it out).

ISA (8 years, 1 month): Like GER, ISA begins in Situation A without inverting the order 1, 2, 3 and turning the forms on both axes at the same time. On the third attempt at drawing what she expects to happen (without trying it out), she inverts the order 3, 2, 1, but she does not succeed any better in the detail of the forms, except that 2 is not reversed.

JAC (8 years, 8 months): At first, JAC inverts nothing, then she corrects herself by reversing the order without turning the forms around. After several trials and errors she gives a double inversion in Situation A. In Situation B, everything is correct.

The analogy between these reactions and those of the same level with respect to the road map is obvious. It is understood that inversions are required, but these are locally executed with a hodgepodge of errors and successes. By contrast, Level II-B is a clear advance relative to the reactions of section 3, because success is general and rapid:

NAT (7 years, 7 months): NAT correctly inverts the forms in Situation A, at first forgetting to invert the order. She notices this immediately: "Oh, shoot! I forgot that." In Situation B, everything is correct after several hesitations.

IVA (9 years, 2 months): IVA immediately succeeds in making the inversions in Situation A, indicating by a movement of his hand where the horizontal bar of Form 1 must be located. In Situation B, he achieves the same success by using his hand to help him with the position of the horizontal bar of Form 2.

BAR (9 years, 11 months): BAR achieves the same success as IVA without any flubs, making a small pivot of his hand at the beginning of Situation A.[1]

CYR (10 years, 0 months): All of the inversions are made correctly without movements but with slow reflection.

SCA (10 years, 2 months): Same reactions. SCA, however, makes a mistake on Form 3 in Situation A but corrects it immediately.

Subjects from 11 to 12 years of age differ from the preceding subjects only in the greater rapidity with which they perform these tasks. This indicates the formation of a system, as we saw in section 4. Thus, the striking convergence that one observes in the evolution of reactions in situations as different in appearance as reading an upside down map and predicting inversions due to turning a page seem to show that the construction of correspondences by symmetry is far from being as easy as one might have supposed from the precocious character of perceptual and figurative symmetries. The reason for this appears to be that in going from bijections between states (therefore intramorphic), which suffice for figurative symmetries, to the intermorphic composition of bijections with inversions, one subordinates correspondences to transformations. In Situation A, these transformations are themselves linked to one another by intertransformational correspondences which is the source of their greater difficulty. This subordination of symmetries to a structure confers on them their character of deducible morphisms. It also explains their tardy formation insofar as it makes appeal to logical acquisitions of the operatory stages.

[1]Apparently there is an error in text. A form rather than a situation is indicated, but it makes no sense to speak of the beginning of a form—Translator.

9 Conflicts Among Symmetries

Jean Piaget
with
Annette Karmiloff-Smith

In order to better analyze the formation of symmetries that are not perceptually given but have to be constructed by the subject in terms of correspondences with reversals, it proves helpful not to stick to isolable symmetries. In other words, it is useful not to limit oneself to symmetries that arise from a single system as was the case with the roadmap presented upside down or the transparent pages of chapter 8. Instead, we need to employ polyvalent systems involving several possible symmetries all of which can be used in solving a single problem but which present quite different relationships among themselves. Once again, the equilibrium of a balance scale provides such a problem. In certain cases, the relationships involved in a such scale are logical in nature, that is the relationship between weight and the number of identical objects; in other cases, the relationships are looser, even at times resting on simply arbitrary conventions. The advantage of variety in relationships as well as in objects is twofold. On the one hand, it allows us to attain greater spontaneity on the part of the subject than is seen when the relationships in play are suggested by the material itself. On the other hand and more important, it permits one to differentiate different forms of symmetries in function of figural, spatial, physical, or logico-arithmetic factors.

1. EQUIPMENT AND TECHNIQUE

A primitive and manipulable scale is provided in the form of a support on which the child can symmetrically or asymmetrically position a long wooden beam at one of 15 holes along its length. Weights can be suspended on either end of the support in order to balance the beam. The weights present four particularities. First, all are plastic and weights numerically close to one another are similar in size. Moreover, they are shaped in the form of the whole numbers one to nine. Each has a hook at the top. Second, they differ quantitively in weight, each number weighing one unit more than the preceding. Thus, number 1 weighs one unit, number 2 weighs two, number 3 weighs two plus one, and so forth. Third, each set contains two each of numbers one to five but only one each of six to nine, so that the subject must use additive combinations of the smaller numbers to compensate for the larger ones. If there is already a set of conventions, arbitrariness is increased even more by the addition of another set of numbers. The set just described is painted red; the second set is painted yellow. It contains elements identical with the elements of the red set and with identical relationships among them, but the yellow numbers weigh slightly more than their red counterparts. The difference, however, is so small that it can only be detected by weighing.

The interrogation proceeds in the following stages:

1. The experimenter asks the subject to place all of the red numbers on special nails at the ends of the beam. The subject can do this as he wishes, but he must do it in such a way that, when he finishes, the beam is balanced. It is the subject, therefore, who decides whether to put the weights on first and then place the beam on the support or to first balance the beam on the support and then distribute the weights. The different methods[1] used by the subject are analyzed as well as retro- and proactive regulations.
2. The same is done using both sets of numbers, red and yellow. For the youngest subjects the number of numbers is reduced to two 1s, 2s, and 3s and one 4, 5, 6, and 7. For other subjects, both complete sets are used. In addition to the problems posed in (1), in this condition the subject has to discover the difference in weight between elements of the red and yellow sets and to find a method to overcome this added difficulty.
3. The experimenter fixes the beam asymmetrically on the support without numbers. It is, therefore, not balanced. The instruction is to balance it without necessarily using all of the numbers. The red set is used.

[1]It is not clear whether Piaget means to distinguish *procédés* from *procédures.* Although generally synonymous, the latter refers specifically to sets of rules whereas the former does not. For that reason, I have maintained the distinction by rendering *procédé,* method, and *procédure,* procedure—Translator.

4. Starting with the result of (3), the subject is asked to move one of the numbers that he has placed at one end of the beam at the opposite end while keeping the beam balanced. Several solutions are possible, the most economic of which is simply to change sides, that is, to exchange the numbers on one side with the numbers on the other side keeping the number of holes from the end to the support constant. (This is equivalent to rotating the apparatus 180°.) When the subject does not change everything but only the number asked for (normally 9, because it has the greatest effect on the longer arm), there are not enough numbers left to effect a solution simply by adding compensating weights. This obliges him to seek another solution.
5. The experimenter places the weighted beam off-center (either Hole six with red weights 9 and 5 or Hole five with yellow weights, 4 and 8 + 2)[2] so that it is in equilibrium. The subject is asked to add two numbers of the same color while keeping the beam balanced, then two more still keeping it balanced, and so on. The point is to determine whether the subject uses only the absolute difference between the two numbers or the proportional relationship between the numbers to solve the problem.

2. INITIAL CORRESPONDENCES

It is a matter of course that the correspondences from which the subject starts will remain at the level of simple figural symmetries. In other words, he will place an object on either side without regard to its weight or the number it represents. In this regard, one can distinguish a Level I-A where the child sticks to doing this and a Level I-B where he does it but corrects himself and begins to be concerned with numerical values, although he still does appeal to additive compositions. Here are some examples of Level I-A:

SOP (5 years, 4 months): For the first part of the interrogation, SOP places the beam on the support at the center hole, therefore balanced, then on Holes six and nine, righting it with her hand. Coming back to

[2]The French manuscript and edition read "hole five with yellow weights 9, 8, and 2." This would be impossible since the beam is too short to allow equal moments with these weights. In the first instance, apparently, equilibrium is achieved because the 9 units of weight at one end are 5 units of length from the center and the 5 units of weight at the other end are 9 units of length from the center. By analogy, in the second instance equilibrium would require placing 10 units of weight on the end 4 units of length from the center and 4 units of weight on the end 10 units of length from the center. I have, therefore, changed the weights to make that possible—Translator.

Hole eight, she puts the 6 on one side and a 2 on the other and is very surprised by the disequilibrium that results: "Oh!" After other attempts with one number on each side, she puts 8 + 6 + 7 on one side and 3 + 2 + 4 on the other, that is, three objects on each side, then 5 + 1 + 1 opposite 4 + 2 + 5, then four numbers on each side, and finally 1 and 2 on both sides achieving balance. She so little understands the reason for the equilibrium thus attained that she believes she can also achieve it with 6 opposite 3—again, therefore, with one object opposite another, but with the objects being arbitrary.

CLA (6 years, 5 months): CLA places the beam at its middle by sight, then puts one weight opposite the another, using whatever weight is handy. After 17 attempts: "I can't do it." The objects are reduced to the first six red numbers, but he still proceeds without any method: "I can't get it; it always leans." He proceeds then with little unequal piles, 1 + 1 and 2 + 2 on one side opposite 6 + 5 + 4 on the other. Then he says, "I put too many on the other side," and goes back to one weight opposite another without any more success and continues this until, after groping for a long while, he puts the same weight at each end: 1 opposite 1, 2 opposite 2, up to 5 opposite 5.

And some cases of Level I-B:

VIN (5 years, 7 months): VIN places the beam at the fifth hole, then tries the sixth, and then sets about counting the holes of which there are five on one side and 10 on the other: "There are a lot too many." Then, by sight, he places the beam in the middle, that is, at Hole eight with seven holes on either side. Next, he places a 4 on one side and a 7 on the other, then a 6 opposite a 4: "No, it doesn't work because you have to use the same numbers." Whence 4 opposite 4, 1 opposite 1, because "they're the same heaviness." He then puts a 6 opposite an 8 and as it tilts, he wishes to complement the 6 by a "tiny, tiny, tiny one" and adds a 2. He goes back to one opposite one, but because there are no pairs beyond the 5s, he does not know what to do from 6 to 9 and, not envisioning the possibility of additions despite previously adding a two, he limits himself to pairs smaller than 6.

OLI (6 years, 10 months): OLI says of the beam: "It can't be at the beginning because that would never work." He then proceeds one weight opposite another while adding from 6 to 9 at the center. Next, he holds the 7 next to the 9, examines their sizes minutely, and says, "yes." Trying them on the balance, he rights the beam with his hand. After again trying one weight opposite another one, he puts the 8 and the 7 on one side and the 9 and a 6 on the other, but this seems to be a pairing up and not numerical addition: "I put a bigger one on one side and a bigger one on the other, and then the smaller ones." On Question 2, he pairs off the yellow weights with red ones without weighing them in his hand then places the red 7 opposite the yellow 7, then the yellow 4 opposite the red 4. "Wait a second" He then tries the red 3 opposite the yellow 3: "What the heck!" He does not understand the inequality YELLOW > RED despite his various attempts. On Question 3 (beam off-center), he attributes his failures to the fact that "there is the wood here (meaning the weight of the longer side)." On Question 5, he uses a 2 and a 3. This fails: "I give up. I don't understand anything. You, you put two different ones and it worked, so I put two different ones, too . . . (and it didn't work)."

It is evident that Level I-A, symmetries only have to do with the number of objects and not with their properties. The only exceptions are CLA who moves to Level I-B at the very end of the experiment and for SOP who balances the scale for an instant but fails to exploit her momentary flash. At the lowest level of the intramorphic, therefore, only figural symmetries are involved.

The progress made at Level I-B is to go on, as VIN says, to the "same numbers," and to do this because "they're the same heaviness," but without additivity, that is, without weights yet being quantified. Thus, symmetry remains figural more than anything else. "A bigger one" on both sides and then "the littler ones," says OLI, and especially "You, you put two different ones and it worked, so I put two different ones, too." It is as if the different ones constitute, insofar as compared in terms of a qualitative relationship, a class of equivalent as well as a class of similar elements.

3. THE QUANTIFICATION OF WEIGHT

Between the qualitative weight of the object, which only permits intensive symmetries, and quantitative weight such as an addition like 5 = 3 + 2, one finds a certain number of intermediaries between Level I and II characterized by this additivity:

EMA (7 years, 3 months): On one side of the centered beam EMA puts (1 + 1) + (2 + 2) + (3 + 3) and on the other either 4 + 5 or 9. She then takes 4 + 5 away and substitutes 7 + 6. Next she uses an ordinal criterion of position, that is, 6 opposite 4, in addition to others: "Yes, look; it's the fourth one."—"And if I take off the 4 and the 6?"—"It'll be straight. There's still one that's a little heavy (5) and then there (behind 5) and (on the other side) they're all light."[3] There is, therefore, very approximate equivalence of sums. Naturally, for the yellow and red sets she first puts a red 5 opposite a yellow 5, and so forth, but after various attempts she does not resolve the problem. Going back to the red with the beam off-center, she puts 2 + 1 + 3 opposite 2 + 1 + 3. After other attempts, she says, "No, you really can't."

ISA (8 years, 11 months): After inequalities, ISA finds the equilibrium for 3 opposite 3, "Because I put two numbers of the same kind, at the same length," then 3 + 2 opposite 3 + 2. For 9 opposite 8: "It's too loaded there (9)." Subsequently: "I put the big one (9) there, then a bunch of little ones on the other side to make the same weight." Comparing red and yellow, she at first assumes equality of the numbers, for example, red 2 opposite yellow 2, and so on. Then, after several failures: "If I changed sides (she tries it)? Yes, on both sides the yellow is heaviest." She believes that she straightens everything out by proposing: "Two on each side and of each color" as, for example, two red 3s opposite two yellow 3s. Finally she declares, "You shouldn't have mixed them. They're heavier than the red ones." For the beam off-center, she tries according to weights and to identities and concludes, "It's impossible."

These facts are interesting with respect to the formation of correspondences by additive equivalences. One does not yet find in them bijections of the form 5 = 2 + 3, but only a symmetry between some heavy ones and "all the light ones," that is, an analogy with the extension of classes (EMA). It is the same with ISA, "the big one there, then a bunch of little ones on the other side to make the same weight." But this quantification remains quite modest, because ISA believe it is possible to cancel out the differences between the reds and yellows by changing their positions to the two ends or by substituting for red and yellow 1s several of each in equal numbers!

With Level II-A, this dawning quantification of weights is consolidated up to the point of attaining symmetries by additive equivalences, but again with numerous gropings or regressions:

NAT (7 years, 4 months): "I'm supposed to put the same on each side?"—(The experimenter repeats the first instruction). She then places the beam at its center and wants to put 1 + 2 + 3 + . . . 8 + . . . "on both sides." Because the equipment makes this impossible, she immediately places 5 opposite 2 + 3, then continues with 9 opposite 7 + 1, "because seven plus one, that makes eight." For n > 5, "You don't have two 6s, two 7s, and so on. Even so, I'm going to try." Whence

[3]Neither the French manuscript nor the French edition is clear—Translator.

7 + 8 = 9 + 6 (equilibrium). With the beam off-center at the seventh hole, she makes a series of trials and errors with a fortuitous success that she does not notice and another which a weight's falling off impedes describing but which provokes the statement, "I'll never be able to put them back right." With the beam off-center at Hole five, she makes even more numerous trials and errors and finally succeeds without understanding: "When it's like that (she shows the end farthest from the support), you have to put a lot there, close (to the support). It's kind of funny." Comparing red and yellow, she quite quickly discovers that the reds are lighter and places one yellow weight opposite another identical yellow, does the same with reds, but fails with mixtures of the two. Question 5: failures and one fortuitous success.

JAC (8 years, 8 months): JAC gropes around for a long time looking for equalization, but she does this in terms of classes of small, medium, and large. This continues up to the moment that she has a sudden insight: "Wait! (5 opposite 2 + 3)." Then, very excited, she places 4 + 1 opposite 5 and 1 + 1 + 2 opposite 4. "Ah! I got it!" Comparing red and yellow, she sees the inequality and devotes herself to numerous trials only to conclude: "The two together, it's impossible. You just saw it!" She comes to the same negative conclusion for the beam off-center.

This discovery of additivity, naturally insufficient to resolve the questions of the beam off-center or of mixtures of red and yellow weights, is nevertheless rife with consequences insofar as indicating an equivalence between weighable and numerical correspondences and, therefore, a beginning of intermorphism. The result is that subjects at Level II-B frequently calculate weighable equilibrium by planning on the basis of an arrangement of weights on the table and, therefore, on numerical correspondences. On the other hand, there are, at this level, other kinds of progress relative to Questions 2 and 3. Before we consider this, however, we need to establish some definitions.

All subjects understand that the series of red and yellow weights obey the same recursive law of n + 1, even though the yellow are seen to be a little heavier. In this regard, then, it is necessary to distinguish two forms of correspondences when the subject succeeds in attaining equilibrium by mixing the two colors. We speak of "direct correspondences" when the equilibrium between two red-yellow combinations have to do with the same reds and the same yellows, for example, with red 5 + yellow 4 on both arms of a beam, which simply amounts to uniting the equivalences "red 5 ↔ red 5" and "yellow 4 ↔ yellow 4." This, of course, is relatively easy. By contrast, we call "crossed correspondences" the more difficult composition where some red and some yellow number balance a different red and a different yellow number and where the first red number differs from the second in the same way that the second yellow number differs from the first red number, for example, red 5 and yellow 6 opposite red 6 six and yellow 5. With respect to situations where the beam is off-center, we call "compensatory correspondences" those that combine weights and distances and "positional correspondences" those that, correct for a beam supported at the center and erroneous when it is off-center, only have to do with weighable and numerical symmetries with equal positions. That said, here are some examples of three cases that remain intermediary between Levels II-A and II-B:

IVA (9 years, 5 months): After trials and errors with the balance, IVA prefers to put the forms on the table in identical pairs (1 ↔ 1 to 5 ↔ 5) or in pairs with additive equivalence (9 + 6) ↔ (8 + 7): "One big and one small . . . the heavy with the light and the light with the heavy." Curiously, however, even though he thus equalizes the numerical sums and the total weights and even though he thereby grants, in fact, an equivalence between numerical and weighable correspondences, he does not take consciousness of this through sufficient conceptualization: "Are you saying that it's the same weight, do you think that it's the same number on each side?"—"(He counts the weights) Yes."—"If it's the same weight, is it the same sum?"—"No, you can't say that, because there is a nine and not there. If there were two nines and two eights then, yes, but I haven't used the same numbers every time." For the reds and yellows mixed, he quickly sees the inequality but even so tries a red 1 opposite a yellow 1, and so forth. Then he says, "I have a better idea. A heavier one and a lighter one together on each side." He begins with a "direct" correspondence (red 2 + yellow 2 ↔ yellow 2 + red 2) then discovers a "crossed" form (red 5 + yellow 6 ↔ yellow 5 + red 6). "Ah! (obvious satisfaction)."—"Same weights?"—"Yeah, because it doesn't go down." Beam off-center: numerous trials and error ending in success. Question 4: "What can you do so that the 9 will be on the other side?"—(He puts the 3s on the other arm and moves the point of contact with the support first to Hole nine and then to the correct hole, ten) "It acts like a pendulum; when there's too much weight, you put it closer."

PAC (10 years, 3 months): Also after several trials and errors, PAC arrives at the correspondence (8 + 7) ↔ (9 + 6). "Is the total the same?"—"No, because at the end (meaning after the pairs 1 = 1, 2 = 2, etc.) you don't have the same thing on both sides."—"But is it balanced?"—"Yes."—"But it isn't the same total?"—"No, I don't think it always is." Later, however, she comes closer: "Same sum? And so on. . . . "—"You don't know unless you count . . . Yes, if it makes 20 here, then perhaps 20 there, too?" For the reds and yellows mixed, she only arrives at direct correspondences, putting "first the reds then the yellows." For the beam off-center, she succeeds empirically after multiple mistakes and says that "when the bar is long, you need less numbers." She does not understand the situation, however, because once equilibrium is attained in the off-center situation, she thinks it is possible to conserve it by adding identical number-weights at the same point on either side.

YVE (11 years, 8 months): Despite his age and his additive successes, YVE does not yet understand the equality of sums: "If it makes 30 on this side, how much on the other?"—"Maybe 28, you have to count. You can't really know without counting."

Despite obvious progress over Level II-A on all questions, these intermediary cases are interesting because of the conflicts among different forms of correspondences or symmetries that they do not succeed in overcoming. In this experiment, it is necessary to distinguish correspondences between the number of weights (figural symmetries as at Level I-A), between their identities (equalizing symmetries as at Level I-B), and between sums (equalizing symmetries as at Level II-A). What one finds is that subjects employ this third form of correspondence without problems but do so only in action and, therefore, operationally. On the plane of consciousness or reflected comparisons (partial conceptualizations), however, they believe it to be solidary with the other two. There still is not the same sum, according to these subjects, if the elements are not the same or identical in number. By contrast, this difficulty no longer exists for clear cases of Level II-B. Here are several examples:

BAR (9 years, 6 months): BAR begins like IVA, also moves to calculation on the table and begins by saying, "The same numbers on each side, except the 8 (opposite the 7)" and discovers that 7 "No, it's the 6 with the 1." This leads to the compositions: 6 opposite 5 + 1 = 4 opposite 2 + 2 and 4 + 3 opposite 5 + 2. He then exclaims: "Ah! I have it; the numbers, they correspond to the weights. That's pretty neat!" Now, unlike the cases of IVA, PAC, and YVE, who already knew this well enough but only in terms of action, BAR thinks in terms of sums which sets him to spontaneously adding all of the reds, from which he concludes: "Sixty, therefore 30 on each side. (He hangs 9 + 5 + 5 + 1 + 3 + 3 + 4 on one side.) Thirty, then the others here (opposite side)" and he attaches them without adding them. "How can you be sure?"—"Because I have 30 here, they make 60 in all, so it's clear: 30 here, too. There is as much weight as the number, so you calculate the same number. For example, three plus three, then (on the other side) six." For the reds and yellows, he says immediately: "I'm going to see if they're the same weight (tries). No, the yellows are heavier." Four equal piles of reds all equaling six are, therefore, needed (6 = 4 + 2 = 5 + 1 = 2 + 1 + 3). He puts them back on two at a time: "That makes 12 on each side." Whence 12 reds + 12 yellows ↔ 12 reds + 12 yellows. For the beam off-center, he succeeds empirically but, lacking any understanding of "moments" attributes inequalities to the fact that "the bar, it weighs something too when it's long." Question 4: In order to put 9 on the other side, he simply turns the beam around.

COR (10 years, 4 months): Confronted with a minor error: "It tilts, so I calculate how much that makes. There (on one side) there is one less."—"Number?"—"No, that doesn't count (meaning the number of weights) I have the . . . the . . . the sum, see!" For the reds and yellows, after several attempts, she moves from direct (yellow 2 + red 2 opposite red 2 + yellow 2) to semicrossed correspondence (yellow 5 opposite red 5 + red 1). With the beam off-center, she succeeds after 17 errors, "Because it's not equal." To remedy this lack of equilibrium between a single weight on one arm and four on the opposite arm, she starts by simply changing sides, then she modifies the internal order of the four and does that twice: "No, that doesn't change anything." Finally, she comes around to changing the point of support. By contrast, she seems to understand that in order to add a new weight to each arm (unequal because off-center), you have to choose unequal weights.

LAU (11 years, 5 months): After additions: "If I have 30 of them here, how many do I need there (a lot more objects)?"—"There are more of them. No! You also have to do 30, because before you had 12 and 12. Yeah, every time you need the same number (sum)." Reds and yellows: Unequal sums are necessary, "Because I think three reds are almost equal to two yellows." He rapidly succeeds with the beam off-center but attributes the inequality of weights to the weight of the arms themselves: "Here there is more bar." By contrast, when adding new weights in the asymmetrical situation, he insists on choosing ones that are equal. First, he chooses a 1 opposite a 1 and, because the balance tilts, he shouts, "It's not possible! I put the same thing. Normally it would work!" He gives the same reaction for 3 and 3, 4 and 4, and so on. "I don't understand. When it's balanced (among different weights), it ought to work. It's not in the middle (the beam), but once you put it quite straight with these two (9 and 5), I don't see why the 1's won't work!"

ANA (12 years, 1 month): Despite her age, ANA still hesitates a moment on the question of sums. After having placed the 14 reds in equilibrium, 7 against 7: "Is it the same number of objects on each side?"—"Yes."—"What is a sum?"—"It's when you count how many it makes in all."—"Is it the same sum on each side?"—"Yes, almost. No . . . yes, the same."—"If there are 30 here, how many there?"—"Thirty also, or perhaps 29 point five. No (she laughs) it has to make 30." Comparing reds and yellows, she makes multiple attempts and then puts yellow 6 opposite red 5 + red 3: "No, not two more." She then moves on to direct correspondences. Question 5 with a 9 and a 5: She adds a 2 on the left and a 3 on the right (fails), then permutes them (succeeds)[4] "And with the others?"—(She places a 3 and a 4 in the same places) (tilts). "I don't understand anything. I put a difference of one here too. (She tries a 6 and a 5; it tilts.) Hmmmm. It's funny! (She tries a 6 and a 4; it balances.) It works, but I don't really understand why because here there is a difference of two!"

To begin with, one sees how the equalization of numerical sums with the beam centered completes the elaboration of intermorphic composition between numerical and weighable correspondences that has been forming since Level II-A. The tardiness in completing this coupled with the existence of intermediary cases as paradoxical as those of IVA, PAC, and YVE is instructive insofar as it indicates the objective gap that separates the intermorphic from the intramorphic. From the intramorphic at Level I-B onward, some subjects like VIN and OLI see that "the same numbers" are "the same heaviness" or speak of "smaller" and "bigger," which seems to imply an intrinsic relationship between a number and its weight in the form of observables being imposed simply through empirical discovery. It happens that in order to get from that point to the deduction of an isomorphism between the equality of two sets of weights and the equality of their numerical sums conceived as metrical equivalences, it is necessary to traverse the whole distance separating Level II-B (9½ to 11 or 12 years of age) from Level I-A five or six years of age). And this is so even though the additivity of the weights and numbers is acquired as early as Level II-A (seven or eight years of age) for small collections! The reason for this disparity is quite clear: This composition presupposes a "deduction" or, in other words, intermorphism between two types of correspondences of the same rank (weights and numbers) is something other than empirical inquiry and calls for construction. We often have said that correspondences are "transformable but not transforming," because they consist in comparisons and therefore must not, in contradistinction to operatory transformations, modify their contents under penalty of falsifying the comparisons they produce. The formation of intermorphic compositions does not escape this rule. They do not modify the findings (here weighable and numerical). By

[4]Karmiloff-Smith assures me that only approximately equal moments were required for equilibrium.— Translator.

contrast, they constitute a higher step in the hierarchy of putting things into correspondence because by being grounded on deductive necessity they transform, even while refining, the very instruments of comparison.

4. TRANSMORPHIC GENERALIZATIONS AND RELATIVIZATIONS

Two sorts of progress characterize the last of our levels, observed from 12 to 14 years of age. Insofar as beams centered at their midpoint are concerned, the correspondence of numbers and weights, sometimes made explicit in its recurrential form, $n + 1$, permits the subject to start directly from sums and to, subsequently, divide them between the two arms. As for off-center beams (we see in chapter 10 that the law of moments is understood at this level), the weights to be added to an equilibrated system are immediately relative, therefore proportional, to the weights already placed ($n' > n$) and no longer absolute, which is to say, equal to one another (as with ANA and the subjects of Level II-B):

MIC (12 years, 3 months): For Question 1, he spreads all of the equipment on the table, makes two piles, and fastens them to the beam without checking details: "Okay, I saw what sort of things I had, I counted, it came to 60, and I put 30 on either side."—"Same number of objects?"—"That I don't know. It doesn't matter. It's whether they're equal that matters."—"Equal?"—"Yes, in total number, like if you have 30 of these little 1's on either side." Reds and yellows: same operation and grouping. For unequal weights on an off-center beam, he adds a 3 on one side and a 2 on the other, then a 6 and a 4: "I doubled it."—"Why not 4 and 5?"—"No, you always have to put twice or half as much," and he also proposes 8 and 12.

ALI (14 years, 0 months): "I make piles of 10. I'm going to add the whole and divide it in two. That way, it will be the same weight."—"Are you sure?"—"Because it seems to me that each one is getting heavier and heavier both in number and weight . . . Even so, I'm going to check whether the weight corresponds to the number (he places 8 + 2 opposite 9 + 1). Yes, each one must weigh one more weight than the one before it (he places 7 + 3 opposite 6 + 4, then 4 + 1 opposite 3 + 2)." For the reds and yellows, he places the support off-center and after two tries finds the equilibrium for yellow 1 opposite red 4 + yellow 2, knowing from the start that one less weight is needed on the long arm "because there it's more sensitive, and I wasn't sure that there (short arm) I had put enough." Then, with the beam exactly centered, he puts 9 yellows and 11 reds on each side. "Careful, the yellow ones are heavier."—"But it doesn't make any difference at all. What counts is that you have the same thing on each side." Laughing, he points out that one could equalize the weights of two buildings to each of which one added a chair and that "it wouldn't matter if the building and the chair didn't weigh same." For a beam off-center but balanced by different weights, he immediately adds a 3 opposite a 2, then a six opposite a 4 "because if I double it, it's the same thing," and, amused, he comes back to his comparison: "If it works with three chairs on one side and two on the other, then it has to work with three buildings on one side and two on the other!"

This relativization substituting proportional numbers for absolute values in the reactions to Question 5 seems, at first sight, to constitute the only progress of Level III relative to Level II-B (see LAU's astonishment, etc.). But it only represents one aspect of a more general transformation, consisting in the utilization of a method of calculation that makes compositions of morphisms both necessary and "free," which is to say capable of bearing on arbitrary contents. Two facts are significant in this regard. The first is that the solution of the problem of the equality of sums (in the case of the beam resting at midpoint) is programmed from the start without resulting from previous and particular additive compositions. By counting the weights on the table before putting them on the beam in order, subsequently, to divide their sum into equilibrated halves, the subject provides himself with a general model that he can later apply to arbitrary sets and subsets. In the second place, this is not just a matter of a simple instrumental scheme, but of a model that includes reasons for doing what you do. ALI sticks to stating them explicitly and verifying them by specifying the law of succession, which is the relationship $n + 1$. It is, therefore, the morphism of numerical successor applied to weight as well as to whole numbers. If one defines the transmorphic as a composition of morphisms subordinated to an operatory instrument of calculation, this deductive subordination coupled with the conquest of the arbitrary and of proportional relationships (themselves due, naturally, to this inferential procedure) permits one to consider these reactions as characterizing a transmorphic level. (A proportion is an equivalence of relationship, etc.) It differs from intermorphic compositions by being a correspondence among correspondencs.[5]

This study gives a new (and good) example of the genetic transformation of correspondences as instruments of comparisons. Nevertheless, it remains

[5]Recall that, etymologically, "*trans*" implies a going beyond (transfinite, transcendent, transfiguration, etc.) and does not simply mean "among or between" except in degenerate usage.

that these instruments, although progressing, conserve and manifest a permanent function, which is precisely that of comparison, a differentiated expression, nuanced in varying degrees, of the still more general function of "assimilation." But this is not the place to discuss the relationships between the relative invariance of functions and the progressive construction of their organs. We come back to that topic in the general conclusions to this work.

10 Correspondences and Causality

Jean Piaget
with
Cl. Voelin
and
E. Rappe du Cher

When we ask children to explain and compare two causal situations, we find ourselves face to face with new problems. The first concerns "lawfulness." Lawfulness is evident in functions different in nature from correspondences among arbitrary forms. This is because lawful functions consist not only in comparisons between the results of two transformations (Tf's)[1] but also add the idea of dependency between the transformations of y and those of x. When the child discovers dependency between covariations by means of correspondences of this sort, he needs to explain them causally or, in other words, to show why such dependency is necessary. According to our previous hypotheses, casual explanation consists in assimilating the transformations observed to some sort of operations analogous to the subject's own operations but "attributed" to the objects themselves. In causal explanations, objects are therefore considered to be operators. That being the case, the correspondences that the subject establishes between transformations he discovers deep within objects and his own operations will constitute a second problem. In other words, the correspondences that the subject finds between the processes he observes and the deductive model to which he is committed present more difficulties. It is, however, a matter of course that this second system of correspondences, while being more or less clearly manifested in notions that the child constructs, cannot be teased out by the observer. This is because the mechanisms responsible for the "attribution" in which it results are not conscious. The psychologist's job is, therefore, to establish how the subject uses his logicomathematical, in

[1]Bijection between x and y, if y = f(x).

particular his spatial and "infralogical," operations[2] in general in order to interpret causal connections among phenomena. Contrary to some people's opinion, it is easy for the experimenter to discern the operations the subject uses without confusing them with those of the adult theoretician. The most noteworthy way this is accomplished is by comparing the child's operations to those of following as well as to those of preceding stages. Nevertheless, a difficulty remains with respect to the distinction of causal operations from those that the subject already employs on the plane of lawfulness. In effect, it is clear that the subject needs a logicomathematical framework even to "read" facts. In that case, however, it is only a matter of operations "applied" to objects as assimilatory instruments; it is not yet a matter of operations "attributed" to objects in the sense just defined. Even if this distinction complicates the analysis, the persisting problem is still to reconsitute the correspondences between transformations that the subject situates in reality and his own operations or conceptual schemes.

1. EQUIPMENT AND TECHNIQUE

The equipment includes two apparatuses:

1. Beam Balance: The beam is a bar of iron, perforated at equal intervals by 24 holes that allow it to be fastened to a support as well as to have weights suspended along it. The even number of holes makes the balance necessarily asymmetrical. The weights are all equal (50; see Fig. 10.1).
2. Wagon on a Rail: The wagon sits on a rail, the inclination of which is variable. It is, moreover, attached by a string and pulley to a counterweight is the form of a balance-tray (called tray). The experimenter can load the wagon and tray with weights, all equal (40 m). The weights of the wagon and the empty tray are insignificant and have little effect. If there is equilibrium, one has the relation $p_1 \cdot \alpha = p_2$, where p_1 and p_2 are the respective weights of the wagon and tray and where α is a trigonometric function which expresses the slope of the rail (see Fig. 10.2).

To begin, the experimenter presents the balance to the child and asks him to do several things in order "to see how it works." Then he asks for a preliminary explanation of the respective and combined roles that the

[2]Bearing on the continuum and its division, on grouping according to neighboring relationships rather than similarities, and so on, and, therefore, on the constitution of objects and not on their classes.

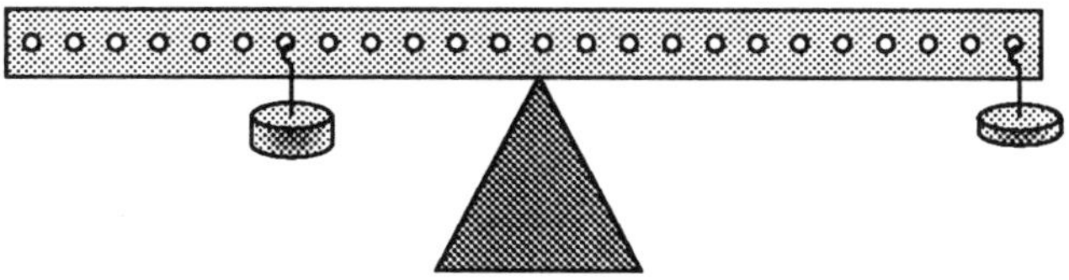

FIG. 10.1. Beam balance apparatus.

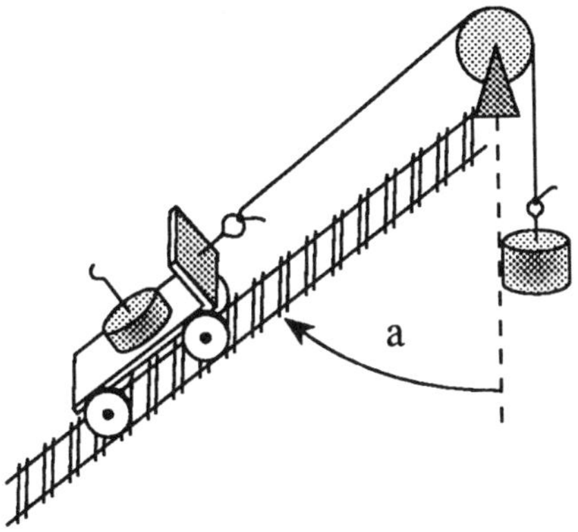

FIG. 10.2. Wagon on rail apparatus.

weights and their distances from the support play. After this, he goes on to the second apparatus.

With the second apparatus, the experimenter again begins with a brief description. He then alternates between asking subject to anticipate what actions will lead to a given result and what results a given action will produce. (An example of the first question might be, referring to the situation shown in Fig. 10.2 with the wagon at the top, "What must be done to make the wagon go down the rail?") The experimenter then asks the subject to link his predictions to his findings and to explain "how it works."

A first comparison of the two apparatuses is followed by a deeper explanation of each, and that in turn is followed by new comparisons. For one comparison, the instruction is the following: "You take this thing (apparatus) and I'll take the other. You have to do the same thing with yours that I do with mine" (e.g., bring a weight closer to the beam's point of support.)

2. INTROMORPHIC CORRESPONDENCES

The first correspondences one sees involve only local and momentary observables without compositions among them. Sometimes they are correct; sometimes they are incorrect (notably when an unforeseen fact is perceived as a perturbation that can be neglected). When anticipations and explanations are asked for, they can end in total contradictions because of the plurality of the factors in play. See the following cases:

TAN (6 years, 10 months): With the wagon, TAN seems to begin with partial understanding: "It went down, because it had more weight (than the tray)"; "You have to add a weight there (tray) and then it (the wagon) will go up because that (tray) is going to go down"; "The wagon would go down if you took the weight off (from the tray)." When the experiment does not confirm her,[3] she reverses the correspondence: "You have to take off the weight on the wagon, and it will go down."—"Why?"—"Because the string (of the tray) will go up."—(Demonstration: The wagon ascends.)"Why?"—"Because it had more weight, because you let it go. It went up."—"And if we put another weight on the wagon?"—"It's going to go down because it will have more weight than there (the tray; she tries). It stayed the same!"—"And if we take off two weights?"—"It's going to become lighter and go down." TAN finally goes so far as to say that if the wagon goes up, it is "because they have the same weight (it and the tray)!"

VIN (6 years, 6 months): Balance: He at first expects that the beam will remain horizontal with a single weight at one end. "What happens if you let go of something heavy?"—"It falls."—"Then if I put that here (a single weight but at the other end)?"—"It will go like that (tilt to the side of the weight) or like that (the side without a weight)."—(The experimenter lets go of the beam, and it swings to a vertical position)—"That's funny!"—"What do you have to do to put it like it was before?"—"You have to put them (two weights) on both sides."—(The experimenter does this, and the beam tilts.)—"It leans!"—"Why?"—"Because there are two of them."—"And this way (second hole, which balances the beam)?"—"Because it's not heavier on one side than the other." Wagon: It goes down when the experimenter puts a weight on [the tray] "because the weight[4] is heavy."—"And if you want to make it go back up?"—"Take off the weight."—"And if you don't?"—"Put one here (on the tray; the experimenter does this)."—"And to make the wagon go down again?"—"Take off this weight (from the tray)."—"Good. What else?"—"Take that off (from the wagon!—tries and fails). No, put one on instead." He establishes that two weights on the

[3]Apparently for quantitative reasons not given in the text TAN's reasoning, essentially correct, is not confirmed—Translator.

[4]VIN says, "*le plaque*" meaning the plank or plate, apparently a reference to the form of the weight—Translator.

tray will make four on the wagon go up: "It's crazy."—"Can you make it go down without putting weight on or taking it off?"—"Like that (he raises the tray by hand) or put five of them on the tray(!)." The experimenter shows him that the inclination of the rail can be changed. He at first believes that by raising it a little he can make the wagon descend.—"Go down?"—"I think so. (The experimenter does it.) Ah no! (The experimenter raises it more.) It [the tray] goes down more, and so the wagon slips."—"And so it will go back up?"—(He puts the rail higher and the wagon again ascends.)—"Why?"—"Because it goes up, the wagon; it doesn't slip."—"And being hooked to this tray, doesn't that help it go up?"—"No, oh yes . . . no. It's that (the rail) that helps it go up." Comparison of the two apparatuses: "It's the same, that (beam) and that (rail). The weight is too." The experimenter tries to have him reproduce on the wagon what he himself does on the balance, but the subject limits himself to giving the same inclinations to the balance and to the rail and to comparing both weights on each apparatus saying, "There's more weight there than there (left and right), but they're the same."

SAN (7 years, 5 months): After supposing that the balance can be balanced simply by putting equal weights on either side, SAN establishes that "it goes down on the side that has more holes" between the point of support and one of the weights. She does not see the analogy with the wagon, however, and begins, in order to make it descend, by loading the tray with weights before putting any on the wagon. That done, she discovers that she has to put four weights on the wagon when there is one on the tray and that three are not enough to make the wagon descend: "Four things on one and one on the other, is that the way it should be?"—"Yes."—"then how many will you have to put on the tray so that the wagon goes back up?"—"Five (therefore, $1 + 4$)!" A moment after trying this, which should have freed her from this misconception,[5] she sees that the wagon descends with eight weights opposed to two on the tray. In order to make the wagon go up again, she then places ten weights on the tray.—"Why?"—"Because there are eight of them there (therefore, $10 = 2 + 8$)!"

The most general characteristic of these reactions is the absence of composition between the correspondences that have been successively established. All of these subjects quite naturally start with the simplest hypothesis. They either assume that there will be equilibrium in symmetrical cases where the number of objects is the same on both sides of the apparatus

[5]Because when she places the first of the additional four weights on the tray, the wagon goes up—Translator.

(using either the wagon or the balance), or they assume that the side with more weight will fall. When the facts disconfirm this anticipation, two attitudes are adopted. The first consists in disregarding the perturbing factor and doing nothing more, which amounts to contradicting the facts. For example, SAN discovers on two occasions that a smaller weight on the tray makes a bigger weight on the wagon go up, but she continues to reason as if that were not at all the case and puts five or ten weights on the tray in order to make four or eight on the wagon ascend. By contrast, the second attitude consists in taking account of the unforeseen fact by creating a new correspondence, but one in defiance of contradictions it produces with respect to prior correspondences. Thus, TAN after having correctly asserted that for the wagon to descend it must be heavier than before (or the tray lighter), says calmly that "You have to take off the weight on the wagon, and it will go down," and explicitly that "It's going to become lighter and go down." Likewise, VIN affirms that one can make the wagon descend by taking weights off of it and even adding five more to the tray! He also predicted that a single weight at one end could make it tilt to either side. It should be noted, moreover, that the absence of composition evident in these two reactions is also apparent in the tendency to link different aspects of a single factual state in terms of immediate relationships. It is as if a more or less necessary relationship obtained among them, even though only contingent encounters are involved. For example, observing that equal weights on the wagon and on the tray makes the wagon ascend, TAN goes so far as to say that the wagon ascends "because they are the same weight." VIN thinks that the balance tilts simply because "there are two" weights. And regarding the ascending wagon, he is led to neglect the role of the tray in favor of the role of the rail "that helps it go up" just as it helps it "slip" in the situation of descent. This amounts to saying that if, in a given state, things are "like that" (as a subject of 7 years, 0 months expresses it), it is that "they must be like that." In other words, in such situations a sort of "pseudonecessity" comes into play. This, in general, is an obstacle to the opening up of new possibilities; in particular, it is combines with the first attitude to slow down any composition among correspondences. With respect to interapparatus comparisons, it is a matter of course that under such conditions, comparisons between the two apparatuses can only be figurative.

3. THE STAGES OF INTERMORPHISM

As we have just seen, subjects of Level I do not integrate unforeseen and perturbing facts. Either they ignore them, or they modify their schemes in ways that the contradiction is not felt as such. There is, therefore, no attempt at composition. By contrast, subjects of Level II-A force themselves to integrate new factors. This indicates clear progress in terms, among other things, of the spontaneous discovery of the role played by the inclination of the rail and in terms of the beginning of compositions. It must be recognized, however, that such compositions as are seen at this level still only consist in local and partial undertakings. More systematic compositions are really only manifest in an indisputable way at Level II-B where stabler combinations between weight and spatial factors are seen.

Here are some examples of the transitional forms seen at Level II-A:

CRI (7 years, 0 months): CRI places some weights on the balance that he thinks are unequal. Disabused, he says that "that one is heavier because it's farther ahead (more distant from the point of support)."—"Has its weight changed?"—"No, but once it goes there (tilts down) and once it goes there (toward the point of support)." He succeeds in finding several states of equilibrium. With respect to the wagon, he sees clearly that in order to make it descend, it is necessary to load it more or to unload the tray and, in addition, he spontaneously finds that "you can lower the rail." However, he remains surprised by the inequalities of the weights necessary for the wagon and for the tray, whence diverse hypotheses. One completely valid one that remains undeveloped by CRI is that "there (wagon), it's sloped." Another is that the weights are spread out on the wagon and piled up on the tray: "Then if you stack them up on the wagon you won't need so many?"—"Maybe (negative effect). I don't know; it's funny." Comparison of the two apparatuses only produces: "That goes down and that goes up."

MAR (8 years, 3 months): MAR thinks that a weight's variable action on the balance is only due to the fact that "it changes holes," but she can find no reason for this. With respect to the wagon, she sees the role of the weights that one adds or takes off well enough: "You can also put that down (the rail)," but she gives no other explanation for the inequality of weights than "here (on the wagon), it is lighter than there," without saying why. From the fact that two weights are not enough to make it descend she concludes by simple extensional correspondence "then it doesn't work with three." After verification, she asserts that "You had to put four on." The interapparatus comparison produces: "It's almost the same problem. One (side) goes up, and then the other goes down."

RIA (8 years, 8 months): RIA gives the same reactions with respect to the difference of weights on the wagon and the tray. She also says that "you could put the rail down; the slope would be faster." But there is progress in that RIA compares horizontal and inclined rails by saying that in this second case it must "be heavier (on the tray) than when the rail is there (flat)." Interapparatus comparison: "It's the same thing. There is more (weight) on one side and less on the other."

SCA (8 years, 4 months): In order to make the wagon go up, SCA says, "You put the rail back up and then take the weights off of the wagon." The tray is "heavier" than the wagon. "But if you weigh them by hand?"—"Yes, but if you put the rail back up, it's heavier . . . because when the rail is more sloped there is more force (élan)." With respect to the balance, "when the weight is in the middle, it is like there wasn't any weight, it's like there wasn't any when it gets close to the middle."

ARC (9 years, 6 months): ARC attributes the inequalities established between the weights on the wagon and tray to the slope of the rail: "When you move the rail, what changes for the wagon?"—"Weight's involved, that's what I think," and he believes that there will be equality with the rail at 45° and the wagon and tray in symmetrical positions. In that case, the wagon "should be in the middle (at midheight) because that makes the weight the same." Interapparatus comparison: "You almost have to do the same thing because (on the balance also), if you put the weight back (toward one end), it makes it go down."

HUB (9 years, 11 months): HUB understands that if one weight on the tray makes three on the wagon ascend it is "because it's not very sloped." When six weights are needed on the wagon to make it descend (with two on the tray), he attributes it to the fact that "when it's sloped, it goes down faster." But he does not see that he contradicts himself when he says subsequently that in order to make the wagon go down with equal weights on it and the tray, it would suffice to put it "very sloped." On the whole, he is on the right road, and in the interapparatus comparison, he correctly says that on the balance "the weights stay the same but you change holes" like for the wagon "you change the slope."

NAT (10 years, 11 months): Like CRI, NAT thinks that in order to equalize the weights, it is necessary to stack them on the wagon as they are stacked on the tray.

ANA (10 years, 11 months): Like ARC, ANA proposes to put things at midheight.

Before commenting on these reactions, let us examine those of Level II-B. The explanations of the latter are not more developed (except with respect to the vertical) but their intermorphic compositions of correspondences between spatial factors and weight are more stable because they occasion the use of a synthetic concept called "force," "strength," and so forth:

ALA (9 years, 0 months): ALA explains variations on the balance by the fact that "if the weight's always the same, it's not the same distance."

With respect to the rail, "it goes up or goes down, there is a certain strength" and "it changes" with the inclination and the weight. But he does not succeed in conceptualizing the difference between "strength" and weight.

BEA (10 years, 4 months): By contrast, BEA says that for equal weights one changes the force by modifying the inclination of the rail or by changing holes on the balance. When the latter is introduced, BEA immediately counts the holes and concludes that "there is no middle," whence the variations in the effects with positions: "If you move these weights [away from the point of support], it gives more force at the ends." For the wagon: "I think I understand: that (the rail) is sloped and that (the string holding the tray) is straight down and then that (the tray) makes more weight because it falls faster, whereas there (the wagon), there is an angle. It doesn't fall as fast."—"Does the tray have more weight?"—"You can't say more weight. It's more force. It (the wagon) has less force because it is sloped."—"And if I do that (lower the rail)?"—"You have given the wagon force and taken it from the tray."—"And here (balance), can you change the force?"—"You have to change holes."

ISA (10 years, 11 months): In order to explain the "real weird" fact that with two weights on the tray more than five are necessary to make the wagon descend, ISA also says that the tray "hangs (vertically) and there not, the rail slopes," whence it results that "it has more resistance here (tray) than there (wagon)." The term "resistance" is in this instance an exact synonym of what BEA calls "force": "Are resistance and force the same thing?"—"No, it's the resistance that does things—it pulls."—(A drawing is made) "Can you change the resistance on a teeter-totter?"—(Yes) "You change places. If you have the same weight, it goes down on the longest side."

MAR (12 years, 11 months): MAR gives the same reactions: "It's the strength . . . the strength of the weights, that's what plays the role."—"What is strength?"—"It's the weight of the weight(!). When you change the descent (the inclination of the rail) it doesn't change the weight, it changes the strength." With respect to the balance: "Because that (one side of the beam) is longer, all the weight bears on this arm. It makes sense." Interappartus comparison: "When it's horizontal, it's like when the arms are equal; when it's (the rail) sloped, it's like when an arm is longer; and when it's vertical, it's also like when the two arms are the same length."—"Can you transform this apparatus into a balance?"—"Yes, when there are six on the wagon and three on the tray, it has the same strength."

YVE (12 years 5 months): "The wagon isn't vertical, so the tray is heaviest."—"That changes the wagon's weight?"—"No, it doesn't change the weight, but it changes the value."[6]—"When does the weight have the most value?"—"Almost at the vertical. The more horizontal it (the inclination) is, the less value the weights have."—"Why's that?"—"You must be able to explain it, but . . . the weights will never be equal (wagon and tray) except when they are vertical." Comparison with the balance: "There, the more you put the weights toward the center, the less value they have."

In contradistinction to the reactions of Level I, where subjects look only for correspondences with respect to successive factors considered separately and without coordinations, from Level II-A onward there is a quest for composition. For the balance, composition between the correspondences of weight and position is immediate, but without causal explanation. Although subjects rapidly discover that slopes can be modified in the wagon apparatus, they do not stick to compensating that factor with the factors of weight or speed. Rather, they also appeal to the way in which the weights are stacked (CRI and NAT), to the position in height (role attributed to the "middle" by ARC and ANA), to the weight of the support or rails, and so forth. As for comparisons between the apparatuses, they only appeal to the ascents and descents and to factors affecting them, for example, slopes or holes, without a general model.

With Level II-B reactions, by contrast, intermorphic correspondences between weights and slopes are stabilized by being generalized and are accompanied by two kinds of progress. One kind is relative to the factors of inclination. The subject discovers that the essential difference between the tray and the wagon is that the first is suspended vertically and the second is sitting on an inclined rail. The second kind of progress is the constitution of a synthetic concept called "force," "strength," "resistance," or "value" which MAR nicely defines as "the weight of the weight." In other words, they come to understand the variable action (according to position or inclination) of a weight that is constant insofar as it is considered a property of an object. But this concept remains verbal in the sense that, if it serves to integrate the facts into a general intermorphic composition, it in no way specifies the "how" or the "why" and therefore does not attain the rank of transmorphic causal model. "Force" is indeed the source of speed, speed being due to the slope; this is perceived at Level II-A. But that does not explain the inequality of the weights that are necessary or sufficient in different situations. In other words, the intermorphic, although used in a general and stable manner at Level II-B, remains on the plane of lawfulness and functional dependency. It does not provide causal interpretation in the

[6]"*Valeur*" sometimes means "force" in French—Translator.

form of attribution of operations to objects conferring internal necessity on the dependencies or connections that up to now have simply been conceived as regular rather than as intrinsically determining.

4. TRANSMORPHIC CORRESPONDENCES

It is at Level III that properly causal explanation begins to be sought. The issue, then, becomes to examine the morphisms that are used to achieve this:

OLI (11 years 0 months): OLI begins by saying that the weight of the tray (one weight on the tray and three on the wagon) "is heavier than the wagon." He then points out that "it can more easily descend when it's steeper; (it is) as if it were heavier," whereas the wagon on the inclined slope, "It would press (on the rail). If it is flat (rail horizontal), it cannot move but presses downward." He explains that the wagon "presses in both directions," one downward, the other sideward, which, therefore, is a decomposition of force. "It's the same weight (on different slopes) but in one case, it presses less than in the other; it's not the same speed." With the rail vertical, the weight would be "the same (in equilibrium) because it will descend the same way."

ERI (12 years 6 months): "The weight there (wagon), it has a point of support, whereas here it doesn't."—"Explain it to me."—"Here (rail inclined) it presses above and that cancels part of the weight."—"It really cancels?"—"If the rail is horizontal, the weight is completely cancelled because there is a point of support, whereas if the rail is more oblique, the weight is less and less decreased and finally, when it is vertical, it is not canceled at all." However, only the weight's actions are involved: "It, itself, does not change." With regard to the interapartus comparison, the beam is compared to the rail and "if you change the inclination, it would descend like here (balance) when you change holes. You add some weight (meaning, the weight increases) because that becomes longer." "The weight is divided in length," which explains a longer trajectory of action.

ENZ (14 years 3 months): For the balance, ENZ explains the greater action of weights distant from the center by saying: "The farther they are, the more they descend, the lower they end up," which amounts to translating the moment or the distances in terms of trajectories (rotation of the beam) and no longer in terms of simple scalar lengths. But for the wagon, ENZ remains close to Level II-B, limiting himself to saying that with the slope, "Less is needed to hold it up," the idea of support remaining implicit.

LAU (14 years 1 month): For the balance, LAU says that a weight situated far from the center "acts on the whole part of the bar from the axis up to the end."—"Then?"—"There is more force." Regarding the wagon, "when it's like that (inclined), there's a force that pulls toward the earth, but also (another) like that (he indicates the direction of the rail)" whence it results that "the force will be greater if it's more sloped because it will pull it more directly, perpendicularly to the earth." From this comes his comparison of the two apparatuses: "the force varies with the steepness of the rail" and "on the balance with the distance from the axis."

CHA (14 years 1 month): Regarding the greater weight necessary to make the wagon descend, "It's because the rail supports the wagon, it slows up its going down. The tray, there's nothing that holds it back." The wagon supported by the rail, "It's the story of the dumbwaiter (*char à commission*)!" With respect to the balance, "It's there (axis) where it is supported (the beam); so if you go closer there, it (the weight) goes closer to where it is supported, so you can't (meaning 'you don't need to') put a lot of weight." On the contrary, "If it's at the end, it strains it more. If I want to lift something, I take a piece of iron (lever), I press at the end, and that has more weight."

VET (15 years 0 months): VET sees immediately that the weights at the end of the beam have more action than the central ones, but he says (correctly!) that "the length of the bar has no importance in calculating the weight of an object." Like CHA, he compares this situation to that of the lever (and again in terms of personal, not just scholastic experience) and concludes that the weight, "all the way to the outside will have more (power of) traction." As for the wagon, "there is a quite steep slope, so the earth's attraction has a greater influence, and there you have it!" Otherwise, the wagon "is retained by the rail."

SCA (15 years 1 month): Comparing weights at the ends of unequal arms of the beam: "It pulls more there where it tilts, and it pulls less when it is less inclined." In effect, the end of the arm gives "a lower inclination" than if nearer the center because, in the latter case, "All the force there (part of the bar between the center and the end) is lost for the weight." It is then, in fact the principle of the lever that SCA describes (and in a way obviously not inspired by school). With regard to the tray of the other apparatus, "It pulls down toward the ground," whereas the wagon: "Uh, no, because it's on the rail, it can't."

RIC (15 years 2 months): "The slope takes some force off of the wagon (he indicates the direction) whereas the tray falls vertically, so it loses all its force."

These various explanations are quite striking because of the number of relationships they add to simply observable correspondences and because of the deductive and necessary subordination of these relationships to the general explanatory model. Such developments characterize the transmorphic level because the explanatory model is added, as a total system, to intermorphic compositions between correspondences of the same rank.

As far as the wagon is concerned, the novelty consists in a decomposition of forces, inclination no longer being limited to modifying speeds, but now implying two components that it is a matter of coordinating. One is attraction, "a force that pulls it toward the earth," as LAU says, and who also adds "perpendicularly to the earth." The result is that vertically it acts alone, as in the case of the tray, whence equality of the weight's actions on both the tray and the wagon. The other component is the fact that if the rail is inclined, the wagon presses on it from another direction, which decreases the action of the weight. ERI expresses this by saying that horizontally, "the weight is completely canceled." The general conclusion is, then, that to the extent that the rail is "more oblique, (the effect of) the weight is less and less decreased" (ERI) because as OLI says, it "presses in two directions." Taking into account the angle (in fact, of the cosine), it seems clear that these subjects's excellent explanations arise from the idea of work defined in terms of the displacement of force.

Insofar as the balance is concerned, things appear to be the same, as we maintained long ago.[7] In effect, if moment is measured in meters-kilogram, that is, d•f, work is expressed in kilograms-meter, that is, f•d. Although these expressions appear to be identical, they signal the essential difference that in the case of work d is a vector and therefore represents a trajectory. It is exactly this difference that makes it explanatory, because an activity rather than a static length comes into play. This is the distinction that VET pertinently expresses when he says that "the length of the bar has no importance in calculating the weight of an object," and that if a weight distant from the center manifests more action, it is due to its power of "traction," as in the case of the lever. The same comparison is explicit with CHA and implicit with LAU. ENZ goes so far as to specify the greatest displacement of the weights when they are farthest from the fulcrum: "The farther they are, the more they descend, the lower they end up," therefore, f•d and not d•f (also, cf. SCA).

5. CONCLUSION

Returning to the problems with which we began, one can wonder what the relationships are between the correspondences or transformations that the child discovers in reality and those that he discovers in his own operations

[7] *Les Explications Causales* (Volume XXVI of *Études d'Épistémologie génétique*). Paris: Presses Universitaires de France, 1971, p. 97.

or actions. In particular, one may ask whether there exists, as we suppose, a correspondence between causality attributed to objects and the subject's operatory structures.

To begin with lawfulness and the functions in whose forms it presents, the question of the respective contributions of the subject and objects is already quite complex. As already mentioned, a function $y = f(x)$ has three aspects: putting x and y into relationship or correspondence; dependency such that variations of y are controlled by those of x and not the other way round[8] (the reciprocal only meaning that the variations of x can be reconstituted mentally starting from y); and a set of transformations (or covariations) modifying x_1 into x_2, x_3, and so on, and (correlatively) y_1 into y_2, y_3, etcetera. True, each of these facts constitutes an observable, and the function as a whole thus results from a reading of observables (therefore from "experience"). It nevertheless remains that the reading itself presupposes the elaboration of reading instruments and is due to the subject's activities from the three points of view just distinguished. In order to establish relationships between x and y, for example, to establish relationships between the weights and the movements of the balance or the wagon, one has to be able to classify, to put into relation, to make more or less systematic comparisons (correspondences), to distinguish "more" and "less" (elementary quantifications at play from sensorimotor levels onward), to spatially organize (inclinations, middle, stacking), and so forth. All of this depends on schemes and coordinators previously elaborated by the subject. Insofar as dependencies are concerned, a certain number of inferential processes are needed just to organize their coherence. The proof of this is that the young subjects in section 2, like TAN and VIN, do not know whether the wagon descends because it is heavy or because it is light. With regard to transformations, we should note, first of all, that the facts whose observables the subject examines are all "experimental facts." In other words, they are ordered, manufactured, assembled, or dissociated. They are, then, facts that already have been "transformed" by the subject. We also should note that their transformations either are due to the subject's actions or are assimilated to his schemes of action (to "press," to "pull," to "help," when "the rail helps," to "counter," etc.).

This leads us to the causality or explanation of transformations once causes and effects are put into correspondence. In this regard, the observer finds a progressive correspondence between the subject's causal explanations and his preoperatory or operatory logicomathematical structures (Levels I to III). At Level I, explanatory "becauses" for the subject are not, in fact, causal and do not go beyond the level of lawful "dependencies," all the while presenting the interest of being traced onto action proper (to "press," to "let go," to "help," etc.) with, of course, a first form of

[8]The *x*'s being the manipulations effected; the *y*'s are their results.

"attribution" to objects themselves. However, they only involve necessity for the subject. At Level II-A, progress in explanation includes, on the one hand, the roles attributed to slope (wagon) and distance (balance), which is an expression of the beginning of operatory spatial structures. On the other hand, it includes logical coherence (including the additivity of weight as is seen at Level II-A in chapter 9. At Level II-B, what is new is the general idea of "strength" or "force," which has explanatory intention but which remains too global to play a role of that kind. By contrast, Level III the decomposition of forces according to their directions and their composition with trajectories in the form of "work" attain the level of a causality at last provided with intrinsic necessity. It is at this level that the correspondences between causal, and therefore physical, and operatory, and therefore logicomathematical, compositions become clearest and most numerous, verifying Leibniz's famous aphorism: "The cause in things corresponds to the reason in truths." In effect, both constitute systems of transformations coordinating the production of novelties with the conservation of invariants, whether it is a matter of material objects and mechanisms or of mental processes. With respect to this production, it can take on, in both domains, the most varied forms involved in structures like those of groups, and so on, common to the physical world and to cognitive compositions. These include forms that allow us to displace and orient, to order, to bring together or dissociate, to compensate or reverse, to optimize (extremal principle), not to mention forms of transitivity, of associativity, of distributivity or reciprocities, of symmetries, etcetera.

Correspondences of this sort between causality and the subject's deductive productions become conscious only tardily, of course. Their conceptualization only starts the moment that scientific thought constructs models conceived as such and raises the question of the extent to which they are adequate to the experimental facts. There is, however, a fundamental reality attesting to the existence of correspondences at all levels and to the "attribution" of the subject's operations to objects. That reality is the continuity that links the experimental manipulations by means of which the subject organizes facts to the final deductive form that these initial manipulations take when they become operatory precisely through progress in the composition of actions. In this regard, the interapparatus comparisons (cf. ERI at Level III and even MAR at Level II-B) are instructive because, without yet conceptualizing the notion of work itself, they give evidence of putting organizing schemes into correspondence with one another, that is, they make weight vary as a function of inclination or distance according to direction.

11 Equilibrium of Moments in a System of Coaxial Disks

Jean Piaget
with
F. Kubli

In this experiment the subject is presented with five disks graduated in size and rigidly affixed to a single horizontal axle. The smallest disk has a radius of 2 cm; each of the others is 2 cm greater in diameter than the preceding. All have a small plug at the same point on their circumference to which 1 of 5 weights may be attached so that it hangs to one side or the other along the circumference of the disk (see Fig. 11.1). The weights vary from 50 g to 250 g and have strings so they can be suspended from the disks. The problem is to conserve the equilibrium of the system by attaching weights to at least two different disks, one weight per disk, as the subject wishes. The law that the child must find is that the sum of the products of the weights and the radii of the disks must be the same in both directions. Situations are represented in the following way: 1↙2 + 2↙5 = 3↘4, where 1, 2, and 3 designate disks; 2, 5, and 4 designate weights; and the arrows designate the direction of rotation. The moment to the left (↙) would therefore be (1 × 2) + (2 × 5) and the moment to the right (↘) would be 3 × 4.

It is interesting to attempt to specify by what correspondences subjects come to discover and eventually to explain this general relationship, and that from several points of view. To begin with, it is a matter of products, even though young subjects tend to want to ensure equilibrium by simply equalizing the sum of the weights pulling the disks to one side with the sum of the weights acting in the opposite direction, as if the apparatus were some sort of balance. Our principal question is, therefore, to understand how the subject goes from additive to multiplicative compositions and what form of abstraction, empirical or reflective, he utilizes to do so. The observables simply indicate that a lighter weight on a larger disk gives the same result as

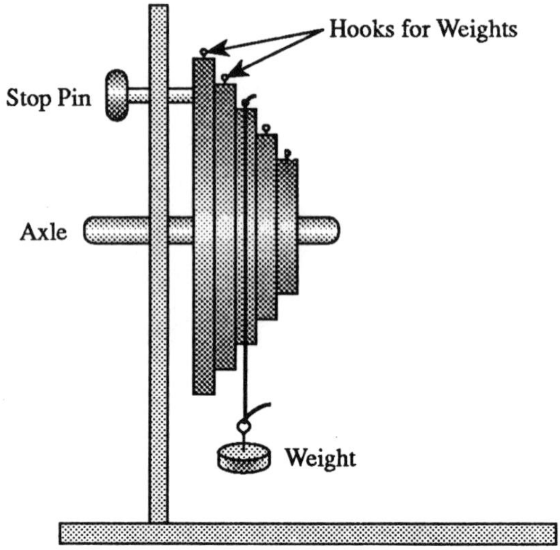

FIG. 11.1. Coaxial disk apparatus.

a heavier weight on a smaller disk. In order to go on from there to a constant product, a reflective abstraction seems necessary, which would be instructive with regard to the formation of intermorphic compositions. On the other hand, the apparatus used allows new weight-disk pairs to be added, as one proceeds, to the pair or pairs with which the subject begins. This can be done as on a balance scale where equilibrium can be conserved by adding equal weights to each balance-tray, the problem then being that of additive composition. For the disks, however, what one adds is a new product pair. But something else is also possible. Once the initial weights are put in place, the subject may simply move them, as in a problem of conservation of substance where one changes the form of the whole object without doing anything else. In this case, it is interesting to compare the processes in play with that of the additive "commutabilities" seen with simple displacements.

1. LEVEL I: INTRAMORPHIC CORRESPONDENCES

Intramorphic correspondences have the double character of being simple readings of observables and of lacking adequate compositions. In general, they represent the reality of preoperatory subjects from 4 to 7 years of age. Although it is obvious that such correspondences are relative to the subjects' level, it is also obvious that they are relative to the degree of complexity of the problem set for them. It is not surprising, therefore, that in the present case, the first level is found in 9-year-old children:

CLA (9 years, 5 months): CLA begins with 1↙1[1] versus 2↘2 by way of exploration and predicts rotation to the right. There are, therefore, two correct correspondences and a third one that is implicit and that is not correct. The first is that of the correspondence between the side to which the weight hangs and the direction in which the disk is pulled. The second is the correct correspondence linking a heavier weight to a bigger effect. The third, of which CLA says simply, "If you calculate the weight, you can predict what side it's going to turn to," consists in believing that rotation depends only on the relationships of the weights (here 2 and 1) without considering the size of the disks. Effectively, when she is asked to conserve equilibrium, CLA first gives 1↘1 and 3↘3 versus 2↙2 and 4↙4, which she corrects to 1↙1 and 4↙4 versus 2↘2 and 3↘3[2] which gives total weights of $1 + 4 = 2 + 3$. As that does not work, she tries 1↙1 and 2↙2 versus 3↘3, which gives total weights of $1 + 2 = 3$ [which still does not work]. Likewise, she predicts that 2↘4 versus 3↙3[3] will turn to the right and continues according to the same principle. Following these failures, she moves Weight 1 to a larger disk: "I told myself that it might be lighter on a larger disk," which is a beginning of putting weights and disks into correspondence, but the correspondence is reversed and without issue, because, in effect, CLA goes back to her initial rule.

MAR (9 years, 6 months): MAR appears to indicate progress and look for some relationship with the disks. He tries 1↘5 and 2↘4 versus 3↙3 and 4↙2 and 5↙1 so that the heaviest weights will be "at the front." Seeing that this fails, he no longer pursues anything but equality of the weights: 3↙3 versus 4↘2 and 5↘1. Stunned by his lack of success, he says, "But two plus one makes three," and he checks this by weighing the weights in his hand. He then returns to a relation with the disks: "I have an idea. I put the lighter weight on this disk (2) and the heavier on the little one (1)," whence 2↘4 versus 1↙5.[4] Then he

[1]Recall that the number to the left of the arrow refers to the disk and that the number to the right of the arrow refers to the weight. The expression 1↙1 would therefore be read as Weight 1 on the left side of Disk 1, 3↘5 would be read as Weight 5 on the right side of Disk 3, and so on—Translator.

[2]There is an error in both the French manuscript and the French edition: 3↙3 and 4↘4. I have changed the notation to make it conform to Piaget's analysis—Translator.

[3]Again there is disparity between the notation and the text, and again the notation has been changed to bring it into conformity with Piaget's analysis—Translator.

[4]In the French manuscript (repeated in the French edition!) there is at this point a total and unexplained shift in notation, that is, ↘ is replaced by ↙, which would mean an upward

thinks of the height of the suspensions. "You have to put the heaviest weights on top, the lightest weights on bottom." Finally, he comes back to the equality of weights on ↘ and ↙.

BET (10 years, 3 months): BET starts with an interesting idea of symmetry: "I put the biggest one in the middle, and to balance the others with each other, I put them so that one pulls in this direction, the other in the opposite," that is, 1↘1 and 2↙2 and 3↘5 and 4↙3 and 5↘4. As this fails, she goes on to equality of the weights: 4 + 1 on the right (↘) and 5 on the left (↙): "Now they're even in both directions." Despite what she finds, she begins again according to the same principle, then: "You probably have to look at the distances from the ground, I mean the heights," whence diverse attempts lead fortuitously to 4↘5 versus 5↙4, and therefore to equilibrium, which she generalizes to 2↙3 versus 3↘2. But she does not see any multiplicative relationship in this and simply says, "You have to look at the number of the weight and the number of the disk," then places 1↙1 versus 3↘2 and is astonished by her lack of success: "But it worked with 2 and 3."

TER (10 years, 11 months): TER begins with the equality of weights going to either side, that is, in directions ↙ and ↘, and then says: "Perhaps it's because of the difference in the height of the weights." He tries 1↙1 versus 5↘1 and concludes: "The weights are heavier on the bottom than on the top."[5] A counterexample in no way convinces him.

PAT (11 years, 6 months): PAT also begins with equality of weight going to either side, ↙ and ↘, and likewise concludes that "the length of the strings must have some effect . . . on the scale in the store, the lowest weight is always the heaviest." The experimenter shows him 5↙3 = 3↘5: "Ah, yes. The perimeter is bigger here (Disk 5)," but even though in this way verging on the correct correspondence, he simply concludes that "the difference in the weights has to be two," whence 5↙1 versus 3↘3. He finally goes on from there to trials of equal weight.

There are two characteristics common to these reactions. On the one hand, the apparatus is initially assimilated to the idea of a balance scale whose equilibrium only depends on the equality of weight on either side. On the other hand, after findings disconfirm that hypothesis, there is a search for some supplementary correspondence capable of complementing the role

---

rotation equal to the downward rotation, ↙, on the other side. Because this is never repeated and makes no sense, I have made the paragraph conform to the definitions given originally—Translator.

[5]Note that because Disk 5 has a larger diameter than Disk 1, a weight hung on Disk 1 will hang lower than one hung on Disk 5. Because of the moments involved, the system will turn to the right which should indicate that the initially higher weights are heavier. It must therefore be that TER makes his judgment after rotation—Translator.

of the weight. But it is obvious that none of the supplements proposed leads to compositions at the intermorphic level. CLA comes round to supposing that a weight "might be lighter on a bigger disk" but does not proceed to verification of any sort. MAR, who has the merit of immediately considering the disks as well as the weights, simply arranges things so that the "heaviest" weight will be more "at the front." He therefore limits himself to a spatial order without understanding the inverse relationships insuring a constant product. Then he appears to approach the idea of constant products by putting a lighter weight on Disk 2 "and the heavier on the little one," but he immediately distorts this relationship by supposing, as is prevalent at his age, that the weight's action increases when it is "on bottom." BET starts with symmetry and comes round to the same hypothesis concerning the "height"of the weights. However, she cannot exploit her discovery of an equilibrium for 4↙5 versus 5↘4, which she only generalizes to 2↙3 versus 3↘2. In fact, she concludes from this that because "it worked with 2 and 3," it ought to be able to balance 1↙1 as well as 3 and 2. Similarly, PAT, establishing that 5↙3 = 3↘5, deduces that "the difference in the weights has to be two"!

But what is instructive in these reactions is that subjects from 9 to 11 years old, whose level is operatory in problems of conservation, reason here as children 5 to 6 years old reason on simpler problems; that is, they show no capacity for intermorphic or intertransformational compositions. The reason for this is that they constantly postulate that equilibrium is to be achieved by equalizing weights in both directions. Other factors that they invoke by turns, they see as perturbations explaining failure, but they do not integrate them as intrinsic variations of a unified system. In other words, they do not integrate them as variations capable of ensuring compensations, as they do in their model of additive "commutability" for conservations (see chapter 4, p. 57). What is lacking, therefore, is the search for a model that, of course, would presuppose reflective abstraction. Instead, these subjects stick to observables and to empirical abstractions belonging to the intramorphic. The reason for this *décalage* is, evidently, that in this particular case the pertinent variations are multiplicative in nature, not simply additive.

2. LEVEL II: INTERMORPHIC CORRESPONDENCES

At Level II the search for compensations begins and there is discovery of inverse relationships between the weights and the disks:

BEA (11 years, 3 months): BEA immediately notices that "the small disk turns faster. I must put the small weight on the small disk (1↘1 versus

2↗2). No, that doesn't work (1↘1 versus 3↗3). No, that doesn't work either. I'm going to try this (1↗2 versus 2↘1). Ah! Yes, it works that way. Weight 1 is stronger because it is higher (meaning on a bigger disk, 2)."— "Any other way?"—(He puts 1↘5 versus 3↗4, then 1↘5 versus 2↗4, etc.)[6] "Weight 4 has a longer string."—"Can we say that it's stronger?"—"Yes."—"Can you prove it?"—"Yes, if you take two equal weights with a longer string (he immediately does this). No, it doesn't work. I thought that the heaviest had to be on the littlest radius (compensation!)." By applying this rule, he then constructs a certain number of quasi-equilibria, the series ending, finally, with 2↗4 versus 3↘3, then 1↗4 versus 2↘3, then 3↗4 versus 4↘3 in equilibrium. "And with 4 on 5?"—"(He tries 4↗5 versus 5↘4.) There you go!" But he does not generalize this discovery and also tries 1↗4 versus 4↘2 and 1↗4 versus 3↘2, then empirically finds 1↗4 = 2↘2. By contrast, for this simple relationship he succeeds in making a multiplicative statement: "The weight's action on Disk 2 is double, it pulls, perhaps, with twice as much force because the radius is double. Weight 4 on Disk 1 pulls with half its force!" But here again, he does not generalize and goes on to try 2↗1 versus 4↘4, then 2↗4 versus 4↘1, and finally again discovers 2↗2 versus 4↘1 which he had seen before. He then repeats: "On the bigger disk, the littler weight pulls harder."

NAD (12 years, 3 months): NAD begins with 1↗1 versus 3↘5 and says like BEA, "I thought 'Weight 5[7] is heavier,' that's why I put the light weight on the little wheel." She makes different attempts, then reverses the relationship: "Ah! I found it. On the big wheels the weights have more force." She makes four more attempts the last of which is 2↗2 versus 4↘1. "Why is there equilibrium here?"—"Maybe it's by chance."—"But is there an explanation?"—"Perhaps, but first I need to find other cases of equilibrium." She then devotes herself to two interesting behaviors.[8] The first consists in modifying 2↗2 into 1↘3 in order to see, she explicitly states, if a heavier weight on a smaller disk will conserve the equilibrium. Then as this is not at all the case, she modifies the positions of Weights 2 and 1, placing them on Disks 3 and 5 instead of on 2 and 4, thereby conserving the distance between them

---

[6]1↘4 versus 2↗5 has been changed to make BEA's actions conform to his statements—Translator.

[7]Again the notational convention is violated and the French sources are in error. I have changed the notation to make the translation coherent—Translator.

[8]Piaget's objections to behaviorism are well known. He used the word behavior (*comportement*) to refer to that doctrine or to purely observable behavior. In this case, he uses the word conduct (*conduit*) by which he means behavior in the broad sense including consciousness. Because conduct sounds unnatural in English, I use behavior, but in the sense of conduct—Translator.

which she measures by the fact that between 3 and 5 as between 2 and 4 "there is one free disk between the weights, so you have to keep that (meaning the same space)." Thus, one finds in this a search for a class of equivalencies between states linked together by transformations that reduce to simple displacements, as was the case of additive commutability. Later however, NAD comes close to a multiplicative relationship (on an apparatus with identical units[9]). She tries 1↙1 versus 1↘(1 + 1), then 1↙1 versus 2↘1, and finally 1↙(1 + 1) versus 2↘1 (equilibrium). "Ah, you have to put twice the number of one's on the disk that has a smaller radius." But there is no real understanding for all of that. She places 4↙(1 + 1) versus 5↘1: "No. I don't know why it doesn't work."

KAR (13 years, 0 months): KAR places the five weights in the order 5 → 1 on disks 1 → 5 alternating the directions, ↙ and ↘, and explains the absence of equilibrium by the fact that the sum of the weights is not the same in both directions. For 1↙5 and 5↘1, he predicts a rotation in the direction of Weight 5 and finding equilibrium says: "I should have guessed." He then generalizes this result to 1↙5 and 2↙3 versus 4↘2 and 5↘1, saying for 2↙3 and 4↘2: "I put a little heavier weight on a small disk and a little weight on a big disk." There is, therefore, compensation but only with additive quantification.

REG (13 years, 11 months): Discovering 1↙2 = 2↘1 after trials and errors, REG says: "Ah, you have to put more weight in front (small disk) than behind. If you move a weight toward the front, you have to increase it. For each unit of displacement, you have to add a unit of weight." She verifies this but only attains quasi-equilibria. By contrast, for 1↘4 versus 2↙2 she thinks "double it," but cannot get beyond additive compensations for other pairs.

GRA (13 years, 11 months): GRA does not succeed in finding equilibria between pairs for the same reasons.

STE (13 years, 1 month): STE is on the way to multiplication when he tries proportions. He tries 1↙2 versus 2↘4 and then finds 1↙4 = 2↘2 but says, "I don't know why there is equilibrium here . . . it must have to do with the path traveled, but how?"

The following subjects indicate progress in the direction of multiplicative compositions by discovering that moving a large weight generates a greater effect than moving a small one:

ELS (9 years, 10 months): ELS says "it depends on the point where the weight is hung and on the size. A little weight has a littler influence

[9]Several one-unit weights which allow Weights 2 to 5 to be replaced by 2, 3, 4, or 5 units.

than a big weight." She finds 1↙4 = 2↘2 and from this concludes that "both actions are equal because the little weight has more effect if you put it behind (disk 2)." Nevertheless, she explains 4↙5 = 5↘4 by the fact that "the difference between the weights (5 and 4) is the same as between the disks (4 and 5). They're both one." If these weights were to be displaced keeping the same difference, for example, onto Disks 3 and 4, "The difference in the big weight's influence is greater than the little one's. The big one will pull harder."

RAP (11 years, 3 months): RAP thinks equilibrium can be conserved by moving two weights, 4 and 2, from 2↙4 = 4↘2 to 3↙4 versus 5↘2, because if one has 2 + 4 = 4 + 2, one also has 3 + 4 = 5 + 2. Disabused by the findings, she explains that "the heavier weight changes more" in being moved from Disk 2 to Disk 3 than Weight 2 changes in being moved from Disk 4 to Disk 5. We have, therefore, a situation intermediary between the invariant of the sum and the invariant of the product. Similarly, for 1↙4 versus 2↘2 she does not predict equilibrium because Weight 2 on Disk 2 is not far enough from Weight 4 on Disk 1 to compensate it.

THO (12 years, 7 months): THO discovers through trials that "the radius of the disk is more important than the weight." In moving Weights 4 and 2 from Disks 2 and 4 to Disks 3 and 5 respectively, he does not know what to predict. After trying it, he says: "If you lower the weights, 2 becomes stronger and if you raise them, it's 4."—"Okay, why?"—"The relationship isn't the same any more."

HAN (13 years, 9 months): HAN discovers 5↙1 = 1↘5 and believes that equilibrium will be conserved with 1↙5 versus 3↘2, then generalizes to 4↙1 versus 1↘4 which he changes to 2↙2 versus 1↘4 and deduces the following rule: "If you increase the higher weight, you must move the weights that were on Disk 1 to Disk 2 in the same relationship," but he gives as an example 3↙5 versus 4↘4 which remains additive (3 + 5 = 4 + 4). Like the preceding subjects, HAN therefore remains in a position intermediary between additive and multiplicative compositions.

KUR (13 years, 0 months): KUR discovers and generalizes the equilibrium x↙4 = 4↘x, but he only understands it in terms of the addition x + y because, asked to deduce something else from it, he puts 2↙4 versus 5↘1, because 2 + 4 = 5 + 1. By contrast, he spontaneously explores whether 5↙1 versus 1↘5 can be inverted to 1↙5 = 5↘1, then deduces from this that "to compensate having Weight 5 on Disk 2, you have to calculate the sum 5 + 2 = 7 and put 7 on Disk 4." Corrected, he discovers that to equilibrate 2↘1 + 3↘1, "You have to put five 1's on [Disk] 1" and goes on from there to "and if you move 5 to Disk 2, it makes it necessary to put Weight 2 on Disk 5 in order to compensate it." These inferences then lead him to multiplicative composition: "The product between the number of the disk and the weight must be the same on both sides (↙ and ↘), but you can distribute these products as you wish!" Thus, KUR has attained Level III.

Both stages in this intermorphic level bring up a whole set of problems. The first is that of the source of this new attitude of composition among two sorts of relative correspondences, one toward the weights (known already) and the other toward the disks insofar as they modify the weights' actions. Because it is observable, this modification was already evident at the intramorphic level. There, however, it was only conceived as a perturbation opposing the regularity of the supposed law of equilibrium where there is equality between the sum of the weights suspended in one direction, 6, and the sum of those suspended in the other, 5. By contrast, the novelty seen in subjects of this level is that changes in the action of a single weight according to its position are immediately considered to play a positive role. The problem being to find a state of equilibrium, these changes are rapidly assimilated to a possible scheme of compensation. Such a scheme is not given in the observables and can only be verified by them if one seeks to find it there. In other words, it only can be verified empirically on condition of subordinating empirical abstractions to a reflective abstraction that directs them by coordinating transformations in order to deduce conservation from them. Thus it is that BEA and NAD, beginning with a direct relationship between the weights and the disks, give in to verification and reverse the relationship, which leads them to near or complete compensations, but again checked empirically. These new and significant behaviors of verification extend to the supposition of "chance" for a favorable case, as NAD expresses it, which makes it necessary "to find other cases" before deciding.

The reactions of the first group (from BEA to STE), although attaining the general principle of compensation (BEA—"on the bigger disk, the littler weight pulls harder"; or NAD—"on the big wheels the weights have more force," etc.), do not, for all that, succeed in interpreting it in multiplicative terms. The only exception is where (BEA, NAD, REG, etc.) the product $2 \times n$ is identical to and confused with the simple addition $n + n$. Thus, NAD thinks equilibrium can be conserved by moving Weights 2 and 1 from Disks 2 and 4 to Disks 3 and 5 simply by "keeping" their distance. REG makes progress by saying that "if you move a weight toward the front, you have to increase it," but sticks to contending that "for each unit of displacement, you have to add a unit of weight." The implicit model that seems to inspire these subjects therefore would be that of additive commutability, according to which what one takes off at one point is found again at another.

With subjects of the second group, by contrast, one observes a situation intermediate between additive and multiplicative compositions. The displacement of a weight not only requires the addition of units, as with REG, but "the difference in the big weight's influence is greater than little one's" (ELS) or "the heavier weight changes more" (RAP). Some subjects' interpretations thus become qualitatively multiplicative, so to speak, as is the case with THO when he says that "the relationship isn't the same any more," or with HAN's expression "if you increase the higher weight, you must move [the complementary weights] in the same relationship." And qualitative multiplicity is implicit in ELS's statement that "the little weight has more effect if you put it behind." The surprising fact is, however, that despite obvious progress, the calculations remain additive: For ELS if $4\swarrow 5 = 5\searrow 4$, it is because the difference is "both one"; for HAN "the same relationship" gives $3\swarrow 5$ versus $4\searrow 4$ because $3 + 5 = 4 + 4$, and so on. Even KUR, who ends up attaining Level III, begins by saying that "to compensate having Weight 5 on Disk 2, you have to calculate the sum $5 + 2 = 7$ and put 7 on Disk 4!" Moreover, the fact that the discovery of $x\swarrow y$ versus $y\searrow x$ gives place to so few generalizations, except additive, is due to the same reasons; that is, RAP concludes from $2\swarrow 4 = 4\searrow 2$ that $3\swarrow 4 = 5\searrow 2$, because $3 + 4 = 5 + 2$, and so forth.

The problem, then, is to understand the reason for the belated character of multiplication. In order to do this, let us designate by A the beginning weight and by A′ the disk to which it is attached, as well as by ΔA a second weight fixed to a different disk ΔA′, the symbol Δ designating the difference to be found so that ΔA and ΔA′ equilibrate A and A′. One then has the proportion:

$$\frac{\Delta A'}{A'} = \frac{A}{\Delta A} \quad \text{whence the lawfulness of the crossed products} \quad A \times A' = \Delta A' \times \Delta A \qquad (1)$$

We have known for a long time that proportions, as equivalences between two relationships, are acquired only belatedly, as are all relationships between relationships. We also have known that it is the same with multiplication itself as addition of additions ($n \times x = x$ added to itself n times, even though there is already addition of units). That is why the preceding subjects and even KUR at the beginning reason as if $A + A' = \Delta A' + \Delta A$ without proportions or crossed products. However, from the second group on (from ELS to KUR, the children come close to the proportionality of multiplicative composition, and it is a matter of understanding how they do it. Evidently, the first reason is that the addition of a radius and a weight has no meaning because these magnitudes are heterogenous. If, instead of sticking studiously to numbers, the subject centers on what they represent, that is, actions or effects to be composed as such, he will understand that it is a matter of "relationships" (THO, HAN), which sooner or later will lead him to products (KUR) because such relationships implicitly involve an interplay of proportions. In effect, comparing actions can be done additively insofar as they are of the same nature, like two weights, but between the disk and the weight there is an interaction, the action of one modifying that of the other and reciprocally, and it is the understanding of this reciprocity that pushes subjects to speak of "relationships." We are, therefore, far from the additive commutability to which the first group of subjects adheres, and that can be seen even better at Level III.

3. LEVEL III: TRANSMORPHIC CORRESPONDENCES

The preceding makes clear that the solution of the problem of equilibrium by multiplicative composition is situated at a transmorphic level. This is because it is the operatory equality of sums of products in the directions ↙ and ↘ that determines the composition of the morphisms of morphisms, of the equivalence classes capable of complementary substitution and an automorphism ensuring conservaton of equilibrium. Unfortunately, subjects from 12 to 15 years old whom we were able to question with regard to this experiment had received, in general, scholastic instruction on the question of moments of rotation. This decreased the interest of their reactions. By contrast, the two cases that follow did not present this drawback:

MAC (13 years, 5 months): "How can you make it balance?"—"Are the distances between the disks the same?"—"Yes."—(He puts 1↙1 versus 2↘1.) "I put them like that to see where you have to put the heaviest. It's on the smaller disk. I'm going to try it (1↙2 versus 2↘1). Yes, on Disk 2 the radius is doubled and the weight is halved. Let's try again (1↙5 versus 5↘1). It's already the rule we're looking for!"—"Which one?"—"If I put a weight on Disk 1 and another on a disk whose radius is n times that of the first disk, that weight must be divided into n parts and one of them put on radius n to equilibrate [the system]."—"Yes, but what do you say about 2↙4 versus 3↘1 and 4↘1?"—"It will turn in the direction of Weight 4."—"Why?"—"The equivalent of Weight 1 on Radius 4 is equal to 2 on Disk 2. Weight 1 on Disk 3 must be multiplied by 1.5. That makes a sum of 3.5 on one side that one must equilibrate with 4 in the other direction (therefore, 7 pulling ↘ and 8 pulling ↙), which makes 4 a bigger weight."—"Can you tell me what you have to add in this situation (1↙5 and 3↘1) to produce equilibrium?"—"You have to add 1 on Disk 2."

THO (14 years, 5 months): THO begins with 1↘3 versus 3↙1. "What was your idea?"—"There are three distances to go up if you come from the bottom. The mass must therefore be tripled (on Disk 1 in relation to Disk 3). For example, 2↘2 versus 3↙1 must also produce equilibrium (he tries). No, it doesn't work. You have to have 2↙2 versus 4↘1." He next makes a series of inversions: 1↙3 versus 3↘1; an error with 1↘5 versus 4↙2 that he corrects to 1↘8 versus 4↙2; then 1↙9 versus 3↘3. He succeeds in equilibrating 1↘1 and 2↘2 by adding 5↙1,[10] and so on. "Can you formulate a general law?"—"In order to compensate a weight of several units on a disk bigger than Disk 1, you have to add to Disk 1 a supplementary weight equal to the product of that weight and the number of displacements that would be necessary to lower the weight to Disk 1."

One sees that MAC (son of a counseling psychologist, not of a physicist) speaks the language of the operations of products and divisions ("that weight must be divided into n parts" in order to equilibrate a multiplication by n). By contrast, THO uses virtual displacements to describe the details of the actions needed to conserve an initial equilibrium with new values. Instead of proceeding by additive commutability, as did subjects of the preceding level, he bases his reasoning on the product $\Delta A = A + nA'$, where ΔA is the weight to be found and n is the number of displacements (=difference of the radii) between the starting disk A′ and the disk to which the weight is moved. Therefore, one could write:

$$[\alpha(A_1)\ \mu\ \Delta(A'_1) = \beta(\Delta A_1)\ \omega\ \beta(\Delta A'_1)] \Leftrightarrow [\alpha(A_2)\ \mu\ \Delta(A'_2) = (\Delta A_2)\ \omega\ \beta(\Delta A'_2)] \Leftrightarrow \ldots^{11} \quad (2)$$

Where α is the starting position of weight A_1 or of disk A'_1 (with union of the two: μ); β is the position of ΔA_1, the weight displaced or added to $\Delta A_1'$ (by union ω); and Δ is the product nA or the quotient A′/n or the inverse.

One then establishes that, as in the formula in chapter 9 section 5, there are commutability and complementary substitutions, because one can permute the directions ↙ and ↘ in the unions μ and ω and modify the pairs AA′ while conserving the equilibrium. But in contradistinction to additive commutability, where only simple displacements come into play, the A's are not constant because their action varies according to the disks A′ nor are the A″s constant because their dimensions and actions are equally modified, whence the necessity of the products insofar as expression of these interactions $A \times A'$.

It is clear, therefore, that these compositions are situated at a transmor-

[10]There is an error in the French text: "*Il réussit à équilibrer 1↘1 and 2↙2 par une adjonction 5↙1.*" I have changed the second arrow to correct it—Translator.

[11]Piaget's notation is obscure, and there are disparities between the French manuscript and the French edition. Nevertheless, it seems clear that Piaget wishes to convey the equality of products necessary to move from one equilibrium to another—Translator.

phic level insofar as they are subordinated to a general system of calculations and insofar as they give rise to combinations that are at once free in their choice and necessary in their results. It is also clear that these morphisms are the expression of operatory transformations, but they are limited to teasing out the equivalence relationships that result from them. They do not engender their construction or their innovative efficacity. From the transformational point of view, the succession of levels we see here allows us to discern an instructive process: Each successive conquest ends in the construction of a local group (such as $x \cdot y = y \cdot x$), whose subsequent generalization makes it into a quotient of the following broader group. This can be translated into terms of local automorphisms that subsequently are included in more general automorphisms. At the end of this evolution, the system then takes (in agreement with Wittman) the form of a category in the sense of McLane. According to McLane, one distinguishes the vertical arrows C_1 (increase of a weight A by one unit at the same point A′) and horizontal arrows C_2 (displacement of a weight), and where $C = C_1C_2$ constitutes a subset of the transitions I possible in states S, given the I of Level III allowing any equilibrium whatever to be achieved. The I's have their inverses T_1 and they are composed $T_1 \circ T_2 = T\Sigma\{I\}$. All the T's are engenderable starting from the C's. On the other hand, one can attribute to the subject, in his predictions or empirical findings, a distribution of effects into -1 (turn to the left), 0 (equilibrium), and $+1$ (turn to the right). Each transition I in the first system determines an arrow in the second system. This constitutes a second category relative to the results, because the relationships between categories S, C, T, o and -1, 0, $+1$ can be considered as a sort of elementary logical function.

12 Comparison of Two Machines and Their Regulators

Jean Piaget
with
A. Blanchet
and
E. Valladão-Ackermann

This experiment uses two machines of quite different configurations. One consists of a piece of wood with a little man drawn on it that has slots opening into holes at both ends (Fig. 12.1) One starts by sliding the upper rung of a ladder through the slot and into the hole on the bottom, so that the man is sitting on the upper rung. The slots and holes are arranged in such a way that when the man is pushed off balance, he rotates to an upside-down position on the next lower rung. By repeating this procedure, one can produce a succession of rotatory movements around the rungs that bring the man to the bottom of the ladder. The second machine is composed of a toothed wheel whose movement is powered by a rubber band fixed to its axle and regulated by means of a cog-arm (Fig.12.2). The cog-arm's axle is provided with a pendulum. As the cog-arm seesaws, one end catches on a tooth on the wheel and thus blocks its rotation while the other end releases the tooth previously blocked. As is evident, the primary causal mechanism is quite different in the two cases. In the first, the man's weight brings about his descent; in the second, a rubber band makes the wheel turn. By contrast, a regulating apparatus intervenes in both situations with the same effect, that is, to produce constancy of the overall speed, and does so by analogous means, the two ends of the man or of the cog-arm acting turn by turn to produce momentary braking of the moving part on one end just as it is let go on the other.

These machines bring up two major problems in establishing correspondences. The first has to do with determining the kind of morphisms that permit the regulation to be understood. This is particularly difficult because the causality involved is looped rather than linear. The seesawing of the

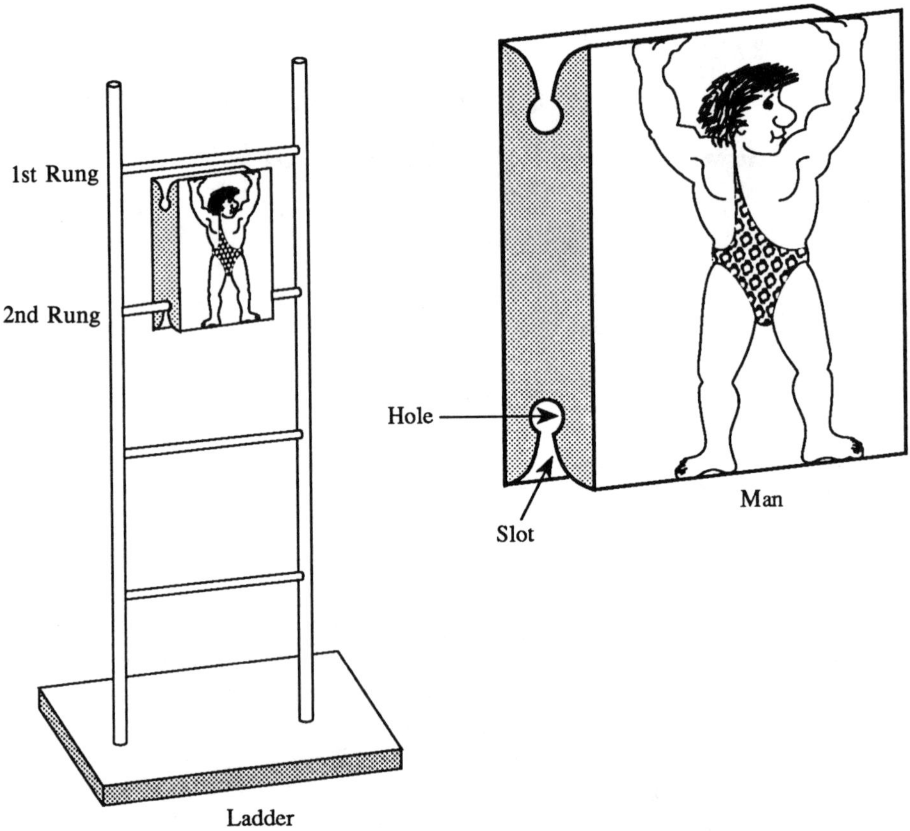

FIG. 12.1. Man on ladder apparatus.

cog-arm and the man's rotation both bring about a succession of brakings and stops T^1, T^2, and soon, alternating with releases $T^{1'}$ $T^{2'}$, during which the mobile advances. In such situations, one has to create a more complex set of correspondences than is required in situations involving simple linear mechanical causality. The second problem has to do with the fact that subjects' reactions again obey the law of succession from intra-, to inter-, and on to transmorphic relationships that we have found in the preceding investigations. When making comparisons between the two apparatuses and their mechanisms, will subjects discover the functional similarity between the two regulators or will they use morphisms like those to explain the machines separately? Will they use correspondences of higher rank for internal analysis of the machines at ages where they still use lower rank intermachine comparisons? Or will they be led by intermachine comparisons of higher rank to improve the internal correspondences that appeared sufficient before intermachine comparisons were made?

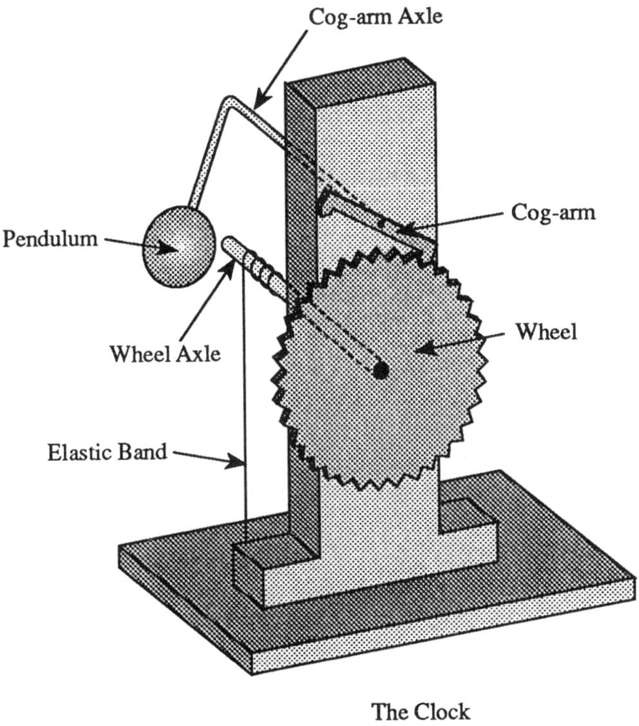

FIG. 12.2. Toothed wheel apparatus.

1. TECHNIQUE

The clinical interviews usually begin with the man on the ladder (I). The child examines the slots and holes and explains how the apparatus works. The central problem is to establish the correspondences that insure transition from one rung to the next. The upper rung can only be let go of at the moment that the other end of the man interlocks with the rung below. Because of the toy's design, this occurs automatically when the slots are oriented in the same direction as the ladder. In order to verify that they child has understood, the experimenter asks whether it would be possible for the man to go home when he is halfway down or whether he would go down the ladder in the same way if the ladder were to be positioned obliquely.

The interview with the toothed wheel (II) raises even more questions. Once it is understood that the wheel turns because of the rubber band, it is a matter of specifying the cog-arm's role in terms of its seesawing and the action of the cogs at either end. When Cog A is inserted between two teeth it momentarily stops the wheel; at the same time, Cog B is off the wheel and has no action on it. But rotatory pressure on the wheel caused by the rubber band makes it push Cog A away. This momentarily frees the wheel but causes Cog B to come down and block the wheel's movement. Then Cog B is pushed away, and the sequence is repeated.

Once these points are examined, the experimenter goes on to comparison of the two machines. This is more complex for the following reasons. In II, the wheel is the principal mobile and is a different object from the cog-arm, its regulator. By contrast, the man is both the principal mobile and its own regulator. As principal mobile, the man moves down the ladder; as regulator, the man's rotation corresponds to the cog-arm's seesawing while the slots and holes at his head and feet catch the rungs in the same way that the cogs on the cog-arm catch the teeth of the wheel. It goes without saying that, in making spontaneous comparisons, the child will assimilate the man sometimes to the wheel and sometimes to the cog-arm and that questions will be needed to specify the model subjacent to the correspondences that he proposes. In particular, it is a matter of establishing the degree to which he dissociates the two aspects of global causality (general movements) and regulation involved in the two apparatuses.

It also proved useful to have children make comparisons with a third quite different mechanism (Fig.12.3). This was a doll whose spread arms successively catch onto zigzagging nails causing an obligatory descent perceptually more similar to the cog-arm's seesawing than to the man's pivoting on the ladder.

2. INITIAL CORRESPONDENCES

Preoperatory subjects 5 to 6 years old elaborate two kinds of correspondences. The first qualify as premorphisms of repetition. They have to do with enchaining actions of the same form that succeed one another. Thus, they describe the global rhythm of events (rotations of the man or of the wheel, etc.). Correspondences of the second kind put particular actions into relationship with their supposed results. Far from being conceived in terms of regulations when that is appropriate, however, these effects are constantly interpreted in terms of their positive actions and, therefore, as favoring the movement:

VAL (5 years, 9 months): For the man: "You have put it in the circle (the hole in the feet), then he goes down, he turns."—"And then?"—"He threads himself onto the other rung, he turns one more time, then he threads himself, he turns again . . . every time he goes into the next." For the wheel: "What's it like?"—"A little clock."—"How does it

FIG. 12.3. Zig-zagging doll apparatus.

work?"—"There's a rubber band . . . and then there's something (cog-arm) that taps on these little things (teeth) and the tapping makes it move."—"Moves what?"—"The circle (wheel) and the little thorns (teeth)."—"And if this piece of wood (cog-arm) weren't there?"—"The wheel would stop turning." Comparing I and II, she does not see any relationship between the cog-arm in II and any part of I. "Why aren't they alike in any way?"—"Because that (cog-arm) must go up higher and turn faster." In that case the cog-arm would be like the man whereas in the state presented, the man would resemble the wheel "because he turns and so does the wheel."

SON (5 years, 6 months): After analogous reactions with the man ("he turns because he's held by that" [rungs] and the wheel, SON compares the man with the cog-arm "because he goes a little fast" and the cog-arm also "goes fast." With the third apparatus: "She holds with her arms and afterward she goes down."—"How does she do it?"—"She bends, she holds on (nail on the left), she falls (to the right), she holds on" (left) and soon—"And does that look like anything here (II)?"—

"Yes, because she (the doll in III) she holds on and she turns, and there (cog-arm in II) it holds on and it's turned."

MAR (6 years, 0 months): "He goes down with his head on bottom and his feet on top, then the feet on bottom and the head on top, then (etc.)."—"And if I give him some force?"—"He's going to fall (this is tried). No, because there are things (rungs) and they hold him." With II: "How does it work?"—"I don't know. (The experimenter puts on the cog-arm.) You might say a clock. It (the cog-arm) makes it work (fact). No, that (the pendulum of the cog-arm)." "There, there's the wood (cog-arm) that makes it turn (wheel) . . . "—"If you take off the wood, the wheel is not going to turn?"—"No."

CEL (6 years, 9 months): Similarly, CEL thinks it is the cog-arm that makes the wheel move "because the wood taps on the teeth." The resemblance between I and II is that the "the man turns and the wheel does too."

JOS (7 years, 6 months): "If you take off the cog-arm?"—"The wheel would stop." Comparison of I and II: "Both make noise."

General rhythms are thus reflected in correspondences of repetition that are also used in intersystem comparisons. Other subjects go quite far in describing details but their descriptions, correct as such, are only drawn from one-way and not two-way causal relationships (advance and braking) in the sense of regulations. The cog-arm does not slow anything down but "makes [the wheel] work" by "tapping" on the teeth. At best, with SON it "holds on" before "it's turned," but as seesawing and not as slowing down the wheel's rotation, which without the cog-arm "would stop turning." With respect to the rungs in I, the two relationships invoked are that the man "holds on" or "holds" or again "it holds" speaking of the rungs themselves, but it is clear that these two sorts of expressions are equivalent and do not convey a braking of the speed but, on the contrary, an auxiliary action of descent. It is also interesting to bring up that these subjects of Level I are the only ones to grant immediately and without hesitation that the same thing would happen if the ladder were oriented obliquely.

It is evident, therefore, that correspondences of this level do not go beyond the intramorphic, because relationships between machines (I-II or II-III) are limited to global characteristics (rotations, speed, noise) with no intuition of braking.

3. INTERMORPHIC CORRESPONDENCES

Progress from this initial level consists in progressively dissociating positive causal actions (general rotations) from regulatory actions affecting speeds (braking), but with multiple difficulties and slowness of coordination. It is appropriate in this regard to distinguish two sublevels II-A and II-B. In II-A, braking is discovered with apparatus II but not yet with apparatus I. This is because all one has to do is simply to read off the observables relative to the cog-arm and the wheel in order to establish the stops for which only one of these objects is responsible. In the case of the man, by contrast, who participates in his own regulation by means of the slots and holes being adjusted to the rungs, braking is only understood at Level II-B. This is because a partly inferential interpretation is needed in order to understand that the interactions of the principal mobile and of the rung are comparable to those of the wheel and the cog-arm. Here are some examples of Level II-A:

FRA (6 years, 2 months): FRA thinks that the man is going to fall the length of the ladder. After a trial: "The rungs hold him on . . . because there are these points (sides of the slot) that hold him on the rungs (which he thought he saw while positioning the man)." In II, the rotation of the wheel is explained by the action of its axle."And why doesn't it go at full speed?"—"Because the wood (cog-arm) holds it."—"How?"—"The little wood catches in the little peaks (teeth), then the wheel turns, then it catches."—"Can you make it go at full speed?"—"Yes, by taking the stick away."—"And without taking it away, can you find a position where it will go fast?"—"No." He finds no resemblance at all between I and II, but after the experimenter has asked, "If you look at how it moves," he makes the rungs correspond to the teeth and the man to the cog-arm, then to the wheel because "they turn," but in no instance does he invoke braking.

PIE (7 years, 11 months): In II, PIE says that the wheel turns "because of the rubber band," the cog-arm "because of the wheel," and the pendulum "because of the cog-arm." With regard to the latter, "There is the piece (Cog A) that brakes on the wheel."—"Is that all?"—"No, also that (Cog B). There is (Cog A) in the teeth, the wheel turns a very little bit and there is the other side (Cog B) in the teeth." In I, by contrast, he limits himself to a description, and when he compares the man to the cog-arm and the rungs to the teeth, he specifies as differences that in II "there is a pendulum and a brake (he indicates the object) and here (I) there isn't any."

HUB (8 years, 5 months): HUB gives the same explanation for II and understands that if one takes the cog-arm off "it's going to turn fast," whereas with the brake "it can never go at full speed because there is always one (end of the cog-arm) that stops it." In I, he expects the man to fall, then he gives a good description of the role of the rungs, but he does not see regulation in this situation. However, he assimilates the man to the cog-arm, but the cog-arm "stops and makes something go, whereas that one (man), he doesn't do anything but turn." On the other hand, he compares the speeds of the wheel and the man, but does not see that their common characteristic is to be globally constant, and that is so even when the man from I is actually laid on the cog-arm in II. Even then HUB does not suggest a functional similarity.

With apparatus II, therefore, subjects distinguish positive causal correspondences (actions of the rubber band, etc.) from braking quite well, but it is not the same with the man on apparatus I. When FRA says that the rungs "hold him on," he simply wishes to explain why he does not fall. PIE even makes explicit that in I "there isn't any [braking]." If the reactions in II announce the beginning of intermorphism, the absence of all reference to regulation in I indicates that that beginning is limited to a reading of observables (and in that sense to an attitude that is still intramorphic) without construction of comparative models.

By contrast, Level II-B subjects present a series of improvements leading stepwise to the idea of a common regulatory mechanism. It is interesting to follow the transition from simple analogies among relevant observables in different situations (I, II, or III) to the construction of a system that has become deductive in diverse degrees:

FER (8 years, 10 months): As do all of the subjects in this section, FER immediately understands the mechanism of the man's descent in I and why he can be neither put on nor taken off halfway down. In II, the wheel turns "because of the rubber band" and "the wood (cog-arm), it brakes," for two complementary reasons: "The wheel hits against that (Cog A of the cog-arm)" like "the piece of wood (Cog A) hits; and after the wheel slips, the piece of wood, it goes up and that (Cog B) comes down." Comparison I-II: "Yes, they're alike. The wood hits the wheel and the man hits the rung." Elsewhere the man corresponds to the cog-arm as well as to the wheel, but on condition of differentiating its global and local actions, that is, rotation versus catching. FER ends up choosing the wheel "because it is the wheel that hits first (and not the cog-arm)."

ANA (9 years, 7 months): At first, ANA does not differentiate the ideas of automatic movement and step by step regularity. In I: "If I put it on the first rung, it turns, then it goes on the other, no, it turns upside down . . . then goes automatically to the next." In II, the cog-arm impedes "turning at full speed. It holds between each little tooth, then it slips, then that comes down again (on the other side) and it starts over." Comparison: "Yes, they're alike because the man, he falls, he falls, and the wheel, it turns, it turns."—"What do they do alike?"—"Each goes once, once, once. They aren't going to jump two little holes, both are regular, one after the other."—"How is that?"—"Well, the wood (cog-arm) which goes in and out, it does the same thing as the man who goes in and out." But with Apparatus III (doll and nails), she generalizes the idea of "holding" expressed with regard to the cog-arm: "In both cases (I and II) there is something that holds, that makes it turn. If the rungs and the nails weren't there, it would go straight."

ANT (9 Years, 8 months): In I: "There are two notches every time (she indicates the holes). If you put him on there (feet), he turns, and then there is another (head) where it goes again . . . " and so on. In II, the wheel makes the cog-arm move: "Because the notches are bigger (than the cog-arm's points), it (wheel) hits that (Cog A) and that makes it rock." Comparison: The man resembles "the wheel because there are holes—there are notches there, and there too"; and the points of the cog-arm correspond to the rungs. Further along, she specifies: "And then that (man) stops at every notch and there too (wheel)." But between the two, the experimenter has shown Apparatus III which ANT compares to II "because the point (of the cog-arm) goes between two notches (teeth) and the doll (III) does almost the same thing. She stops at every notch (nail)."—"And is that (III) like that (I)?"—"No, I don't think so. Ah yes, if that (III) is like that (II), [it's] like that (I), too, because that (II) is like that (I)." Correspondence, therefore, is here imposed by transitivity! "What is like what?"—"The hole stops at each notch and there too." In I, "the man is replaced by what here (II)?"—"By the points (cog-arm) and by the wheel."—"By the cog-arm, the wheel, or both?"—"Both!"

MAT (10 years, 0 months): In II, MAT decomposes the cog-arm's mechanism as follows: "The wheel makes the ends of the wood lift up—when it turns, there are teeth. The end of the wood is held back, and when it lifts . . . there is the other that comes down." This, however, brakes the wheel: "For me, it catches them (teeth)," and in order to increase the speed, it is necessary to put "both arms in the air." In I, the man "is held back by the rungs" then "he turns . . . because he gets pushed back by the rung . . . because it slips. Here there is a circle (hole on the other side) and then that hooks in (onto the following rung)." There is, therefore, with MAT both distinction and interaction between braking and the active dynamism, but his comparisons between I and II remain global and only stress superficial repetitions: "They're a little bit the same because the man, he turns and the wheel does too, and he makes the same noise as the pendulum."

PAU (10 years, 5 months): In I, the man "is always held by the upper rung, automatically," and so on. In II: "The teeth on the wheel make the wood (cog-arm) rock and the wood makes the pendulum rock." The cog-arm "is a little like a system with two teeth (of the wheel) but

> it's the opposite;" that is, "it catches there (A) and then it's going to catch here (B)." For the comparison, he begins with the idea that the mobiles (wheel and man) must have a common speed "because they are regular, both of them." His diverse comparisons with the pendulum start from this false idea, but his conclusion is correct: "For both, it can't go faster because there is something that catches." With respect to Apparatus III: "If the man (I) is like the wheel (II) and this doll (III) is like the wood (cog-arm), they [man and doll] can't be alike." But he proposes to make them work together by coming back to the idea of comparing speeds, and, as the man on I arrives at the bottom of the ladder more quickly, he says: "Maybe if you had more rungs, it would get there at the same time."

Each of these subjects succeeds, therefore, in discerning a braking effect or stop in I that corresponds to the same action exercised by the cog-arm II. FER, it is true, does not use these words but is content to say only that the man "hits" the rung. However, he clarifies that he does so in the same way that the wheel hits the wood of the cog-arm. ANA speaks of "holding" in the sense of making the wheel "turn" instead of "jump two little holes." By contrast, ANT explicitly speaks of "stops" and MAT of "hooking" or "pushing back" in addition to "holding back." And finally, PAU goes so far as to say that "to catch" amounts to decreasing the speed.

At Level II-A (from FRA to HUB), subjects have not discovered the mechanism of braking in I because it is not isolable as the man plays the double role of active mobile by his descent and regulator by his slots and holes. For this reason, their intermachine comparisons only involve global repetitions (turning, etc.) as was the case at Level I, or details of form and action. When the man is put into correspondence with the cog-arm, it is only in virtue of their rocking, and so forth. By contrast, Level II-B subjects do compare the major mechanisms, that is, general movement and braking, that I and II have in common, but they do not yet arrive at the idea of transmorphism that becomes central at Level III. In other words, they do not yet arrive at the idea of different speeds, each of which is rendered fairly constant by regulation. Nevertheless, they are, in different ways, headed in the direction of that interpretation. The principal notion evoked in this regard is that of "regularity," used by ANA and PAU. To ANA regularity means step by step, "each goes once" without jumping any little holes; to PAU it means the same speed for the different mobiles. This regularity as well as the automaticity understood by all of these subjects and expressed by ANA are applied to braking as well as to the primary dynamism. Because, at this level, this regularity and automaticity are distinguished from one another and put into relationship, it is clear that one can qualify the compositions internal to each apparatus as intermorphic. As for the nature of intermachine comparisons, the contrary assertions of ANT and PAU on the subject of transitivity between I, II, and III shows clearly what is still lacking in the construction of a general system. The discovery of constant global speed will, in effect, be a matter of better dissociating the details of the actions of braking and moving forward, which is complicated by the fact that II involves four mobiles (rubber bands, wheel, cog-arm, and pendulum) and I only one mobile with two distinct functions. (ANT partially succeeds in this situation but without conclusions regarding speeds.)

4. INTERMACHINE COMPARISONS OF TRANSMORPHIC LEVEL

These characteristics relative to speeds and to the distinction of two causalities, mechanical and regulatory, appear to us to differentiate a third level where the construction of a general intermachine system is imposed. Here are some examples, beginning with an intermediate case:

PIE (11 years 6 months): "It's a spring system that makes a wheel turn and a pendulum swing. The wheel turns and that pushes (the cog-arm), it raises its tooth (Cog A) and it comes back because of the weight of the pendulum. The tooth pushes on one side and when it no longer pushes there, it pushes on the other side," and so forth. After giving a detailed description of I, PIE concludes: "II is a spring system and I works all alone when you put the man at the top. II is a system of gears and I of rungs. In both there is recovery and in both there is (action) of the weight throughout. In both, instead of falling free, something brakes; in both it turns, and in both you can't stop the wheel or the man."

RIC (12 years 6 months): After making detailed descriptions, RIC distinguishes the causality of motive force from regulation. The first is due in I to heaviness and in II to "a rubber band, like a spring, that makes the wheel move," and the wheel "makes the cog-arm and pendulum move." The second is formulated explicity: "The cog-arm is so there will always be the same speed—so it lasts longer," just as in I, the ladder imposes "always the same speed." With respect to the detail of the compensations, RIC vacillates between the two systems. At first the man corresponds to the wheel and the rungs to the cog-arm; then the man resembles the pendulum and cog-arm. "Which comparison is better?"—"Both, maybe." With respect to III, there is little comparison except that the nails "make the movement quite monotonous, always the same, then . . . that's all!"

PHI (12 years 0 months): PHI also vacillates between both types of comparisons. The two certain correspondences are that, for global movement, "you have to rewind the rubber band and you have to put the man back up" and that for the speeds, "the rung brakes a little and the cog-arm, too," such that each of the mobiles, man and wheel, "always goes at the same speed, because it takes the same time to turn and, moreover, the rungs are spread the same and the teeth are the same size." In other words, both systems "they both have the same rhythm." But with respect to details, one can compare "the man and the cog-arm, a tooth stops each one; the ladder, it was teeth." Or again, "the man with the wheel and the rung with the cog-arm." PHI refuses to consider one of the forms of comparison as better.

JUA (13 years 5 months): JUA immediately focuses on the speeds: "If you say that the man resembles the wheel and the rungs the cog-arm, you see right away that the cog-arm slows it down and the rungs do too." The man, like the wheel, "always [goes] at the same speed." With regard to III, "It's the nails that brake."

ERI (13 years 3 months): After correct descriptions for I and II: "They're the same kind of system. That (man) would sort of replace the wheel and the cog-arm would sort of replace the rungs."—"What functions do they have?"—"To brake, because if there were no notches, it would go at full speed." Further on, he says that their speeds are constant without acceleration because after each stop, the mobile starts off again "with the same weight." But one can also compare the man to the cog-arm: "What comparison do you prefer?"—"For me, both systems are useful; both are comparisons."

VER (14 years 1 month): VER immediately compares the man to the wheel not because they both turn but "because for both there is something which slows it down," whence the conclusion for each that "then it goes at the same speed."

SAL (14 years 1 month): SAL begins with a remarkably correct analysis of the relationships between the teeth of the wheel and those of the cog-arm, which adds to the usual correspondences inherent in the rocking of the cog-arm a series of correspondences concerning the successive and relative positions of the two kinds of teeth. He then draws what follows from this insofar as the constancy of global speed is concerned. For the man, "There is a certain acceleration when he falls, but when he arrives at the next rung, he is braked again, then the speed increases, then it is braked, then it increases. So, that makes the speed constant."—"And for the pendulum?"—"The same. The wheel accelerates each time and is braked. You have to average the little accelerations and the brakings." Whence the global constancy produced by the composition of alternating correspondences. As for comparisons relative to the man, "It's funny. A little bit ago, I was talking (about him) with the wheel and now with the cog-arm (because of the braking of the slots). I think that there (II) there are two moving elements and there (I) only one." He thinks, therefore, that the man fulfills both functions of advancing and braking which are separate in II.

FRA (15 years 4 months): Similar in this regard, FRA makes comparisons between the man and the wheel and declares: "I like both. The pendulum (II) is this movement (in I) but split up. There is a main part (the wheel) and a part that brakes (cog-arm) whereas there (man in I) the part brakes itself."

It is clear that one could group these responses into sub-levels (III-A and III-B) according, for example, to whether subjects simply grant two sorts of possible comparisons between I and II, based on mechanical causality and regulations or whether, like SAL and FRA, they break down the man's double functions. What is more interesting, however, is to establish that these subjects coordinate the two systems, motor and regulatory, and that they discover a general property engendered by their composition, that is, the constancy of the global speeds of the man and the wheel.

In order to understand this composition, essentially transmorphic in nature, it is useful first of all to recall that the regulators at play in these situations have two functions: (1) guidance with respect to the directions to be followed, and (2) braking without forward pulsion with respect to speeds. In effect, when the man effects a rotation after having been stopped or when the wheel starts turning again after a brief stop, the resumption of movement is due to the weight of the first or due to the rubber band in the second. It is due, therefore, to the motoric causality that is freed up by the rung or the cog-arm momentarily ceasing to brake. In such cases, therefore, regulation consists in the alternation of negative actions (brakings) and cessation of these actions (freeing up). This is different from a homeostat or negative feedback loop, the function of which is to maintain variations around a given norm. Such devices brake an action when it goes beyond the norm but, inversely, reinforce it when it falls below the norm. To coordinate the mechanical action of the man or wheel and the regulatory action of the brake is then, as SAL says so well, "to average the little accelerations and the brakings" that succeed one another in a morphism of alternations. The rest of the Level III subjects do not make the transmorphic composition of these two sorts of correspondences (of motor and regulatory character) so explicit, but they all succeed in doing so in fact. After all, they end up coming to the same conclusion of a product presenting the property of uniform global speed in II as well as in I (and in III).

Of course, this transmorphic synthesis (in the sense of construction of a total system with heterogeneous components) is not effected without difficulties. We could cite all sorts of hesitations and even momentary contradictions, but it would make the analysis too long. Our goal being to study the construction of inter- and contransformational morphisms and not the anatomy of individual reactions and levels, it appears more useful to tease out the beautiful succession of intra-, inter-, and transmorphic correspondences described in sections 2 to 4 than to detail trials and errors that vary from one subject to another.

These three levels are clearly distinct with respect to relationships between motoric causality and regulatory braking, but that says little about the respective roles of the correspondences internal to the machines and of the intermachine comparisons in the successive solutions from Level I to Level III. At Level I, we have distinguished correspondences between global repetitions from attempts to establish particular correspondences between a differentiated action and its effect. Under these conditions, it is a matter of course that intermachine correspondences are essentially limited to global repetitions: "It holds on and it turns" (SON), "both make noise" (JOS), and so forth. By contrast, comparisons between particular objects or actions are limited by lack of understanding. The cog-arm is not similar to anything in I, according to VAL. For it to correspond to the man "that (cog-arm) must go up higher and turn faster," and so on. In short, because intramorphic correspondences only have to do with observables,[1] it results that the level of intermachine comparisons is inferior or occasionally of the same rank as internal premorphisms, but they are never of higher rank. It is the same with Level II-A because, in this case, braking is only discovered in II and remains absent and is even explicitly denied in I (PIE and HUB).

At Level II-B, by contrast, intermachine comparisons indicate great progress by the fact that braking is recognized in every situation. Nevertheless, one still finds cases such as MAT where correspondences are teased out better during analyses of individual situations than during final comparisons where they remain clearly inferior. For the most part, however, these subjects attain the same level of analysis in the intra- and intermachine domains, and in some cases analyses even begin to be slightly

[1]There appears to be an error in the text which here reads: "*les correspondances intramorphiques ne portant pas sur les observables* . . ." ("intramorphic correspondences not having to do with observables"). This clearly contradicts the statement on page 174: "*l'absence de toute référence à une régulation en I montre que ce début se limite à une lecture d'observables (et en ce sense à une attitude encore intramorphique)* . . . " ("the absence of all reference to regulation in I indicates that that beginning is limited to a reading of observables [and in that sense to an attitude that is still intramorphic]"). I assume that "*pas*" has been substituted for "*que*" in the first passage and have translated accordingly ("intramorphic correspondences only having to do with observables")—Translator.

superior in the second domain. Consider, for example, ANT, who by explicit appeal to transitivity is led to accept the two systems of comparison, man-to-cog-arm and man-to-wheel, as equally valuable.

At Level III, intermachine comparisons are constantly of a higher level than internal correspondences. This can be seen from the fact that it is intermachine comparisons that lead to the discovery (and in certain subjects like VER, even to the demonstration) of the invariance of global speeds. Construction of transmorphic systems is, of course, already underway when motoric causality and braking are coordinated for the machines individually. What is interesting here, however, is that, on the plane of intermachine comparisons, this construction is duplicated by a construction that one might conceive as the elaboration of "logical functors," because it involves linking two "special categories" (I and II) together into a more general category. The latter is characterized by the common property of compensation between accelerations and brakings that are both small and local. In other words, it is characterized by composition whose product is a globally constant speed.

It should be remarked that the two situations, I and II, already constitute a categorical system. There are two reasons for this. The first is that the subject himself constructs three sorts of morphisms. Some bear on mechanical causality with its tiny accelerations T_1, T_2, and so on. Others bear on the brakings, $T_{1'}$, $T_{2'}$, etcetera, separating them. And the third bear on the alternations $T_1T_{1'}$, $T_2T_{2'}$, and so forth, with composition of the first two (without forgetting the variables belonging to the adjustments of the man and the cog-arm on the rungs or teeth and ensuring these regular alternations). But a second reason is added to the first. This is that every regulatory system is both causal and categorical insofar as both imply intrinsic comparisons effected by the material apparatus in its own mechanism and insofar as each correction (here the brakings) presupposes a putting into relationship between the momentary state of fact and the norm prescribed by the programming (here the constant global speed).[2] To be sure, this program and the comparative operations that its execution bring about are due to the constructor of the machine and not to subjects. But subjects are asked to understand them, which amounts to reconstructing them in thought. This is why explanations of regulatory mechanisms are doubly categorical in nature and why, consequently, understanding them takes more time than understanding linear causal relationships. Moreover, the difficulty increases with intermachine comparisons, because they require teasing out a common program in addition to comparable processes. There

---

[2]See the more extensive analysis of categorical and cybernetic causal models that I have presented in an "*Essai sur la classification des modèles*" (*Comptes-rendus de l'Association française pour l'Avancement des Sciences* [Bruxelles, 1975]).

is, therefore, an increase in the number or “power” of the comparisons needed.

To this is added the question of the relationships between morphisms and transformations. In effect, the correspondences necessary for conceptually modeling a cybernetic system are not just inter- or cotransformational, but are in a certain sense protransformational because they precede transformations. Although correspondences do not generate transformations, properly speaking, they nevertheless and more generally amount to specifying the conditions for the effectuation of the program.

13 Morphisms and Transformations in the Construction of Invariants

by
Gil Henriques

A theory as rich and original as the mathematical theory of categories holds special interest for genetic epistemology and imposes at least two tasks on the epistemologist who considers it. The first task is to trace its genesis in the movements of ideas that initially made it possible and that eventually made it necessary. The second is to evaluate its import on the various kinds of knowledge with which it is connected.

Some mathematical theories reflect the result of recent conceptualization but have to do with general forms of cognitive organization whose instrumental role begins very early in psychogenesis. For this reason, their meaning and scope go beyond the restricted framework of the history of scientific ideas. Such theories interest genetic epistemology in several ways. Questions having to do with explicit conceptualization[1] have not often been posed until recent times and do not concern us here. The decisive point is to understand how such theoretical results grow out of the instrumental structures from which, from the genetic point of view, they necessarily begin.

The mathematical theory of categories constitutes a remarkable example of what is observed on the plane of possibilities in the studies presented in this volume. This fact is reflected in the directive hypotheses of this chapter.

The structuralist movement and the great currents leading up to it assigned "instrumental categories" the central role they continue to play in mathematics. That, however, only recently has become apparent through

[1]At Professor Henriques's suggestion, I have translated "*thématiser*" as "explicit conceptualization" throughout this work—Translator.

developments stemming from the structuralist movement and ending in the conceptualization of categorical instruments.

Quite rightly, the critical analysis of this great reflexive movement in the history of mathematics remains the fundamental anchor point for all epistemological reflection on categories. According to our hypotheses, however, the meaning and scope of categories extend far beyond questions raised by historico-critical analysis. For this reason, I set aside everything having to do with the explicit conceptualization of categories, while at the same time recognizing that such questions are interesting in themselves and merit special study.[2]

Instrumental categories play a very important role in certain processes of explicit conceptualization that, in general, have nothing to do with categories. Such instruments of explicit conceptualization often remain unconceptualized. Categories, however, have their own structure that a particular mathematical theory undertakes to make explicit. I make reference to that theory in studying the structures it lays bare, because such structures are of central importance for my analysis.

I use "precategory" to characterize certain forms of mental organization involving instruments for transferring forms. I assume that such instruments play an important role in psychogenesis. I am particularly interested in the genetic relationships between precategories (and categories) and the construction of invariants, and I introduce several necessary distinctions relative to this question.

The chapter has three parts. The first two have as their goals: (a) to characterize the two large types of invariants in question, that is, "invariants of replacement" and "invariants of transformation," and (b) to indicate the systems of cognitive instruments by which they emerge. The third part of the chapter, expanding the set of problems previously discussed, is devoted to questions of mathematical epistemology. On the whole, I concur with Piaget's general conclusions.

INVARIANTS OF REPLACEMENT AND PRECATEGORIES

Let me begin by stressing two general and closely interconnected functional preliminaries. On the one hand, they concern the subject's actions; on the other, they concern the objects on which such actions bear. From the very beginning, these preliminaries are prerequisite to any possibility of con-

[2]E. Ascher's chapter in this volume, "Theory of Categories and Genetic Epistemology," presents category theory as a "theory of mathematical constructions" and expresses a carefully nuanced opinion concerning the contribution of the "categorical style" relative to other possible styles in which genetic epistemology may be done.

structing invariants and, in fact, belong to the most general conditions of cognitive functioning:

1. Actions that play a role in the subject's cognitive functioning are essentially repeatable. The set of aspects capable of being transferred from one context of action to others constitutes what Piaget called the "scheme" of the action at issue.
2. The objects that the subject integrates into his cognitive functioning play the role of functional nutrient for the corresponding schemes. In consequence, they are essentially replaceable by other objects within limits imposed on accommodation by assimilatory functioning.

According to these beginning postulates, all of the subject's cognitive activities are capable of repetition and transfer accompanied by obligatory accommodation when their initial objects are replaced by others functionally equivalent to them. The resulting functional equivalence classes allow progressive extension which can bring about modifications of the schemes themselves. This is what Piaget calls their "accommodation."

Genetic epistemology recognizes no absolute a prioi outside of the general conditions of cognitive functioning. These constitute what one might call, following Piaget, "the functional a priori of knowledge." Undoubtedly, they include the repeatability of actions and the replaceability of objects just discussed. Invariants properly so-called must be distinguished carefully from this purely functional a priori. They are always the object of a true construction and, by that fact, only constitute a relative a priori for subsequent cognitive functioning.

It nevertheless remains that, from the psychological point of view, the most elementary invariants are closely connected with the functional a priori of knowledge. In order to stress this fact, I call them "invariants of replacement" because they are based on abstracting out meanings that, potentially, are common to several objects. These, of course, are meanings for a subject and vary widely with that subject's level of cognitive development.

According to Piaget, it is assimilation to the subject's schemes that confers meanings on objects. From the beginning, this attribution of meanings implicitly embraces all of the objects found successively to be assimilable to the same schemes. Already, then, the very first meanings are intrinsically relative, because they imply consciousness of objects' assimilability to schemes of action and, consequently, assimilability of objects to one another. This does not, in principle, interfere with schemes remaining sources of meaning of which the subject is ignorant. He uses them but, even so, does not take full consciousness of them, as is later the case with reflexive reworking of previous cognitive labor.

The primary attribution of meanings to objects inherent in assimilation to the subject's schemes makes it possible to establish correspondences in function of coassimilability to the same schemes. This represents considerable progress in the objectification of forms that later become invariants of replacement for the subject. However, such invariants are not yet explicitly abstracted and, for that reason, the forms cannot yet be said to be constituted. When I consider this elementary level of mental elaboration, I speak of "premorphic putting into correspondence," because I see in the instruments of interobjective assimilation thus constituted the genetically necessary preliminaries of forms and morphisms.

If one compares morphisms to the preceding premorphic correspondences, their special property is to identify the form to be transferred in the terms they link together and to recognize that form's meaning for the correspondence to be established. Whereas correspondences established premorphically are only based on a commonality of meanings essentially linked to functioning, morphisms in the broad sense in which I take them here are establishments of correspondence that transfer a form. Thus, through construction, the terms of correspondences become "enformed[3] objects" because their explicit conceptualization is determined by the form that is transferred by the correspondence in question. On the plane of consciously conceptualized thought, forms reflect the primordial functional invariants that served as the foundation for preceding correspondences. Their role is to determine what is inherent in objects. As such, they are transferable from one term of a correspondence to others. In that sense, they are invariants of replacement because, through construction, they are transferable from one object to others. Thanks to forms, the subject establishes that the terms of various morphisms are identical from the point of view of such invariants. Invariants of replacement have no function other than that of making it possible to establish such identities. It goes without saying that it is not a matter of simply recognizing indices.

The transfer of forms is not situated on the same plane as that of actions based directly on the corresponding schemes. It is a consciously conceptualized transfer requiring specific instruments. It is these instruments of transfer that, inspired by mathematical terminology, I call "morphisms." They are strictly solidary with forms from a genetic point of view.

Morphisms serve to isolate forms as objects of transfer, but, reciprocally,

---

[3]Henriques uses *informé, information,* and so on, in the first sense of "inform," that is, "to give form or character to." Because the word *information* more strongly suggests "knowledge acquired in any manner," it seems best to use the obsolete forms "enform," "enformation," and so forth, to make his meaning clear—Translator.

the transfer of forms distinguishes morphisms from other forms of correspondences. There could be no form without morphisms that transfer it, nor reciprocally could there be morphisms without forms they transfer. I symbolize a well-defined form by F. When one wishes to speak of instruments for transferring F, it is sometimes useful to speak of F-morphisms.

Naturally, understanding the genetic circle of forms and morphisms requires going back to the premorphic correspondences leading up to it. All that I have just said presupposes that the abstraction of forms and the decisive cognitive progress resulting from it depend on three fundamental coordinators: repetition, identification, and replacement.[4]

In a very general way, the search for greater cognitive coherence pushes the subject to construct invariants of replacement. Such coherence is considerably reinforced the moment the subject constructs isolated and transferable forms that, on the plane of explicitly conceptualized thought, give evidence of complementary substitution of objects relative to schematically repeatable actions. This was only implicitly prefigured on the plane of premorphic correspondences. Nevertheless, from the moment the subject constructs his first premorphic correspondences, the problem of explicitly conceptualizing the invariants of replacement that later correspond to them is potentially posed.

As was just said, I propose to accept the term "morphism," borrowed from the mathematical theory of categories, in a very broad way, but one that I believe is still faithful to the profound meaning given this term by mathematical analysis. When I discuss "structural morphisms" later, I have the opportunity to add several useful conceptual clarifications. I will postpone discussion of the corresponding terminological choices until then.

Every morphism implies active conceptualization, but it does not follow that the subject is always or even most often conscious of the morphisms he uses. What is explicitly conceptualized is the form that is transferred, not the transfer instrument constituted by the morphism itself, nor does explicit conceptualization of the first bring about explicit conceptualization of the second. Insofar as morphisms remain instrumental—and that is always the case at the beginning—they are not explicitly conceptualized, because taking consciousness of transfer instruments cannot be simply an automatic consequence of the fact that there is transfer.

For the subject using them, the totality of morphisms involved in constructing a form constitutes the beginnings of a system. I call such initially rough systems of morphisms "precategories." Their cohesion is

---

[4]Concerning the notion of coordinators and their functional role in the genesis of knowledge, see Jean Piaget, "Introduction," *Recherches sur les Correspondences, Études d'Épistémologie Génétique,* Volume XXXVII, Paris: Presses Universitaires de France, 1980.

based on the identity of the form transferred, which for them constitutes a sort of ideal principle. It depends on certain elementary possibilities of composition that are the most important characteristics of precategories from the structural as well as from the genetic point of view.

The rudimentary organization of morphisms into precategories is not entirely devoid of developmental possibilities, but these by nature remain very limited. A first variety only manifests such an organization's lack of closure and, in fact, betrays the fundamental imperfection of precategories. In effect, because of the unfinished character of the processes that generate them, precategories remain open to the addition of new morphisms insofar as they all have to do with the same invariant of replacement. From the moment that this invariant is acquired by the subject, the morphisms that will eventually come to be incorporated into the precategory only play a secondary role with respect to the morphisms initially employed in explicitly conceptualizing the invariant.

The organization of precategories depends on increasing possibilities for composing morphisms in an elementary way much more than it depends on increasing the number of morphisms. Mediate transfers of the form in question come to be added to immediate transfers by the primary morphisms. Obviously, for development of this sort to occur certain conditions are necessary.

In the first place, it is necessary that a suitably enformed intermediary object be accessible to the subject and that the subject have morphisms at his disposal that have that object as source goal or object. In addition, there must be reasons that the subject feels compelled to compose such morphisms. On this point, experimental information is indispensable. Thanks to the studies systematically undertaken here, information on the evolution of systems of morphisms is available. For further details, the reader may consult the different chapters of this volume serving as the basis for Piaget's synthetic exposition in the chapter, "General Conclusions."

The weak organization of precategories remains remarkably homogeneous over the immense expanse they cover. This is astonishing if we consider the differences in the terms put into correspondence, on the one hand, and in the forms transferred by morphisms, on the other. Doubtless, there is an intrinsic reason for this which has to do with the laws governing the composition of morphisms into precategories of any sort.

Solely with respect to these laws, all precategories resemble one another. They involve an associativity that is progressively constructed and subject to conditions of contiguity which restrain the possibilities of composition. Let it be said in passing that due to this fact, one can construct the form expressed by the invariant organization of all precategories, that is, the form of precategories in general, which is an invariant of replacement having to do with the class of precategories.

INVARIANTS OF TRANSFORMATION AND STRUCTURES

Transferring forms involves finding in new objects what has already been found in previously considered objects. Of course this is true only on condition of an active construction of that something that lets itself be transferred as an invariant of replacement. By contrast, another large type of mental activities aims at modifying objects and, therefore, plays a crucial role in the psychogenesis of knowledge.

All of the subject's effective actions subordinate objects to internal or external modifications by way of physical causality. In principle, however, this requires no underlying intentionality. It is the presence of this sort of intentionality that characterizes, among all of the subject's activities, those that I call properly transformational. In several respects, transformational activities are complementary to morphisms. I analyze this complementarity from the point of view of the construction of invariants.[5]

Whereas morphisms are, by definition, instruments for transferring invariant forms, transformations modify objects, imposing changes of form on them that are desired by the subject. In other words, transformations change the enformation encountered at the start, replacing it with another enformation actively imposed by the subject. Obviously, the subject's active intervention is more restricted in the case of morphisms and other activities establishing correspondences. In those activities, it does not go beyond abstracting and transferring forms, because the enformations of the objects put into correspondence must be kept invariant.

It should be noted that I use the word "enformation" in two related technical senses, neither of which has any but a distant relationship to the current meaning of the word *information*. Here I take "form" in the technical sense already indicated. In the first instance, then, "enformation" designates the active imposition of a form on an object by the knowing subject. In a derived sense, the same word designates the epistemic state or situation that results from this active imposition; that is, it designates the fact that some knowledge content is subsumed under a well-defined form. These two meanings come successively into play when one says that transformations modify the enformations of the objects on which they bear ("enformation" in the second sense) or, making the source of such modifications explicit, that transformations of objects arise from new enformations imposed by the subject ("enformation" in the first sense).

That being agreed, I can schematically express the duality and comple-

---

[5]Concerning the general relationships between morphisms and transformations, compare Piaget's "General Conclusions" in the volume *Recherches sur les Correspondences* already cited [Footnote 4]. Here, we limit ourselves to aspects related to our theme.

mentarity of morphisms and transformations by the following diagrams where F and F′ designate forms and X and X′ designate enformed contents:

The diagram on the left symbolizes the transfer of an invariant form by a morphism. F designates the form; X and X′ designate the contents between which the transfer takes place. The source term, X, is put into correspondence with the goal term, X′, and the enformations in terms of a common form are delineated explicitly. The lines descending form F to X and X′ symbolize these enformations. The horizontal arrow between these lines symbolizes the morphism having to do with the enformed objects and the enformations themselves and not just with contents and their common form.

The diagram on the right symbolizes the change in enformation during a transformation. X designates the object that is subjected to and conserved under the transformation; F and F′ designate the forms that enform X in its initial and final states respectively. The transformation makes X pass from the initial state characterized by F to the final state characterized by F′. The lines descending from F and F′ to X in this case symbolize successive enformations of a single object, and the horizontal arrow symbolizes the transformation that effects transition from one to the other.

What pushes the subject to engage in transformatory activities is, at the beginning, only a simple extension of his tendency to satisfy functionally his ability to act. It leads to his subordinating the objects on which he acts to his intentions. On first view, this might make one believe that transformatory activities move away from all immediate concern for cognitive coherence and that their genetic relationship with the construction of invariants is weak or nonexistent.

This is decisively not the case. It is precisely through structuring transformatory activities that knowledge goes beyond the elementary level of invariants of replacement. Through an interplay of compensations, it sets about constructing what I call "invariants of transformation," in order to distinguish them from the preceding. Like all invariants, they are the product of active coordinations of the subject who constructs them, although the level of these coordinations is not the same for the different types of invariants. Still, it is coordinations that in every case guarantee the coherence of cognitive functioning, and that coherence would be especially threatened by transformatory activities that were poorly coordinated with one another.

Piaget has long pointed out that preoperatory subjects grant privileged status to the final states of transformations in an unduly systematic way. This abusive frequency of centration on final states occurs for two mutually reinforcing psychological reasons. The first is obvious; that is, only final states are present once the transformation is accomplished because the initial states are changed. The second reason is more subtle but no less important. It is that final states only result from an enformation actively imposed by the subject in function of his goal. By contrast, initial states generally are imposed from the outside, even if the subject often has the liberty to choose those agreeable to him.

Access to the invariants of transformation requires going beyond these habitual centrations to more evolved levels. This is because such centrations unduly privilege states that nothing distinguishes by right from other possible states of the objects transformed. Their privilege is of an exclusively factual nature. Nonetheless it is highly effective, indicating the difficulty of the obstacles that the child must overcome on his way to constructing invariants of transformation.

In fact, he must retreat from exclusively considering current states of objects to considering their possible states. This implies a transition, to which I will return, from actual transformations to virtual ones. From the moment the subject is capable of a reflexive return to initial states that, precisely because transformatory activity is involved, no longer have real existence for him, progress of a decisive sort becomes possible. The distinction of initial and final states is itself dialectized and ceases to be absolute. The initial state of a transformation can, at the same time, be the final state of another possible transformation and vice versa. Only by taking all of these possibilities into consideration can one achieve the decentration necessary to construct invariants in a transformational context.

In sum, subjects must replace the consideration of states as absolutes by their consideration as terms in a process of transforming objects. This process can in principle proceed in both directions, at least mentally. To succeed in doing this, the subject must move from considering states to considering the transformations that connect them instrumentally. This is very important because of the new possibilities of coordination it opens up. In opposition to states, transformations can be composed among themselves, thus giving birth to systems.

An important difference between invariants of replacement and invariants of transformation resides in the fact that with invariants of replacement each morphism, taken individually, transfers form. With invariants of transformation, on the other hand, no transformation taken individually is sufficient; only an interplay of complex compensations, at first partial then complete, gives access to the invariant. Invariants of transformation are constituted only where systems of transformations are involved. This marks an important difference of level in relation to invariants of replacement.

It is instructive to compare systems of transformations with precategories. The construction of these two systems brings up different problems, and the nature of their relationship to the corresponding invariants is not the same. In this respect, it is important to discuss the relationship between the actual and the virtual, which forces one to consider very significant difference between precategories and systems of transformations.

To begin with, systems of morphisms are, so to speak, situated beyond the distinction between the actual and the virtual. This is because, even though establishing correspondence like all other activities is temporal, it nevertheless ends in systems of atemporal relationships that can be considered simultaneously. By contrast, systems of transformations are not simply objects that the subject can consider, but are instruments that he uses to modify objects according to goals he sets for himself.

It is clear that the transformations of a system as well as the compositions linking them to one another can never all be actualized simultaneously. In general, there are some whose simultaneous actualization would be completely incompatible. Only the transition to virtual transformations and compositions allows systems of transformations to achieve the status of simultaneous totalities in every case. To do this, the subject abstracts out the effective enchaining of activities and their temporal succession, only retaining atemporal compositions of virtual transformations. This results in those perfect compensations on which the construction of invariants of transformation depends.

Identical transformations, directly linked to the construction of these invariants, lead systems of transformations to completion. I reserve the name "structures" for relatively completed systems of transformations that imply the presence of identical transformations. I call "prestructures" the less complete systems of transformations that constitute their psychogenetic antecedents.

Here I take structures in the sense in which they are taken in the operatory theory of Piaget, that is, as cognitive instruments based on coordinations of transformational schemes. They must not be confused with the structures at issue in certain advanced developments in formal mathematics. Mathematical structures have their origin in the processes of reflective abstraction bearing on operatory structures. They are, therefore, initially embedded in and must be teased out from operatory structures. As objects of pure mathematical theories, however, they belong to a totally different context and arise from specialized processes of construction.

Although the meaning and role of identical transformations are clear from the mathematician's point of view, such transformations pose a major problem for the psychology of knowledge. It goes without saying that an identical transformation cannot be confused with the absence of transformatory activity and nothing justifies the abuse of language committed when such absence of activity is called a transformation. Identical transformations, which in no way modify the objects on which they bear, can only have a very special epistemological status. Their sole justification—and it is a strong one—resides in completing the transformatory systems into which they are incorporated.

In the final analysis, the psychogenetic problem of the meaning of identical transformations reduces to a problem of completion. As such, it concerns what I have elsewhere[6] called an "operatory generalization." Identical transformations are always the result of syntheses that start from other transformations of the system and their inverses. In effect, so long as these direct and inverse transformations are not composed in the form of identical transformations, operatory interplay remains unduly restrained.

Thus the construction of identical transformations is the most exhaustive expression of operatory reversibility. In order to achieve it, the subject must be capable of going from temporal reversal[7] of transformatory activity to the atemporal relationships linking direct and inverse operations to one another. The key to understanding inversion as such lies in the fundamental reciprocity of these relationships. Like the distinction of the initial and final states of transformations, the distinction of direct and inverse transformations is also dialectized. In other words, every transformation ends up being the inverse of some other transformation that is equally necessary for the completion of the system, and the latter transformation is itself and for the same reason the inverse of the preceding transformation.

The subject does not construct invariants of transformation by stopping his transformatory activity to reflect dispassionately on the permanent identity of the object. If that were the case, invariants would always have the character of statically transferable forms. Invariants of transformation manifest the conceptual enrichment of objects in terms of the identical transformations bearing on them. What the subject identifies as an invariant of transformation is only the result of this conceptual enrichment.

The understanding of the genetic circle of invariants of transformation and of transformations themselves requires going back to the construction

[6]Gil Henriques, "Généralisation opératoire et généralisation formelle en mathématique," in Jean Piaget, *Recherches sur la Généralisation, Études d'Épistémologie Génétique,* Volume XXXVI Paris: Presses Universitaries de France, 1978.

[7]*Renversement,* here translated as reversal, refers to Piaget's distinction between *renversabilité,* elsewhere translated as "empirical reversibility," and the *réversiblité* associated with equilibrated systems. (See Jean Piaget, *The Equilibration of Cognitive Structures,* Chicago: University of Chicago Press, 1985, p. 95.)—Translator.

of identical transformations starting from prestructures. This is especially true in the case of the classical conservations studied by Piaget and his collaborators. Operatory reversibility rests on this same circle, and one would seek in vain to discover the principle of its psychogenesis elsewhere.

In sum, we see that, despite the essential diversity of the two types of invariants that I have distinguished, fundamental similarities subsist that permit one to speak of invariants in both cases. At root, they depend on fundamental coordinators to which I have already referred, because it is always a matter of identifying what remains unchanged throughout replacements or transformations of objects.

GENERAL STRUCTURES AND CATEGOREIS

Up to now our analysis has concerned genetic relationships between two general types of invariants, that is, invariants of replacement and invariants of transformation, and the systems of morphisms and transformations that I have called precategories and structures. Both types of system allow a relatively autonomous internal development in which the invariants associated with them are involved.

These parallel developments are based on generalizations that occasion, among other things, a transition to activities of a higher level, notably to correspondences among correspondences, to operations on operations, and so forth. The superimposition of cognitive activities of different orders leads to series of invariants that are themselves superimposed. This is what one expresses metaphorically when one speaks of higher and higher forms or of deeper and deeper invariants of transformation.

The autonomy of each of these two series of invariants and systems of cognitive instruments is, however, very relative because of multiple interferences found at every level. They cannot function at all without local subordinations which may go in either direction. Broadly speaking, one finds these interferences, at first occasional, then systematic, remarkably intensified as cognitive development progresses. In the simplest cases, it is a matter of constructing morphisms between transformations or of constructing transformations bearing on morphisms.

The coordination of the two general types of invariants attains its highest state in mathematics. Beyond the separate development of structures and precategories on their own planes, perfectly systematic coordinations between the two come into play. All of this must be analyzed more closely and the history of mathematics put in relation to certain psychogenetic facts concerning the subject's activities.

I focus on the transitions from structures to general structures and from precategories to categories. In the first case, it is a matter of constructing invariants of replacement bearing on structures. This is especially worthy of attention, because, due to their psychogenetic origin, structures are cognitive instruments used in constructing invariants of transformation. In the second case, it is a matter of constructing invariants of transformation within categories. Such construction extends precategories and orients their development in a new direction. This is equally remarkable because, due to their psychogenetic origin, precategories are cognitive instruments used in constructing invariants of replacement. I end with some considerations related to the explicit conceptualization of categories.

Forms of Structure

The mathematical theory of structures represents the natural endpoint of a long process of reflection on the systems of transformations used in classical mathematics. In that domain, structures are seen as constituted totalities, which allows them to be compared to one another without explicit reference to the constructive processes on which they depend genetically.

Such, let me underline, is the origin of general structures that are structural forms rather than structures properly so-called. Among many concepts of this type constantly employed by mathematicians at the present time, let me mention as particularly noteworthy those of the group, the lattice, and vectorial space. There is a difference of logical type between a general structure and the special structures that can be subsumed in it. That difference prevents the automatic self-application of structural forms. A certain kind of general structure is not to be conceived as just another structure of the kind in question.

Within the analytic framework developed here, I interpret the genesis of general structures in terms of certain processes for constructing invariants of replacement of a particularly abstract type. The activities of comparison and reflection implied by these processes bear on completely elaborated structures. The latter have at their core all of the operatory instruments necessary for the construction of corresponding invariants of transformation. When one constructs the corresponding general structure, however, one only retains certain general aspects of the internal structure of systems of transformations. These aspects underlie the partial identity of meaning of the structures from which they are abstracted.

Thus, such activities of comparison and reflection make fundamental aspects common to different systems of transformations evident and, by that fact, enter into the general framework of the processes by which forms are constructed. That is why I have stressed that, in reality, general structures are structural forms. Like all invariants of replacement, structural forms require their own instruments of transfer. I call these "structural morphisms" in order to distinguish them from all the other morphisms.

The genetic circle of forms and morphisms finds paradigmatic realization in the mutual dependence of general structures and structural morphisms. Its understanding requires going back to the premorphic correspondences leading up to a structural morphisms. It is at the level of such correspondences that the transition from structures to general structures begins. This transition depends, therefore, on processes that are essentially different from those governing the internal development of structures.

The mathematical theory of structures is where, historically, one finds the concept of "morphism," which in its original context had the restricted meaning that I give to structural morphisms here. The history of mathematics clearly indicates that structural morphisms were explicitly conceptualized only a long time after they began to be used instrumentally. In a way analogous to all other morphisms, they imply no conceptualization other than that of the form that they transfer, which in the event is a general structure. Explicit conceptualization of the instruments of transfer does not follow necessarily.

Subsequently, the concept of morphism, issued as just said from the mathematical theory of general structures, has been powerfully generalized in the mathematical theory of categories. That theory, like the preceding, is the product of a theoretical progression requiring a higher degree of explicit conceptualization. The result of this new explicit conceptualization is, however, much more general and differs from the preceding on two fundamental points.

What one calls "morphisms" in the theory of categories are no longer exclusively structural morphisms, whatever type of structures may be at issue. Rather, they are abstract entities subjected to rules that generalize the laws of their composition. The abstract morphism at which one thus arrives, in contradistinction to the morphism of structure, is nothing but an undefinable implicitly determined by the axioms that introduce it.

One cannot exaggerate the importance of the fact that we currently have available two mathematical concepts of morphism that are equally well defined from the point of view of their mathematical rigor. Their profound relationship as well as their radical distinctness cannot escape the attentive epistemologist. Both are mathematically important and rich in ever changing applications. The second general concept generalizes the first without, for all of that, rejecting it.

For my part, I have sought to generalize the notion of morphism by starting, as was natural for historical reasons, from the concept of morphism of structure but have taken my inspiration from that mathematically undefinable something that is the object of the theory of categories. My object has been to create instruments of analysis that permit me to attain and to characterize certain cognitive instruments at play from the most elementary levels of psychogenesis onward. The functional role as well as the general organizational form of such instruments prepare the way for structural morphisms.

On a number of essential points, therefore, this investigation receives decisive inspiration from a highly abstract mathematical theory. The fact that this is possible provides a new example of the remarkable convergence, often brought out by Piaget, between the genetically elementary and certain higher forms of explicit conceptualization that one encounters in advanced scientific theories.

The degree of abstraction to which scientific theories are elevated does away with many of the limitations inherent in elementary forms of knowledge, but does not radically alter their fundamental meaning. This means that if appropriate precautions are taken, the epistemologist can greatly profit from the explicit conceptualization provided by scientific thought as it clarifies important meanings that are only implicit at elementary levels of cognitive development.

If structural morphisms are thus only one particular kind of morphism, they nevertheless present remarkable characteristics distinguishing them from other morphisms, and that is true even when the historical priority of their explicit conceptualization is forgotten. Bearing on structures and for that reason maintaining close ties with transformations, structural morphisms tend naturally to initiate more or less intimate syntheses with them.

Taking into account the varied examples offered by mathematics, it is necessary to distinguish two broad types of situations in this respect. In the first, the morphism rests on and follows transformations. In that case, I speak of "cotransformational morphisms." These are based on a comparison between initial and final states for the transformation at issue and express the result of that comparison by putting initial and final states into correspondence.

In the second type of situation, morphisms provide a plan for possible transformations before they actually are carried out. In that case, I speak of "protransformational morphisms." These offer the remarkable possibility of generating the goal-object starting with the source-object from the transformation associated with them. However, they do this only on the condition that the plan determines the transformation anticipated in an adequate way. Moreover, protransformational morphisms can be used as substitutes for transformations. In that case, the subject contents himself with envisioning the plan without worrying about realizing it effectively. From the etymological point of view, this corresponds to one of the classical meanings of the prefix *pro*.

In every case, structural morphisms are closely associated with interstructural transformations. This often gives rise to transformations bearing on structures in addition to structural morphisms properly so-called. This is so whether structural morphisms are based on and follow transformations or whether they provide a preliminary plan for them. In certain extreme cases in mathematics, the synthesis of morphisms and of transformations is so intimate that one can speak of a veritable fusion. In such instances, only different aspects of a single synthetic activity are distinguished, and one might say that morphisms and transformations constitute virtual components of that activity.

Categorical Structures

However much the two processes may differ otherwise, the transition from precategories to categories is analogous to the transition from structures to general structures on at least on one point. Both involve a relative rupture of continuity with new mechanisms coming into play that differ in essential ways from those that presided over the internal development of precategories and structures. Because, however, these new mechanisms are syntheses of instruments already at work, the new developments are only possible because of the preceding ones. In fact, what is found to be broken is the pseudoclosure of two developments that initially were separate.

Essentially, categories are sets of morphisms organized into operatory systems. In addition to morphisms themselves with their rudimentary organization into precategories, they include instruments fostering their operatory composition. These instruments can only be transformations operating on morphisms.

For systems of morphisms indirectly structured in this way to assume the status of categories, it is necessary that the transformations organizing them in turn be organized into structures. By contrast, morphisms cannot alone and independently of the transformations bearing on them usher in structures in the sense reserved for that term here, that is, in Piaget's sense of well-equilibrated systems of transformations. By definition, morphisms are instruments for transferring forms having no transformatory power with respect to the terms they link together.

Every category contains morphisms that have been constructed or reconstructed starting from others alongside morphisms directly based on the comparison of terms. These constructed or reconstructed morphisms depend genetically on operations of composition which themselves are not morphisms but transformations bearing on morphisms and that generate new morphisms.

By that fact, the status of morphisms in a category implies an essential duality with a distinction of level. This is the principal source of the great complexity of categories in relation to elementary precategories. On the one hand, morphisms are activities of arrowed character bearing on terms that they do not transform; on the other, they are terms of actions with arrowed character of another order that transform them.[8]

This duality and solidarity of morphisms and transformations have general import, but they are particularly striking in the domain of categories. There, without ever being confused with one another, these two activities require each another on pain of limitation in each domain. This accounts for the profound psychological differences between behaviors based on precategories where morphisms are relatively poorly coordinated among themselves and behaviors where categories come into play.

From a psychogenetic point of view, the principal problem raised by such considerations is to know how the subject brings himself to operate on morphisms and to construct new ones that are not based on immediate or mediate comparisons of terms. The history of mathematics suggests a general hypothesis in this respect. Specifically, I suggest that the subject operates on morphisms by transferring operations initially constructed with respect to their terms to the morphisms themselves. This hypothesis is plausible in light of some beginning of experimental verification.

One reservation must be made however. For purposes of simplification, I have spoken as if it were sufficient to consider the simple transfer of previously constructed operations in order to account for the situations at issue. That, of course, is not the case. A transfer of unchanged schemes, such as occurs when invariants of replacement are constructed, could not explain the complexity of the operatory relationships in play. My hypothesis must be understood in the sense of a generalizing transfer of operatory schemes that enlarges their domain of application while at the same time profoundly changing their functional conditions. This considerably reinforces the intrinsic meaning of the schemes in question. The history of mathematics presents many examples that can easily be interpretated in terms of generalizing transfers of this sort.

The first example that I cite springs to mind because of its historical priority as well as its intrinsic importance. From the present point of view, functions are cotransformational correspondences linking sets of numbers. The example has to do with the construction of operations on numerical functions. Notably, several operations initially defined on numbers themselves were transferred onto functions. This led to an arithmetic of numerical functions which later was completed by specifically functional operations. In contrast to the original operations on numbers, these functional operations were from the beginning only defined over functions.

This apparently modest starting point was rich in possibilities which were subsequently explored. From a modern point of view, the elementary operations that have for a very long time been transferred onto numerical functions arise from very different structures. Their systematic exploration

[8]Piaget's "General Conclusions" are particularly illuminating on this point.

was pursued up to the creation of modern functional analysis. In turn, modern functional analysis opened onto general analysis with its immense richness of algebraical-topological structures and so many others. All of this provides a beautiful example of the dynamism of mathematical construction which is never limited to just transferring available operatory schemes to new domains by generalizing them. It constantly constructs new schemes through creative syntheses that often consist in completing generalizations.

Let me move on to a somewhat more specialized example, but a very simple and beautiful one, of the generalizing transfer of operatory schemes to morphisms starting with the terms they link together. A case in point is the construction of the ring of endomorphisms End (Z) of the additive group Z of whole numbers. End (Z), with the structure of the additive group subjacent to its ring structure, has the remarkable and very exceptional property of being isomorphic with Z. That permits the object Z to be recovered from the category of additive groups, at least up to isomorphism, as an operatory subsystem of the system of all the morphisms of this Abelian category. On this new and higher plane, however, it has the ring structure that is stronger than its initial structure of additive group. As is well known, this implies that the initial structure of Z allows reinforcement into a ring structure. This example is a special case of the example of numerical functions mentioned previously. In all probability, it has genetic meaning.

Currently, the categories one uses in mathematics bring into play monoids, groups, rings, vectorial spaces of morphisms, lattices of morphisms, and sets of morphisms furnished with topological structures, to cite only a few examples of well-known mathematical structures. Certain whole categories thus become the bases of structures that, for obvious reasons, I call "categorical structures." They include all of the structures just mentioned but go beyond them in generality.

The multiform richness of categories is as striking as the uniform poverty of precategories. In effect, there is not just one kind of categorical structure that is mathematically interesting. If such were the case, that unique kind of structure would define a universal form of category exhausting all potentialities of categorical construction.

Recent developments in mathematics show a situation diametrically opposed to this. Such developments are marked by a veritable explosion of categorical structures, each conserving its own interest but always open to new possibilities of construction. Taken as a whole, the different categorical structures present relationships of genetic filiation similar to those found in other domains where there is construction of structures. The immense potentialities of this construction hold great interest for the mathematician who works to realize those he considers significant. The epistemologist, by contrast, seeks to sketch out the broad developmental lines of these mathematical constructions after the fact.

From the moment that the subject proceeds to operate on morphisms in order to construct categorical structures, he is on the way to constructing invariants of transformation within categories. This is especially true of structural morphisms, systems of which almost never remain at the level of precategories but tend toward the degree of elaboration belonging to categories. Naturally, any characterization of these goes back to categorical structures.

The invariants of transformation in categories depend genetically on identical transformations that are based on the endomorphisms of the category. The invariants of transformation linked to the category's objects stand in close relationship to these special morphisms. The characteristic property of the endormorphisms is, in this respect, that composing them either to the right or to the left does not change the source and goal objects of the morphisms with which they are composed.

Under their usual definition, categories always include endomorphisms and even automorphisms, at least only identical automorphisms. By contrast, precategories are always devoid of endomorphisms and, in consequence, also devoid of invariants of transformation. The reason for this is that, initially, the transfer of a form cannot be realized or conceived except between distinct objects. Later, by composing morphisms with distinct terms with one another, the subject constructs other morphisms with identical terms, that is, endomorphisms. Because of their origin, these always go beyond simple instruments for transferring forms.

The epistemological status of systems of morphisms serving to support categorical structures changes fundamentally the moment the subject begins to construct such structures. The objects of the category can only lose their relative importance. This is because the transformational organization in which the subject engages bears henceforth on morphisms.

The tendency of the mathematician subject who undertakes theoretical developments involving explicitly conceptualized categories will, of course, be to try to recover as many as possible of the properties characterizing the form of structure of the objects from within categorical structures themselves. From there, it is tempting to go one step further and, reciprocally, only to retain those aspects of object's structure that allow them to be characterized in terms of categorical structure.

There is, however, a surprising fact which for nonconstructivist epistemologists comes within a hair's breath of paradox. Supposedly, form is the most initmate property inherent in objects, even their essential meaning. Yet it is precisely form that lets itself be transferred from one object to others not identical to it, thus allowing for realizations that go beyond the object enformed. In precategories objects are already only supports for a transferable form connected by morphisms, and in categories even more profound abstraction is undertaken. Of the forms of objects, only that which can be characterized in terms of the structure of instruments of transfer is retained. Because of its origin, this reflects the object's forms; at the same time, it generalizes them.

THE EXPLICIT CONCEPTUALIZATION OF CATEGORIES

In the preceding sections, I have let myself be guided by the mathematical theory of categories but have tried not to limit myself to categories constituted as mental objects through explicit conceptualization and theoretical analysis. Just as constituting structures precede the constituted and explicitly conceptualized structures of mathematics, it is plausible that, starting at a certain level, constituting categories come into play in an instrumental way in cognitive functioning. They, therefore, constitute the indispensable starting point for the eventual explicit conceptualization that makes possible their becoming objects of mathematical theorizing.

In the historical elaboration of the mathematical theory of structures, categories have served as instruments in the explicit conceptualization of structural forms. Without doubt this is the most remarkable example of constituting categories's instrumental intervention in mathematics. The constituting categories of structural morphisms and the general structures constituted through their agency provide a new example of duality between structures and categories with levels being distinguished between the two.

This time the relationships are opposite to those characterizing categorical structures where the structure organizes the morphismic system. Here, on the contrary, the category organizes a class of structures arising from a single general form with an aim toward generalization and systematization. In all of this, structural morphisms play an essential role as instruments for comparing and transferring structural form.

Initially, constituting categories remain conceptual instruments that have not themselves been explicitly conceptualized, but nothing stops the subject from doing so later. The explicit conceptualization of categories constitutes new progress comparable to the transition from intuitive constituting structures to general structures that are the object of an explicit mathematical theory. Thus, the mathematical theory of categories is found to be the endpoint of an activity extending the activity leading to the mathematical theory of structures.

The historical continuity of these developments is as evident as the epistemological kinship of the theories stemming from them. A new reflection on the instruments used in classical mathematics is added to reflection on the systems of transformations used in that field. The order of conceptualizations appears to have been determined by the instrumental relationships of the objects conceptualized. It is not surprising, therefore, that the general categorical form came to light relatively late.

This fact is no less meaningful when one compares the profound character of the invariants brought out in the theory of categories. Moreover, it should be remarked that the process of explicit conceptualization was spectacularly accelerated by the use of categories that constitute structural morphisms. The temporal gap between the elaboration of mathematical theories of structures and those of categories is, in fact, extremely short compared to the immense duration of the period extending from the appearance of constituting structures to their explicit conceptualization.

As with all structures, conceptualizing categories requires the intervention of new constituting categories on the instrumental plane. Morphisms transfer the form of the constituting categories being conceptualized. There is, however, more than a simple functional analogy between the processes for explicitly conceptualizing structures and categories. Both processes employ cognitive instruments enjoying an essentially identical form of organization. In effect, the constituting categories used to conceptualize categories are only categories of a particular type of structural morphisms, the structural form transferred being a form of categorical structure.

The mathematical theory of categories is engaged in the explicit conceptualization of a certain species of general structure, in the present case of the most general form of categorical structure, as can be seen from its very marked algebraic aspect and especially from the way in which it treats morphisms. Only those aspects of the morphismic complexities found in constituting categories permitting them to be integrated into categorical structure are retained. These are, notably, their susceptibility to composition through the intermediary of operations subjected to laws explicity determined by the theory.

Thus, the only thing retained from the transfer instrument initially expressing a comparison between two terms is the form, general and devoid of content, of the composable arrow. In this one sees the characteristic traits of the axiomatic and structural method in its application to categories. Movement of forms upward brings the morphism, emptied of qualitative content, to itself play the role of content in an explicitly conceptualized inclusive structure.

In the following stage having to do with the constituting categories used in conceptualizing the forms of categorical structures, the process of conceptualizing instruments of explicit conceptualization continues. Remarkably, this process does not lead beyond categories because the instruments of explicit conceptualization of constituting categories are new constituting categories.

Because it is through the intermediary of constituting categories that the subject attains higher levels of explicit conceptualization, the possibilty of an indefinite recursive process of successive conceptualizations remains open. Effectively, morphisms of each level transfer the forms of the preceding level. By always constructing new forms of categories, the subject only displaces the result of his previous explicit conceptualizations upward by generalizing them. The reason for this is that all such "categories of categories" of more and more elevated levels involve a single form of abstract categorical structure.

One calls structural morphisms that bear on categorical structures "functors." All of the categories of categories just mentioned are, more precisely, categories of functors transferring a common form of categorical structure. Like every other category, categories of functors possess their own categorical structure. Consequently, there is reason to distinguish the categorical structure of the category of functors from categorical structures whose form is transferred by those functors.

This superposition of several levels of categorical structures belongs to categories of categories and prepares the way for their organization. Like the other structural morphisms and with even greater reason, functors are typical cases of cotransformational or protransformational morphisms. They are closely associated with intercategorical transformations.

It is remarkable that all of this organization still lets itself be formalized in an adequate way within the framework of the theory of categories. This indicates the power of the theory which, in fact, has the unique capacity of providing the means for analyzing the instruments of its own explicit conceptualization.

It is not surprising that people have dreamed of taking one further step and seeking an adequate foundation for the whole of mathematics in the theory of categories. It has been established that that enterprise is feasible. To achieve it, it has been necessary to reformulate the theory of categories and to make its internal logic generally explicit. Thus it becomes capable of playing a role analogous to the role that set theory played for the first time in history.

I do not retrace this quite recent development, the vast implications of which are currently being explored. It brings together influences from different sectors of mathematics, and the results of such exchanges are appreciable. They appear to steer category theory and the whole of abstract algebra toward more enriching interactions with the different sectors concerned.

At the present time the most remarkable product of this great reflexive and unifying current in mathematics is topos theory. In a number of ways, this original synthesis goes beyond Lawvere's already promising preliminary results on "the" category of sets and "the" category of categories as a foundation for mathematics.[9] Topos theory appeals to intuitions initially developed in algebraic topology and in algebraic geometry which gave birth to sheaf theory and its successive generalizations. The latter theory arose out of attempts to axiomatize the notion of local systems of coefficients originally resorted to in the context of the former theories.

Topos theory develops these intuitions and extends them to the universe of mathematical discourse. This results in a new general perspective profoundly characterizing the theory flowing from it better than any other strictly formal property. In the theory, objects are envisioned in a way that embraces the conditions of their own continuous variation. This is in fundamental opposition to the manner, until then general, in which objects were conceived.

In effect, it was once traditional to consider every mathematical object as determined a priori in a necessary way. Assuming that, one formalized the notion of variation by a method for which the theory of sets provided an adequate axiomatic basis. In its broad lines, the method consists in fixing a domain of variation. The latter is an arbitrary but, in principle, determined set most often provided with a topological structure. One then associates each point of this space with a set provided with a suitable structure but, again, a structure that can only be conceived as determined within the traditional theoretical framework.

Thus, the set theory reconstruction of the mathematical notion of function has separated the definition of the domain of variation from the law of correspondence. However, only the latter can define a variable structure as such. The new conception is completely different in this respect. In it, the very idea of determined set is only an extreme case of the much more general and fecund idea of variable structure, and one would be wrong to wish to restrict oneself to that extreme case in every circumstance. Naturally, people sought to characterize the more general idea in an intrinsic way.

These considerations, necessarily very incomplete, are insufficient to make apparent all of the new developments in mathematics brought about by the explicit conceptualization of categories. The multiple tendencies observed respond to exigencies of very diversified operatory functioning. In every case, current developments in mathematics appear to refute the disdainful criticism of those who see the theory of categories as a sort of worrisome "abstract nonsense."

With respect to the object of our study, operatory functioning reveals numerous invariants corresponding to very different functional tendencies.

---

[9]Cf F. W. Lawvere, "An Elementary Theory of the Category of Sets," *Proc Nat Acad Sci,* 1964, *52,* 1506–1511 and "The Category of Categories as a Foundation for Mathematics," *Proceedings of the La Jolla Conference on Categorical Algebra,* Springer, 1966, pp. 1–20.

Happily, the fear of dispersion that proliferation of such invariants might lead to is counterbalanced by the accompanying deepening of reflection. The explicit conceptualization of categories has marked a decisive turning point of this deepening process. Again, this bears witness to the dynamism of mathematical construction which is constantly illuminating analytically the conditions of its own operatory functioning.

14 The Theory of Categories and Genetic Epistemology

by
Edgar Ascher

I would like to make some simple remarks—that to certain people will even appear simplistic—about the theory of categories in the hope that its relationships with genetic epistemology will emerge spontaneously or almost spontaneously. Before doing so, let me stress that, although I do not pay much attention to them here, the subtle distinctions introduced by Henriques appear to me to be interesting and also useful for genetic epistemology. In contrast, however, I would like to have us look at the theory of categories through a veil so that we perceive only its important contours—at least those contours that appear important to me.

Here, to a first approximation, are the conclusions at which I end:

1. Categories are the least important thing about the theory of categories.
2. Precisely for that reason, the theory of categories is particularly close to genetic epistemology and can be useful to it.
3. Even so, the categorical style is not the only style adequate for or useful in genetic epistemology.

In preparing this chapter, I began by asking myself what it is about the theory of categories that interests me. I am a physicist who has been led, albeit infrequently, to use some of the techniques of this theory and who wishes to assimilate genetic epistemology. I see in the theory of categories a theory of mathematical constructions. What interests me is to be able to say with some precision, "This is what people are doing in a certain field here and now, and it is the same thing that they were doing in another domain, at first glance very different, on another occasion." A kind of analogy is therefore involved, but one whose interest lies not in the analogy itself but in the constructions to which it leads and also in the possibility of transferring those constructions from one domain of experience to another. In the perspective from which I view the theory of categories, what are called "universal constructions" are central. Certainly, other perspectives are possible. Mine, however, is more or less that of mathematicians who are not interested in categories in themselves but, rather, in what they offer mathematics generally. I believe this to be an attitude that one can recommend to those interested in the theory of categories as a branch of applied mathematics.

In what follows, I try to make plausible the thesis that the theory of categories is a macroscopic theory of mathematical constructions proceeding by stages. It is a beautiful example of reflective abstraction, a process that itself goes back to a constructive principle present from the sensorimotor stage onward. Thus, the categorical style is a way of envisioning an important aspect of the genesis of cognitive faculties. For that reason, it is an adequate style for describing that genesis.

The history of the theory of categories begins in 1942 in an article by Eilenberg and MacLane entitled *Natural Isomorphisms in Group Theory.*[1] In that work, the authors set out to give a precise definition of the term "natural," sometimes employed in mathematics to designate an apparently unarbitrary correspondence between a given mathematical object and another constructed from it. The word "canonical" is also often used to speak of such constructions. The idea of natural correspondence between two objects is made precise by means of the notion of natural transformation between two functors.

Interestingly enough, whereas the notion of functor is defined in the article mentioned, the notion of category does not appear explicitly until 1945 in Eilenberg and MacLane's great work, "General Theory of Natural Equivalences."[2] In his 1971 book,[3] MacLane says that the reason for this is that the notion of "category" was introduced in order to define the notion of "functor" and that the notion of functor was introduced in order to define the notion of "natural transformation." "Our theory," said Eilenberg and MacLane in 1945, "provides the possibility of comparing certain constructions and the isomorphisms that one encounters in different branches of mathematics with one another."

---

[1]Samuel Eilenberg and Saunders MacLane (1942), "*Natural Isomorphisms in Group Theory,*" *Proceedings of the National Academy of Science* (U.S.A., 1941), *28*, 537–543 —Translator.

[2]Samuel Eilenberg and Saunders MacLane (1945), "*General Theory of Natural Equivalences,*" *Transactions of the American Mathematical Society, 58,* 231–294—Translator.

[3]Saunders MacLane (1971), *Categories for the Working Mathematician.* New York: Springer-Verlag—Translator.

The notion of categories, therefore, is important as a starting point and not as an endpoint. It is an auxiliary notion which allows us to put order into what we wish to do. We, therefore, must choose the categories we want carefully according to our interests. For example, one has to decide what morphisms to select. The correspondence associating a group with its commutator group is a functor starting from the category of groups and group homomorphisms and ending in the same category. If one wishes to display the functoriality of the center of a group, he must take as morphisms only surjective homomorphisms, but to accomplish the same for the group of automorphisms of a group one must consider only isomorphisms as morphisms. In this example, we encounter three different categories of groups that are distinguished only by morphisms.

It is also a matter of choosing the objects of the category. Thus, the two cyclic groups of order two, Z_2 do not have a product in the category of cyclic groups, but they do have a product, Klein's group, D_2, in the category of groups.

In short, it is necessary to choose categories in light of the goals one is pursuing. Formulated in the other direction, this proposition reads: "Show me what constructions you make and I will tell you what categories you are using." By preference, this is the working rule I adhere to when doing genetic epistemology.

In Eilenberg and MacLane's 1945 article, one also reads that "the theory of groups studies functors on well-defined categories of groups with values in another similar category. One can consider this as a continuation of Klein's *Erlanger Program* in the sense that a space with its group of transformations is generalized into a category with its algebra of mappings." I believe that this quote confirms in very clear fashion the auxiliary role that categories play in the theory of categories. If Euclidean geometry is determined, according to Klein's program, by the Euclidian group, and relativist physics is determined by the Poincaré group (inhomogeneous Lorentz group)—if such is indeed the case—the fact that these groups of transformations are given still does not exempt one from constructing the theories in question.

I believe, therefore, that I can say that the ideas of construction, similarity, and transference of construction are the essentials of category theory. Hence, it is not astonishing to see appear, from 1948 onward, descriptions of mathematical constructions detached from their original contexts and retaining only their transferrable and generalizable aspect (e.g., Samuel's *universal arrow,* MacLane's *Cartesian product*). In order to illustrate this way of doing things, let us start with the notion of the product of two objects.

First let us consider the product of two sets, $A_1 \times A_2$. The well-known *usual definition* is as follows:

$$A_1 \times A_2 := [(a_1,a_2) \mid a_1 \in A_1,\ a_2 \in A_2] \tag{1}$$

Here, now, is the *categorical definition* which only uses what can be generalized or repeated in another situation, that is, a scheme or diagram. Let:

$$A_1, A_2 \in \mathrm{Ob}\ E. \tag{2}$$

The product

$$P = A_1 \times A_2 \in \mathrm{Ob}\ E \tag{3}$$

of these two sets is an object of E furnished with two morphisms

$$\pi_i \in \mathrm{Mor}_E(A_1 \times A_2, A_i)\ i = 1,2. \tag{4}$$

This product has the property that for any object

$$X \in \mathrm{Ob}\ E \tag{5}$$

with two morphisms

$$\xi_i \in \mathrm{Mor}_E(X, A_i)\ i = 1,2, \tag{6}$$

there exists a unique

$$\phi \in \mathrm{Mor}_E(X, P) \tag{7}$$

which renders the diagram (S1) commutative.

(S1) 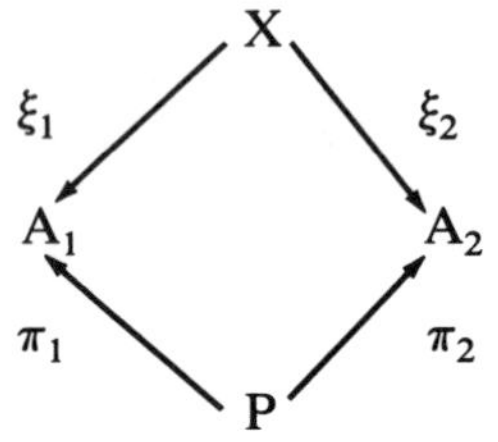

$\xi i\ \pi_i \circ \phi,\ i = 1,2$

"All messages emitted toward A_1 and A_2 can be transmitted by P" (according to Papert[4]).

Before showing how this scheme represents what can be generalized in constructing a product and how it is transferred to other situations, let us mention another schematization recombining some of the elements of the preceding scheme in less differentiated form. On this new level, a pair of coinitial morphisms of category E are taken as objects (of a category C):

$$\mathrm{Ob}\ C = \left\{ A_1 \xleftarrow{\xi_1} Z \xrightarrow{\xi_2} A_2 \right\} = :\{\hat{Z}\} \tag{8}$$

[4]Remarks made at the 19th Symposium of the Centre International de l'Épistémologie Génétique.

The morphisms of the new category C are triplets $\hat{\phi}$ of morphisms of E which connect two objects of C in the following manner:

(S2)

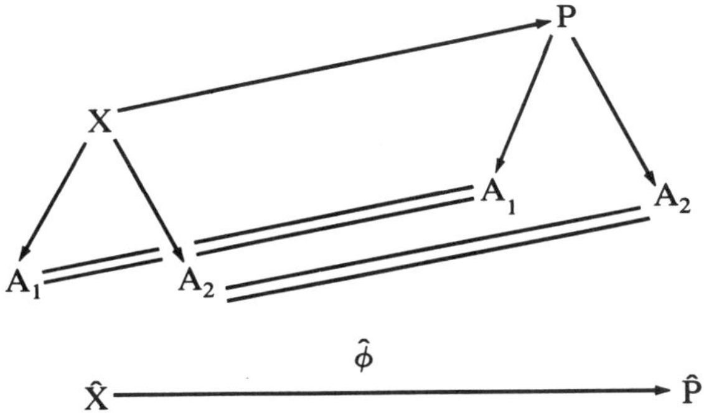

Identical morphisms can be taken as morphisms connecting the two factors A_1 and A_2. On this new level of category C, the product $\hat{P}$ has an extremely simple definition: it is the terminal object, viz. for every object $\hat{X}$ of C, there is a unique morphism $\hat{\phi}$ from $\hat{X}$ to $\hat{P}$

(S3)

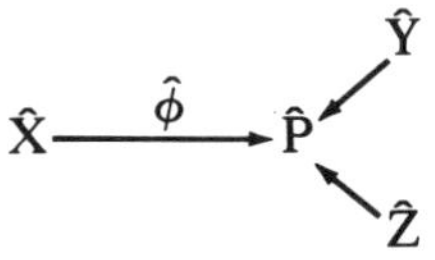

Thus, one has first of all freed the definition of the product from reference to elements chosen at random in the two sets. What is common to all possible choices is a scheme of relationships between sets, that is, a diagram in the category E of sets. However, this scheme can be simplified even more. To do so, one moves to a new level by recombining morphisms of category E into a less differentiated form. Thus, morphisms or even schemes of morphisms become objects.

For me, then, morphisms represent actions, for example, comparing, putting into correspondence, putting into relation, transforming, and so on. Here, however, I do not want to be more specific. The advantage of the categorical style, in my opinion, is precisely that morphisms can signify all of these types of actions according to the situation in which they are found. Schemes of action become objects on which one can again act, and so forth, from level to level. That permits (a) the definition of constructions to be simplified, and (b) constructions to be made detachable and transferrable.

Let us summarize. There are three architectural principles that one might call *globalization, abstraction,* and *reification.* Globalization consists in forgetting the elements on which one acts and only considering the action. Abstraction permits us to forget certain characteristics of action; those characteristics become morphisms (or arrows), and we only study the way in which they are or can be connected. Finally, through reification one transforms actions into things, which is to say new objects on which one acts through new morphisms. The initial objects have disappeared completely; actions and operations become always more abstract; we are really in the domain of abstract operations. In mathematics the theory of categories represents the stage of abstract operations.

By way of example, let me mention the category of positions and its morphisms, displacements, or in other words changes (exchanges) of position. As I just showed this winter, the structure of this "*groupement* of displacements" is a structure known under the name of "Brandt groupoid" (1940). Such a structure is obtained each time one has to consider pairs of objects with a quite natural law for composing pairs which associates a new pair to a pair of pairs.

With the theory of categories, we seem to have reached the most abstract extremity of abstract operations. We cannot say, however, that this theory exhausts everything that one does in mathematics nor that it constitutes the summit of this activity. A great creative activity is unfolding at the level of more concrete mathematics. Certainly, it was that activity that MacLane was thinking of when in 1971, he entitled his book *Categories for the Working Mathematician* (as if those who, like him, busied themselves with the theory of categories did not work).

One can also say that, in psychology, creative thought does not necessarily move on the most abstract level, but can also evolve on the level of concrete operations. In that domain, one is tempted to bring the reification of which it has just been question together with the social phenomenon discussed by Lućacs under the name of "*Verdinglichung*" in his famous book of 1922 and with the social pathology that can be connected with it. Moreover, certain aspects of the individual pathology of reified thought have been studied by the French psychiatrist Joseph Gabel.

Let us now go back to mathematical constructions and show what their generalization by transference consists in. We had defined the product for the category of sets and general applications. Exactly the same schemes can serve as definition for any category. One must be careful, however, not to take this to mean that the product thus defined exists for all categories. In order for a product to exist for every pair of objects, the category must fulfill certain conditions.

We can go even further and use the same schemes to define the product of two categories. To do that, it is necessary to consider a category of categories that contains the categories in question. Such a construction is, as you know, completely legitimate. There are several ways of going about it without falling into the abyss of set theory's paradoxes. In my view, the way that best corresponds to the theory of categories, viewed as a theory of constructions proceeding from level to level, is the one based on Grothendieck's extension of the customary Zermelo-Frenkel set theory.

Having thus obtained a category of categories, nothing hinders us from continuing, if we need to, from level to level.

Another interesting transition from one level to another is obtained in the following manner. One takes two categories, C and D, and considers all of the functors from C to D. These functors are the objects of the new category [C,D]. The morphisms of this category are precisely the so-called *natural transformations* that gave birth to the theory of categories. In consequence of this new interpretation, they are also called *functional morphisms,* a label that suits them better.

If it is possible to construct them at all, the products of all such categories are constructed in the same manner, independently of their origins and independently of the fine structure of the objects and morphisms. This is also the case for the many other so-called *universal constructions.* Today they are defined starting from the notion of *adjoint functor* (introduced in 1958 by Kan[5]). The product that we have spoken so much about thus appears as right adjoint of a particularly simple functor, the diagonal functor.

What one takes as objects and the morphisms that one chooses in order to constitute a category can be very complicated in detail. Because one does not look at them through a microscope, however, the details are forgotten. One simply has objects and morphisms. For example, in a recent work that chance placed in my hands, it is shown that the "behavior" (of a machine) is the left adjoint of the "minimal realization" functor; that is, realization is a universal construction. To achieve this, one introduces, among other things, the category of machines. Its objects are sextuples that consist of three sets, that is, input, output, and state, and three applications among these sets, etcetera.

The notions employed, for example, machine, behavior, realization and so forth, are not notions of the theory of categories. In order to make what one does clear, generalizable, comparable, and transferable, one uses the theory of categories. This also illustrates the underlying working plan: "Show me your constructions, and I will tell you what categories you employ."

In all branches of mathematics, the theory of categories is used more and more and is spoken of less and less. Interestingly, although category theory has become a very useful tool, the mathematical problems approached using it are rarely posed in terms of categories nor are the answers arrived

[5]Daniel M. Kan, "Adjoint Functors," *Transactions of the American Mathematical Society, 87,* 294-329—Translator.

at expressed in such terms. In the process, however, in order to see clearly the meaning of what one wishes to do and to take account of what one can do, one appeals to category theory as a theory of constructions. It is useful because, thanks to its macroscopic character, it permits what one does to be set out without superfluous detail.

I wanted to make plausible, in broad outline, the idea that the theory of categories, considered as a theory of mathematical constructions, reflects the genetic constitution of man's cognitive tools, that is, the detachment of transferrable schemes from a set of actions, then similar operations on those schemes, then similar operations on schemes of schemes, and so forth. Hence it seems clear to me that the categorical style, as a way of envisioning an important aspect of the genesis of man's cognitive faculties, is not a style imposed on genetic epistemology from the outside but is a style that, by nature, is adequate for describing the constructions discovered by genetic epistemology. Obviously, it would be necessary to show this adequacy in detail by introducing the necessary nuances.

One knows that the categorical style is not the only mathematical style possible in genetic epistemology. Neither is it the only style desirable. Without wishing to be exhaustive, I would like to mention at least two styles: the logical style (of formal systems) and the style of the qualitative study of dynamic systems (of which catastrophe theory is an example).

With regard to the logical style I will say only that, unlike the categorical style and the style of qualitative dynamics which would both be macroscopic, this style appears to be essentially microscopic. This, perhaps, is why one sometimes sees a temptation toward atomism and a desire to start from a level called "elementary" or "fundamental." As for the style of qualitative dynamics, it appears to have a bright future before it.

15 General Conclusions

Jean Piaget

Although most of the questions studied in this work are approached in terms of psychogenesis, they are closely related to fundamental epistemological problems. Insofar as one is inclined to consider knowledge in general as a more or less schematized copy of reality and logicomathematical truth as an adequation to entities given in advance,[1] the role of correspondences or morphisms as instruments of comparison will be overestimated whereas transformations themselves will be reduced to metaphors expressing relationships given in reality in the form of "operations" (an idea that Couturat qualified as anthropomorphic). By contrast, if one is neither empiricist nor apriorist but rather constructivist or paritsan of dialectic as source of novelties, the problems of relationships among comparisons and transformations and in particular among operatory and morphismic transformations acquire a new meaning of some importance. That is why we have sought to clarify the extent and nature of their respective contributions in the continuous elaboration of knowledge from elementary levels onward. That is also why we have sought to elucidate the coherence between the psychogenetic facts and the analysis of the same questions on the plane of scientific thought (see the chapters by G. Henriques and E. Ascher). All of these analyses aim, therefore, at more closely encompassing these two aspects of knowledge, adequation, and construction, at once inseparable and apparently opposed.

The facts have in no way disappointed us. The study of elementary

[1]Whether it is a matter of Platonic "ideas" or whatever else one might wish, including linguistic connections.

premorphisms[2] have already made us aware of a progressive reversal between correspondences and transformations, the first initially paving the way for the second and subsequently becoming subordinate to them. Now, morphisms are increasingly composed with one another, that is, as morphismic transformations are formed, we see an even more spectacular reversal. This occurs with the transition from intermorphic to transmorphic correspondences. The reasons for it are that intermorphic correspondences help pave the way for general operatory systems and also that their transformations are the source of transmorphic compositions. The initial process of composition leading from intramorphic correspondences[3] to intermorphic correspondences has shown itself to conform to expectations. In that case, it is only a matter of putting correspondences themselves into correspondence and, therefore, of creating second-degree correspondences that involve nothing beyond the construction of a single mechanism of comparison or assimilation. By contrast, in order to pass from the intermorphic to the transmorphic, which is to say, from the intermorphic to a general system with its intrinsic variations, its generality, its free and necessary compositions, or, in a word, its closure, a new mode of construction is needed. In order to compose intermorphic correspondences with one another, the subject sets himself "to operate" on these morphisms, or, in other words, he sets himself to use a generalization of the operatory transformations on which prior morphisms bear. Thus it is that in Chapter 11, the subject, having discovered inverse relationships and compensations between the diameters, D, and the weights, W, using intermorphic correspondences, goes on to the transmorphic level with equality of the products $D_1W_1 = D_2W_2$, and so on, in order to attain equilibrium. In this instance, the new composition rests on numerical multiplication, which is an example, albeit very elementary, of what Henriques calls "operations (or 'a certain calculus') on functions." By this "certain calculus" he means a composition due to generalization of an operatory scheme "already at work in the terms (the content) of the (preceding) morphisms." It is the same in chapter 2 with transmorphic compositions due to comprehension of the group of rotations, itself issued from intermorphic progress. In chapter 3, it is the external system of reference that plays this operatory role in transmorphic compositions. In chapter 4, it is the calculation of sums, and so forth.

This reversal in the direction of actions is, therefore, no longer effected between simple correspondences and transformations, as in the volume

[2]J. Piaget, *Recherches sur les Correspondances: Etudes d'Epistémologie et de Psychologie Génétique, XXXVII.* Paris: Presses Universitaires de France, 1980.

[3]Simple recording of certain of the observable facts without composing them with one another.

cited in Footnote 1. Rather, it is effected between operatory transformations and new compositions of morphisms, which is characteristic of the highest level of morphismic transformations observed in our subjects. Such a reversal, which seems general at our "transmorphic" Level III, is instructive from several points of view. To begin with, it constitutes a paradoxical exchange of forms and contents, illustrating what we said of their relationships in the Introduction: An extramorphic (i.e., operatory) content of Level II inserted into a morphic form of the same level becomes, in the present case of Level III, the form of this Level II form. The new form is equally morphic, but it follows from operatory generalization of the content of Level II or from reflective abstraction which teases out the reasons for it.

More than anything else, this reversal is important as an example or instrument of progressive convergence and, one might even say, of the gradual interpenetration of operatory and morphismic transformations. In the particular case of our levels, it is still only a matter of a collaboration, but a collaboration such that, at the transmorphic level, the composition involved is at once operatory and morphismic. Thus it reproduces the analogue of cotransformational situations between simple correspondences and operations on the plane of compositions. Naturally, at higher stages such as those of scientific and formal conceptualization, one again finds intra-, inter-, and trans phases, because these are essentially relative notions and because the same ternary process is reproduced at all stages. More interesting in the present context, however, is the fact that at these stages the convergences just discussed lead to a fundamental consequence: If morphisms, functors, and categories conserve their local autonomy, categorical compositions can, according to the case, take the same forms as operatory structures; that is, they can take the form of monoids, groups, rings, lattices, vectorial spaces, and so on (see Henriques's chapter). This amounts to saying that, despite differences of nature between "mathematical entities" of every sort and even though conserving the functional distinction of instruments of comparison and instruments of transformation, the modes of construction converge toward general structures in the form of laws or forms of organization necessary for all coherent construction. The reason for this is that operatory structures are constructed within a domain and categorical systems transfer such constructions to other domains in order to bring out common forms, but "in terms of the structure of the instruments of transference" (Henriques). There must be convergence, then, between the structures and constructions compared and the structures and constructions of the instruments of comparison, otherwise comparison and transference would fail. This follows from the fact that transference is a dynamic extension of comparison which consists in analogically projecting one structure onto another in order to increase the scope of the common characteristics. The remarkable result of this evolution is twofold. On the one hand, it ensures the autonomy of operatory and categorical constructions with respect to their methodological requirements, and, on the other hand, it ensures convergence with respect to their forms of organization. The autonomies of the two forms of construction are conserved by the fact that even if comparisons have become transferences, they do not generate the structures or the modes of construction to be transferred, and still there is convergence. This convergence stems from the fact that, if the "structure of the instruments of transference" were not molded on that of the constructions to be transferred, the process would miss its goal.

But there remains a final stage. Once elaborated, instruments of comparison and transference, naturally, can be composed with one another. From the beginning, they are molded by the structures to be compared that impose their frameworks on them, and this remains true when constructions are transferred while their forms are conserved. It results from this that categorical compositions, although involving nothing more than morphismic or functorial content, again take the form of general structures belonging to operatory transformations. But despite this remarkable convergence, their purely categorical content reinforces their autonomy, whence the current upsurge in the construction of categories as well as in the construction of categories of categories up to the (nonantimonic) point of the construction of the category of all categories.

The development of morphismic and operatory transformations presents two characteristics that are apparently opposed and paradoxically solidary and that are both increasing. These are the characteristics of respective autonomy and of convergence, and they bring up two general problems that need to be discussed. The first is to understand why these solidary aspects exist; the second is to understand why, in the history of mathematics, the conceptualization of morphisms and categories has been so slow in coming relative to the elaboration of operatory theories from Galois and Klein up to the Bourbaki.

The explanation that we propose for the autonomy and solidarity of both forms of construction can be summarized in a few words. On the one hand, all correspondences, operations, and compositions are manifestations of the assimilation of objects or situations to schemes of action or of the coordination of such schemes by compound assimilations. On the other hand, however, simple or compound assimilations can present as one of three types distinguishable by their directions. These directions can be envisioned by means of a graph of the genealogical tree. In that frame of reference, longitudinal or vertical filiations express operations and operatory transformations in a diachronic way. This is because it is precisely a matter, in that particular case, of real productions, called even in biological language "reproductions"! Transversal (or "collateral") connections or kinships express, more or less synchronically, all kinds of correspondences or morphisms that do not modify anything but that describe the result of filiations or compare them among themselves. The third type we have to consider is the superposition of stages or stratification linking transversal systems distinguished by successive generations. This superposition, vertical and therefore again diachronic, of horizontal stages quite adequately symbolizes morphismic transformations and the solidarity of filiatory and transverse kinship relations. Taking inspiration from this graph, we therefore may speak of longitudinal, transversal, and stratified assimilations, but we still have to discuss these notions.

Let us recall, first of all, that assimilation, as incorporation of objects or facts of any sort whatsoever to schemes of action, constitutes the functional mechanism common to all knowledge at every level. In this conception, the term "scheme" expresses what is repeatable in actions, actions being conceived in the broadest sense from perception (which is an activity) or sensorimotor behavior up to operations or conceptualization of the highest levels. In addition, let us recall that the various functional aspects of assimilation can be described in terms of coordinators.[4] By being focused on action, these functional aspects will be those of repetition, identification, and replacement. The assimilation of discrete objects will take the form of putting into relationship (of similarities or differences), of grouping (properties or objects[5]), and of succession (order of movements, etc.). With respect to spatiotemporal continua, their assimilation will involve directions (toward a goal, etc.), enclosures (neighborhood, etc.), and positions or their changes.

That said, it is clear from the single fact of the application of schemes that, in its different aspects, assimilation is the source of correspondences. From the baby who nurses as soon as he can (or happens to suck his thumb) to Cantor discovering the power of the denumberable, one can speak of a permanent function despite the difference of organs. With respect to operative or operatory transformations, they begin with the construction of new schemes and, above all, with their reciprocal assimilation or interscheme coordination (grasp what is seen, etc.), which is almost as precocious as direct assimilation and becomes more and more frequent in the course of all development. One sees right off, however, that if assimilation to schemes and reciprocal assimilation of schemes are entirely general characteristics of action, they are oriented differently from the start. Transformations are successive and are generated by filiations; their

[4]As we have explained in *Recherches sur les Correspondances: Études d'Épistémologie et de Psychologie Génétique, XXXVII.* Paris: Presses Universitaires de France, 1980.

[5]This does not involve additive operations but, in effect, joining together, for example, a 2-year-old child sees a pipe and says "Papa."

succession, however, is characterized, among other things, by the fact that using the product of a prior transformation does not, in itself, constitute a transformation. Rather, it constitutes only a simple mapping. In this respect, therefore, one can speak of longitudinal coordinatory (interscheme) assimilations. By contrast, correspondences do not proceed by filiations[6] and are simultaneously compatible among terms of varied origins at distances of any sort which are then "transversal." Thus, they benefit with respect to their genesis and elementary forms from an initial autonomy relative to transformations, while being able to connect transformations when a need for comparison is felt. It is precisely because they fulfill such a general function of comparative assimilation that their orientation remains at every level. It is, therefore, not without reason that their common bijective, injective, and surjective forms are found again at every stage in the freedom inherent in analogies of all sorts. And, because terms and their relationships remain undifferentiated during the initial stages, every assimilation can be extended into correspondences.

By contrast, this initial duality of longitudinal transformations and transversal correspondences can only result in growing solidarity. This starts at levels where operatory transformations begin to be coordinated to form structures and where correspondences begin to be composed with one another and thus generate morphismic transformations modifying the instruments of comparison themselves. On the one hand, operatory structures give rise to new morphisms, but morphisms that henceforth are deducible with necessity and not just derived from the comparison of observables. On the other hand, comparative assimilation which at first was only extended into intramorphic correspondences now begins to compare morphisms among themselves. In doing so, it provokes the first morphismic transformations in the form of intermorphic correspondences having a first degree of necessity derived from this very composition. These two sorts of constructions tend, therefore, to be coordinated, because operatory structures generate new correspondences and intermorphic compositions tend to organize all correspondences, old and new, into new systems. In such a situation, the combination of morphic transversal relationships and operatory longitudinal relationships, results in the constitution of a new stage. This occurs through stratified superposition, as we said earlier, which is a beginning of synthesis between the transversal and the longitudinal.

Once this level of morphismic transformation is attained, a final step can then be taken, that is, that of transmorphic reversal discussed previously. In transmorphic reversal, the generalization of operations bring about new compositions among morphisms and this henceforth assures a narrow solidarity between these two great systems without acting against their

[6]Except in their compositions which are then, in their turn, transformations.

relative autonomies. Although it is not necessary to do so, we can complete our graph of the genealogical tree by generalizing it to animal evolution (in its totality). This furnishes a good example of the collaboration between the biogenetic transformations and the morphisms studied in comparative anatomy, where action by the first has enriched the work of the second from stage to stage. The temporal and extensional dimensions of this tree are considerable. In it, transformations are marked by the longitudinal filiation of successive branchings that are as different as the *Vertebrates* or the *Arthropods* are from the *Bacteria* from which they are both descended. As for correspondences, they bear on the characteristics that groups or subgroups of animals have in common, for example, the front legs of tetrapod mammals and the wings of birds or the varieties of nervous systems which have developed since the *Coelenterates*. The remarkable fact is that the richness of these morphisms increases with the hierarchical level of the branchings,[7] even though neither the anatomic or functional homologies nor the genetic filiations are due to comparisons or reconstructions that an observer can make but are the product of the organisms themselves. One sees, therefore, the extent to which the constructive character of transformations by filiation and the richness of combinations among "homologous" characteristics (in the biological sense of morphisms issued from natural kinships) are solidary in such an evolution. Now, ontogenetic, including psychogenetic, development provides a comparable picture, although this is of extremely reduced proportions up to the moment that scientific thought, reinforced to a very high degree by its collective character and its historical continuity, can take the baton and open itself onto an evolution that, in certain respects, is analogous to the evolution involved in the filiation of operatory structures and morphismic and categorical transformations.

Let us go on to the questions of conceptualization. It is necessary to distinguish three sorts of putting into correspondence according to the nature of their terms and uses. The simplest and most easily conceptualized is the expression of direct comparisons among isolated objects or actions. The second, much less conscious, links the subject's behaviors in two different situations when he uses the same method to solve problems that are in some way analogous. In this case, it is a matter of "transferences," but it is important here to distinguish carefully between two processes. One, the transformation of one structure by means of another, is operatory and does not involve morphisms. The second consists in completing some analogy between two situations, perceived or judged possible, by transferring additional characteristics or modes of construction as aspects that become common because they are transferable. It is in this case alone that

[7]If one judges by the increase in the number of genetic units.

we speak of "transference" and, as we have already said, it is then a matter of a dynamic comparison consisting in "comparing certain constructions" as MacLane and Eilenberg (cited by Ascher) expressed it in 1945. As we pointed out earlier, the conceptualization of such analogies has been slow in the history of mathematics. Similarly, when the child is asked for constructions, even very simple ones, it is up to the observer to bring out analogies before the subject may notice them. This is even more the case with morphisms comparing two structures in their totalities as we saw with the intermachine comparisons in chapters 10 and 12. In this last case, the discovery of common operatory mechanisms precedes taking consciousness of the morphisms linking the two situations and permitting the comparison as such.

Whence a related problem, that is, how to explain why for a very long time in the history of mathematics morphisms were used in constructing the theory of structures and yet they themselves were conceptualized only recently. Recall in this respect that the theory of functors and categories was elaborated after, not at the same time as, the theory of structures. The explanation of this fact that we have proposed elsewhere[8] is quite simple. Conceptualization being a reflected abstraction and, therefore, both a current and retrospective conceptualization, it naturally involves a content and a form. In the case of operatory structures, its content is the set of compositions and transformations along with their dependencies. The form of this conceptualization cannot modify this content without becoming inadequate; it therefore consists in correspondences and comparisons that tease out the general properties of the system without adding anything to them but their simultaneous union into a coherent whole. This form, therefore, only arises from morphismic and categorical instruments that are not, themselves, conceptualized and that only serve as a tool at this level. From such a point of view, the conceptualization of operatory systems can be said to be of first degree, whereas the conceptualization of the instruments of this or of any other conceptualization can be said to be of second degree. This is precisely what happened subsequently and could not have happened otherwise. It suffices to examine how the Bourbaki constructed their mother or included structures to reach what MacLane and Eilenberg called "a general theory of natural equivalences" (their title of 1945), and it is this new conceptualization that has led from structures to categories. With respect to their formation, the latter indeed result from a reflection on a reflection or from a conceptualization of the very instruments of conceptualization and, therefore, from a conceptualization to the second power.

[8]Jean Piaget, "Structures et catégories," *Logique et Analyse* (Bruxelles), 1974, *67-68*, pp. 223–240.

There is, however, an important theme in all of this that we have just seen and that this work has shown as early as the prescientific levels of psychogenesis. On the one hand, morphisms are used to compare structures (even up to the point of constituting the condition for their conceptualization); on the other hand and independently of conceptualizations, the progressive convergence of operatory and morphismic transformations generates a fecund solidarity between the two without standing in the way of their respective autonomies.

These reflections on conceptualization needed to be made before we could approach two final questions. The first is whether or not categories that can be generated at the transmorphic levels studied in our chapters really do exist; the second is, if they do, what is their nature? In effect, discussion of these questions was subordinated to that of establishing whether one of the conditions necessary for the constitution of a category is its conceptualization by the subject himself. This problem is complex and has already come up with respect to structures.

We have always considered an operatory structure as a system of operations that the child can effectively elaborate and compose with other operations (solving a problem, etc.) independently of whether he thinks of it as a system or even as a procedure. A structure, therefore, can exist without implying explicit conceptualization. For example, it is easy to decide whether a subject uses a structure of proportions before he has been taught to do so, even if he does not take consciousness of this proportionality as a double relationship or only reasons in terms of absolute numbers. By contrast, there exist structures that the subject is consciously aware of through some figurative aspect that they can take on, for example, a seriation, a classification (with inclusion), a double-entry table for multiplicative systems of classes or relations, and so on. And in chapter 7 we saw some subjects of Level 3 construct complicated relationships between kinships while clarifying that one could arrange them within a tree diagram, although they felt no need to do so. As for structures lacking figurative representations like the INRC quaternality group of inversions and reciprocities, the subject can use them with precision (as in systems of actions and reactions) without conceptualizing them explicitly.

There is, therefore, no a priori reason to exclude similar situations with regard to categories. The subject is not restricted to constructing operations and composing them into structures. Moreover, he elaborates all sorts of correspondences, applications, and morphisms that he coordinates according to the intra-, inter-, and transmorphic steps described in each of our studies. But, one might ask, why wish to attribute the possession of "categories" to the subject in the same sense that we claim that he possesses structures that are not just inventions of the observer? And, more particularly, why wish to do this even though the observer is the only one who, in most cases, can conceptualize consciously and in any case the only one who can formalize them? There is an epistemological reason for this that we hold to be fundamental. A genetic epistemology only has meaning on two conditions. One is that it demonstrates a continuity between "natural" thought and scientific thought. The other, just as essential, is that it explains natural thought in terms of its biological formation by linking it to the organic processes of life itself. In all probability, operations and operatory structures have their roots in the genetic, morphogenetic, and autoregulatory mechanisms belonging to the living being. Now, a parallel reason forces us to consider categories as "natural" in an analogous sense. Recall, in this respect, the distinctions we have introduced between the longitudinal direction of transformations and the transversal direction of correspondences with superpositions by stages for the morphismic transformations. Recall also what we have said about genealogical trees and the generalization of morphismic transformations in the tree of unlimited dimensions constituted by the evolution of animals. If all of that is admitted, it seems obvious that, in addition to filiations in the longitudinal direction, there exist a considerable number of transversal relationships that have been enriched in stages and that have not been "invented," but "discovered" by comparative anatomy and physiology. These relationships, therefore, express "natural kinships," which amounts to saying that they express categorical organizations. Moreover, as said at the end of chapter 12, every cybernetic system (and every organism comprises such a system at every level) implies comparisons or putting into correspondence (in relation to its norms) as well as transformations, whence again the "natural" character of morphisms.

That said, the problem is to establish whether in the course of his development the child, by himself, succeeds in establishing categories in concert with the structures he constructs. Among the latter, the most interesting are not those that he discovers or reconstructs when some situation implies them (like the rotations of chapters 1–3), but the structures of levels so elementary that they have not acquired the right to be put at the heart of scientific thought. *"Groupements"* constitute a case in point. These elementary structures are interesting because they involve all of the intermediaries between Henriques's "precategories" with their "invariants of replacement" and at least "special" categories, as Wittman has demonstrated with MacLane's approbation.

Effectively, additive *groupements,* like simple classifications or seriations, only arise from precategories. When the subject transposes the way in which he has classified or seriated a first collection onto other objects, the common form obtained constitutes only an "invariant of replacement." By contrast, with classifications, the *groupement* of "complementary substitutions," which, on the plane of relations, corresponds to that of symmetrical relations, is headed in the direction of categories. In effect, if a class B is divided into two subclasses A_1 and A_1' and if that classification is modified to A_2 (including part of A_1') and A_2' (including part of A_1), one will consequently have $A_1 + A_1' = A_2 + A_2' = B$. This kind of operation, generalizable to all scales, leads to the "power set" of a given set. But independently of this possible generalization at the level of combinatory operations, simple complementary substitution is already oriented in the direction of endomorphisms.

It is, however, only with the multiplicative *groupements* that the categorical form with all of its characteristics appears to be constituted, as in the case of a genealogical tree with indefinitely growing generations. Certainly, if the subject limits himself to comparing a particular family ABC . . . to another A′B′C′ . . . composed of the same relationships in restricted numbers (father, etc.), only precategories with invariants of replacement bearing on the same form with another content are involved. If, however, one considers the whole tree (while abstracting marriage out so as to consider only men), the compositions are unlimited and become richer with each new generation, always retaining the possibility of univocally determined calculation. One finds in this, then, the three characteristics indicated in chapter 7: (a) complementary substitutions with conservation, that is, X + P (his kinship including Y) = Y + P′ (his kinship including X); (b) all of the arrows are invertible (reciprocities) either with symmetry, for example, brother, or without, for example, uncle and nephew, in relation to the longitudinal axis; (c) a growing number of possible paths, the simplest form of which is $\downarrow g \overset{c}{\leftrightarrow} = \overset{c'}{\leftrightarrow} \downarrow g'$ (where g, the generations, and c, the transversal cosurjections, are calculable by conserving the same starting and endpoints, X and Y).

The reason for these compositions is quite simple but merits being teased out because it demonstrates their equivalence with "complete" classification. In effect, to the ordinal of the generations that we designate by I (= father), II (= grandfather), and so on, correspond a cardinal number of degrees of transversal kinship between the descendents: 1 (= brothers as sons of I), 2 (= brothers or first cousins as the grandsons of II), and so forth (see Fig. 15.1). But it is the same for a complete classification, like that of zoologists, with one important difference. What were filiations on the plane of evolution become inclusions on the plane of classification: I =

I	1
II	1, 2
III	1, 2, 3
•	•
•	•
•	•

FIG. 15.1. Correspondence of ordinal and transversal kinship.

a genus and its species (degree 1 of collateral kinship); II = a family, its genera, and its species (whence 1 = relationships between species of the same genus and 2 = relationships between species of different genera, second degree of transversal kinship comparable to being cousins); III = an "order" (in the zoological sense), its families, their genera, and the species of these (collateral degrees 1, 2, and 3); IV = a class (in the zoological sense), its orders, their families, the genera and species (degrees 1, 2, 3, and 4); V = a phylum, its classes, and so on.

Thus, one sees the generality of this structure of *groupements,* the transformations of which are filiations (or inclusions) with their invariants of transformations and the morphisms that result from them. Those morphisms are well defined in themselves and in their compositions and derive from the transformations without being reduced to immediate or mediate comparisons of their terms, because their terms can be linked together by varied paths as a function of filiations.

In short, *groupements* can take on a categorical form, but without that form exhausting their meaning. That is, moreover, the case with all categories applied to operatory structures, maximum convergence only being encountered in the case of the category of sets because, from the very beginning, sets result from putting into correspondence that ensures coordination.

Author Index

Subject Index

V